Latin American
Philosophy

Latin American Philosophy

Currents, Issues, Debates

Edited by Eduardo Mendieta

INDIANA
University Press

Bloomington & Indianapolis

This book is a publication of

Indiana University Press
601 North Morton Street
Bloomington, IN 47404-3797 USA

http://iupress.indiana.edu

Telephone orders   800-842-6796
Fax orders   812-855-7931
Orders by e-mail   iuporder@indiana.edu

© 2003 by Indiana University Press

The paper used in this publication meets the minimum requirements of American National Standard for Information Sciences—Permanence of Paper for Printed Library Materials, ANSI Z39.48-1984.

Manufactured in the United States of America

Library of Congress Cataloging-in-Publication Data

Latin American philosophy : currents, issues, debates / edited by
Eduardo Mendieta.
p. cm.
Includes bibliographical references and index.
ISBN 0-253-34180-9 (alk. paper) — ISBN 0-253-21563-3 (pbk. : alk.
paper)
1. Philosophy, Latin American. I. Mendieta, Eduardo.
B1001 .L38 2003
199'.8—dc21
2002008760

1 2 3 4 5 08 07 06 05 04 03

Contents

PART 4.
(RE)DISCOVERING THE POLITICAL AND ETHICAL IN HISTORY

Acknowledgments

This book would not have been possible without the diligence and patience of all the contributors and, above all, their trust in the editor. I want to especially acknowledge the help, support, and guidance that I was fortunate to receive from two great philosophers, Enrique Dussel and Jorge J. E. Gracia. At the University of San Francisco, where all the work for this book was done, I was supported by a unique group of friends: Pedro Lange-Churión, Lois Ann Lorentzen, and David Batstone. I also want to acknowledge the financial support from the Faculty Development Fund at the University of San Francisco, which helped to pay for some of the translating for this book. I want to thank Elaine Katzenberg, editor at City-lights, for permission to use some images from the beautiful book by Guillermo Gómez-Peña, Enrique Chagoya, and Felicia Rice, *Codex Espangliensis*, which are now on the cover of this book. Acknowledgment is also due to David Pellauer, editor of *Philosophy Today*, for permission to reprint the essays by Jorge J. E. Gracia, Walter D. Mignolo, and Ofelia Schutte that first appeared in the journal. Above all, however, special thanks are due to Dee Mortensen, at Indiana University Press, who for years had been asking me for something, and who with great enthusiasm and verve took this project under her wing. I am also particularly indebted to Käthe Roth, who worked on this manuscript beyond the call of duty, and has thus made it more readable, and Jane Lyle, who saw it through production efficiently and in a timely fashion.

Eduardo Mendieta
Stony Brook, New York

Latin American
Philosophy

Introduction

EDUARDO MENDIETA

In the imaginary worlds of Jorge Luis Borges, from which spew forth—as if by magical incantation—improbable but not impossible creatures, antinomian but not ontological contradictions, there exist encyclopedias that, by virtue of having entries on improbable subjects, such as the cities of Tlön and Uqbar, make these subjects real. In Borges's world, books become gateways to other worlds or, as in the recent Pixar production *Monsters Inc.*, portals through which the dream world irrupts into the "real" world, which is but a fiction anyway. But the reality of the world system of book publication seems to operate in reverse fashion to Borges's world. In this "real" world of nicely packaged books, prodigiously advertised and peddled tomes, and hefty volumes of "companions," encyclopedias, and dictionaries, the absence of entries on Latin American philosophy and philosophers suggests, as if by conspiracy, that neither existed or exist.[1] An unsuspecting young philosopher, browsing wide-eyed, pliant and expectant, naive and eager, trudging and flipping through numerous pages of recently published volumes on everything from Asian philosophies to world philosophies, would walk away without having noticed what she was not looking for, which betrays precisely what these sorts of books are all about. As I have documented elsewhere, one of the most amazing things about the bibliographical work on philosophy published in English over the last decade or so is its utter silence about Latin American philosophy and philosophers.[2] Of course, if our young philosopher were to venture beyond these volumes, and beyond the mainstream venues of publication, she would find numerous books, articles, and anthologies on Latin American philosophy and its practitioners. There are therefore conceptual and philosophical reasons for publishing a book like the one that you, the reader, hold in your hands—reasons that have to do with the logic of exclusion and erasure that has resulted in a loud silence about an obvious topic. Further, this book is intended to be a resource that can be useful to both scholars and teachers.

Latin American philosophy has a history of at least five hundred years of production and an accumulation of reflections covering all major areas of philosophy. Thus, philosophical thought has a very long lineage on this side of the Atlantic. Latin America has generative sources in meso-American and pre-Columbian forms of wisdom. Aztec, Maya, and Inca thought have slowly filtered through not just the imaginary of Latin American peoples and their lingua francas, but also

through that of organic intellectuals, party functionaries, and university professors. In fact, some of the most interesting work in Latin American thought has
emerged from a confrontation with these indigenous philosophical traditions.
Latin American philosophy became the crucible for many philosophical currents
and methods that originated in Europe and were later forced into exile in the New
World. Some of these currents arrived in Latin America before they arrived in
North America. Thus, Latin American philosophy was and is the place for both
creative synthesis and innovative initiative. It has participated in and chronicled
the projects of continental and national liberation from European colonialism and
has grown to be the continental and spiritual sibling of North American liberal,
democratic, and revolutionary ideals. Finally, Latin American philosophy is one
of the primary veins of New World thinking, which combines Old World thinking with pre-Columbian thinking. The parallels with North America—that is, the
United States and Canada, with apologies to those who insist that Mexico is also
in North America—are unmistakable. As philosophers try to make sense of the
traditions, currents, and forms of thought that have emerged in the New World,
we will begin to speak of "American philosophy." From this geo-historical and
geo-political vantage point, Latin American philosophy is an integral chapter in
the history of American philosophy, along with those on pre-Columbian, American, and Canadian philosophies. In Latin America, as a continental unit, notwithstanding the internal subdivisions, we find a series of common preoccupa-
tions, themes, questions, even forms of writing and communicating (and here the
obvious parallel is so-called Continental philosophy, which can and should be
studied in terms of its geographical units—Germany, Italy, Spain, England,
France, and so on—without detracting from its unmistakable unity and identity).
The reasons for studying Latin American philosophy are indeed many, and only
obdurate ideological blindness and stubborn provincialism can render those of us
in the English-speaking academic and intellectual world immune to its challenges
and insights, as well as its vigor and creativity.

    Anthologies such as this one are not unlike city maps: they are circumscribed
by the aims of their potential users and designers. This book is aimed at English-
speaking audiences, who may use it to broaden or sharpen their knowledge of
Latin American thinking. But the goals of the work can be couched more simply:
to offer the reader a sampling of the most recent topical and creative work in philosophy being produced by Latin Americans, reflecting on Latin America, even if
they are not in Latin America. This is not a historically oriented anthology. It is
an anthology about what is most contemporary in Latin American thinking. Further, it is meant to interject in the debates about the sources and chronology of
Latin American philosophy by offering a version of the way that works of Latin
American philosophy should be analyzed. For this reason, this anthology introduces a new and tentative division of, or way of cataloguing, Latin American currents in philosophy.

    We can study Latin American philosophy, especially after the serious turns and
paradigm shifts it has undergone over the last two decades, under three subhead-

ings. I would like to call the first the *institutional* or *disciplinary* study of Latin American philosophy, by which I mean the orientation of philosophy as a university discipline, a *Fach*, a faculty, a discipline ensconced within the tree of knowledge, or the mapping of knowledges bequeathed to us by the French and German enlightenments. Under this rubric we find three types of works, or currents of thought, concerning questions about where Latin American philosophy has come from and where it is going. Following Jorge J. E. Gracia, arguably the don of Latin American philosophy in the U.S., these currents can be identified as universalist, culturalist, and critical.[3] The universalists resolutely reject the idea of a Latin American philosophy, for philosophy is about the universal, and the contingent and geographical do not enter into it. The culturalists affirm the existence of a Latin American philosophy, for all philosophy is its time and culture comprehended in thought. For the culturalist there is no universal philosophy, and to hold on to this view is to succumb to one of the most pernicious forms of ideology and self-delusion. The critical current affirms that there is no Latin American philosophy not because there cannot be one, but because, due to the historical baggage of colonialism and neo-imperialism, Latin Americans have not been able, or have not had the opportunity, to think of philosophy as Latin American. In other words, because Latin America was first a Spanish colony, and after independence came under the domination of France and the United States, its philosophy has reflected only the interests of the colonial and neocolonial empires.

Most of the debate about Latin American philosophy over the last one hundred years has taken place under the *institutional* or *disciplinary* approach. Its longevity and institutional dimension have made it productive and entrenched. Yet, its very institutional context and its narrow conception of what constitutes philosophy and the institutions of philosophy have made it rather ineffective in its treatment of the question. The possibility of and need for a Latin American philosophy is a meta-philosophical question, one that puts the very forms of crystallization of philosophy in jeopardy not just in Latin America, but also in the Western world. Indeed, it is the institutional and disciplinary orientation of these three currents, or schools, that has led to the juxtapositions that Gracia enumerates so well in *Hispanic/Latino Identity: A Philosophical Perspective* (1999). Samuel Beckett's Molloy, constantly waffling, I can, I can't, I can, I can't, comes to mind as one reads this work, for Gracia can be seen as saying, There is Latin American philosophy, but there can't be; there can't be, but there is.

It is precisely in response to the inability of the institutional and disciplinary approach to break through the stalemate on the question of the existence of Latin American philosophy that a second type of thinking has emerged within Latin American philosophy, which I would like to call *genealogical* and *anarchical*. This type of thinking is heterodox and heretical because it crosses all established and sacralized disciplinary borders between philosophy, sociology, political theory, cultural history, and the history of ideas, and because it suggests that the question "Is there a Latin American philosophy?" is less important and insightful than a question that is meant to remind us of Michel Foucault: "What are the institutional conditions for the possibility of asking these questions, and in tandem, what are the effects of asking whether there is, or should be, a Latin American philosophy?"[4] This new school of Latin American philosophy reflects as much the crises of Western philosophy as it does the maturation and internationalization of Latin American philosophical thought. The crises clearly have to do with the failure of the socialist and communist movements throughout Latin America, which are related to the Cold War and the concomitant crises in the discipline of area studies. For, just as disciplinary boundaries in American universities were drawn in accordance with Cold War imperatives—namely, détente and containment of the communist menace—in Latin America the agenda was set by similar geopolitical concerns. Area studies, it should be remembered, were those fields of study related to United States foreign policy. The idea was to prepare American scholars to provide in-depth and useful knowledge on and information about societies in what was then called the Third World—that is, potentially socialist nations. This model became anachronistic with the fall of the Berlin Wall and the Soviet Union.[5] The maturation and internationalization of Latin American philosophy, on the other hand, are related to the trans-nationalization of Latin American philosophers and intellectuals, some voluntarily exiled, others violently uprooted by dictatorships and dirty wars. These factors have led to a greater intellectual independence and rebelliousness on the part of a younger generation of thinkers, who have disavowed either the mantle of historical materialism or the protective flag of historicist Latin Americanism. Not surprisingly, this current's heterodoxy has had a rejuvenating effect on the study of that which it set out either to call into question or to dismantle altogether. Classical authors are unearthed and reread with a new focus: did they participate in the construction of certain disciplinary regimens that were complicit in colonial and national projects? Was their philosophy at the service of the state, even when it purported to stand against the state? The works of Carlos Rincón, Roberto Salazar Ramos, Beatriz González Stephan, and Santiago Castro-Gómez are examples of thinkers in this school.[6]

A third and final group has begun to surface on the intellectual horizon of Latin American philosophical thought, which I would like to call *geo-political* or *world-historical*. Like the genealogical and anarchical school, this school challenges the rigid disciplinary boundaries that have determined the ways in which the questions about the origins and purpose of Latin American philosophy get asked. But in contrast, it opts for a world-systems approach to the issue concerning the building blocks of knowledge. In an extremely provocative and generative fusion, thinkers in this tradition have brought together mid-century ideas on world history, expressed by foundational figures such as Darcy Ribeiro, Leopoldo Zea, José Gaos, and Germán Arciniegas, with work on the world system developed by Immanuel Wallerstein and his school at the Braudel Center in Binghamton, New York. For them the question is not simply, "Is there a Latin American philosophy?" but what kind of philosophy developed in Latin America during the twentieth century specifically in response to the global processes of decolonization, the Cold War, recolonization under international finance capitalism, and the emergence of post-

Occidentalist forms of thinking.[7] Notwithstanding the difference in approach from that of some thinkers in the critical school of thinking, there is continuity with this type of questioning and form of research. Thus, figures such as Enrique Dussel and Anibal Quijano, who otherwise might have been placed in the first school, have made a smooth transition to this new school of thinking. In fact, one may argue that they have been heading in this direction all along, but because of the lack of a more generalized lexicon, their message had been lost or misunderstood. Both Dussel and Quijano are veterans of a type of questioning that sought to place Latin American thought on a world-historical plane.[8] Perhaps in the near future, as a new generation of scholars and philosophers begins to develop, mature, and conceive of a greater America that includes all of its subcontinents, we will begin to think of Latin American and North American philosophies as chapters in a larger geo-political and world-historical school of American philosophy from this hemisphere.[9] This younger generation will read Emerson along with Rúben Darío, Peirce with Ingenieros, Dewey with Vasconcelos, Zea with Wilson, Rorty with Dussel, as they become so many canonical figures in one larger continental tradition.

This book is divided into four parts. The first part deals with the historiography of Latin American philosophy. Enrique Dussel provides a vast and detailed analysis of eight Latin American currents of thought and the problems that they address. His is perhaps the most comprehensive overview of philosophical production in Latin America in the twentieth century. The chapter is annotated with a chronology and an indicative bibliography, and it serves as a compass for future directions in Latin American philosophy.

The next part revisits the question, "Is there Latin American philosophy?" and goes on to ask, more critically, "Should there be?" This part brings together representatives of the three schools of Latin American thought discussed above. Jorge J. E. Gracia asks whether there can be "ethnic philosophies" in this age of the proliferation of both ethnic philosophies and continentally named philosophies (Asian, African, etc.). He takes Latin American philosophy as a special case to illustrate the problems and contradictions intrinsic to projects of ethnic philosophies. He advocates a "family resemblance" approach to the issue of ethnic philosophies, in which no essences are presupposed or postulated and what counts is the continuity of a historical experience and the stability of a series of philosophical concerns.

The essay by Santiago Castro-Gómez can be read as a manifesto for the genealogical or anarchical school of Latin American philosophy, and he provides the briefest, clearest, and most explicit description of the development of this school's philosophical agenda. The essay acts as a postscript to his scandalously untranslated critique of Latin American reason, which stands as one of the most important philosophical texts to have come out of Latin America in the last twenty-five years.[10]

Walter Mignolo raises questions about the relationship between Latin American philosophy and indigenous Latin American forms of thought. He contrasts

Latin America's situation with similar challenges faced by African philosophers, who contend with the question of what makes African philosophy *African*, especially if the philosophy produced in Africa by Africans continues to perpetuate investigation of the same philosophical ideas that European philosophy has enshrined and entombed in the mausoleums of its philosophical canon. Behind Mignolo's insightful juxtaposition is his concern with the crises of disciplinary boundaries and turfs. If philosophy is not, and can no longer be, what geo-politics dictated as the maps of knowledge, then why shouldn't Latin American philosophy acknowledge and benefit from its own sources? This is not a call to some form of Third World–oriented authenticity movement that can accept only what is indigenous; instead, it is a call for self-reflexivity on the part of practitioners of Latin American philosophy.[11]

The third part presents three chapters that differ in their subject matter and format. Alfonso de Toro focuses on the work of Jorge Luis Borges and argues for a nuanced reading of Borges's relationship to postmodern literary and philosophical production. De Toro details the literary techniques used by Borges and the way that they inspired, not only evocatively but also, and perhaps most especially, conceptually the work of postmodern theorists. De Toro's suggestion, to put it hyperbolically, although not entirely inaccurately, is not so much that post-structuralists, postmodernists, and deconstructivists found a perfect ally and exemplar in Borges's texts, but that, in many ways, these movements emerged in response to Borges. Borges was post-structuralist, postmodern, and a deconstructivist before such movements existed.

Amós Nascimento, a Brazilian philosopher, offers a carefully annotated discussion of recent debates on modernity and postmodernity in Brazil. He argues that Brazil's internal debates have helped to conceal a reality that is more fractious and complicated than many philosophers will acknowledge. Nascimento focuses on the question of racism—in particular, on Afro-Brazilian contributions to a prepostmodern Brazilian culture.

Ofelia Schutte takes up similar questions, but from the angle of postcolonial theory. In a gesture that might surprise some readers, Schutte urges familiarity with key Latin American philosophical and intellectual figures as foundational postcolonial figures. Her text acts as a double chastisement: to North American philosophers for fetishizing the Indian and African postcolonial, thus erasing the United States' painful colonial history, and to Latin American philosophers for failing to acknowledge their lineage within anti-colonial and postcolonial struggles.

The fourth and final part turns toward rediscovery of the political within Latin American thought. The three chapters gathered here come from an expanding library of Latin American works in political philosophy. The essay by Maria Herrera Lima looks at the constitutional challenges that the Zapatista movement presents to the Mexican government. The challenges are positive ones in Herrera's view, and represent the revitalization of the Mexican public sphere and the development of a new form of constitutional patriotism. Her goal is to relegitimate the Mexican commitment to the rule of law and democratic procedure.

Norbert Lechner's essay looks at the relationship between political culture and postmodernist sensibilities in the Latin American contexts. He states that while postmodernism might have catalyzed, at best, or given rise to, at worst, the end of a certain type of modernist thinking that allows for the emergence of new social actors, postmodernism as a historical and political sensibility might be hindering the emergence of a post-statist popular politics.

An essay by Beatriz González Stephan closes this part with an exquisite exhibition of what can be done with Foucauldian tools to rejuvenate the discourse of citizenship in the land of God and soccer nationalism. González's work is emblematic of a new type of research agenda that will challenge both the old schoolbook narratives and the mid-century identification by intellectuals with a national project of liberation. In her work, as well as works by others in her school, there is a turn toward social actors, away from the great *caudillos* and *letrados* of the colonial and national liberation periods.

While this selection of essays covers expansively and indicatively the ground of Latin American philosophy, essays by Franz Hinkelammert, on political economy and psycho-history; Luis Villoro, on cultural rights and the autonomy of peoples; Raúl Fornet-Betancourt, on inter-cultural dialogue and globalization; Miguel León-Portilla, on Nahuatl and Spanish; Iris Zavala, on Bakhtin, Lacan, and feminism; Octavio Ianni, on globalization and the enigmas of the world modernity; Hugo Zemelman, on social actors and forms of knowing; Mauricio Beuchot, on postmodernity, religion, and analogy; Roberto Salazar Ramos, on a Latin American post-philosophy; Renato Ortiz, on the artifices of a global culture; and Néstor Garcia Canclini, on the imagined globalization and the citizen as consumer, are just a few that could have contributed to a volume of this nature. Indeed, Latin American philosophy exists and it is prodigious in its production and creativity. It is only that the encyclopedias, dictionaries, and books that summarize or survey world philosophy have unknowingly orchestrated the exclusion of a rigorous tradition of thinking that so incites and challenges us in the English-speaking world.

NOTES

1. See Johan Heilbron, "Towards a Sociology of Translation: Book Translation as a Cultural World System," *European Journal of Social Theory* 2, no. 4 (1999): 429–444; André Schiffrin, *The Business of Books: How International Conglomerates Took Over Publishing and Changed the Way We Read* (London: Verso, 2000); and Eduardo Mendieta, "Of Language and Encyclopedias: On the Institutions of Philosophy and the Geopolitics of Knowledge" (forthcoming).

2. Eduardo Mendieta, "Is There Latin American Philosophy?" *Philosophy Today*, SPEP Supplement 43 (1999): 50–61.

Eduardo Mendieta

3. Jorge J. E. Gracia, *Hispanic/Latino Identity: A Philosophical Perspective* (Malden, Mass.: Blackwell, 1999), chapter 6, "The Search for Identity: Latin America and Its Philosophy," 130ff.

4. For an exemplification of this new school, see Benigno Trigo, ed., *Foucault and Latin America: Appropriations and Deployments of Discoursive Analysis* (New York: Routledge, 2001).

5. See Noam Chomsky et al., *The Cold War and the University: Toward an Intellectual History* (New York: New Press, 1997), and Immanuel Wallerstein et al., *Open the Social Sciences: Report of the Gulbenkian Commission on the Restructuring of the Social Sciences* (Stanford, Calif.: Stanford University Press, 1996).

6. See also Santiago Castro-Gómez, "The Challenge of Postmodernity to Latin American Philosophy," in Pedro Lange-Churión and Eduardo Mendieta, eds., *Latin America and Postmodernity: A Contemporary Reader* (Amherst, N.Y.: Humanity Books, 2001), 123–154, and "Latinamericanismo, modernidad, globalización. Prolegómenos a una critica postcolonial de la razón," in Santiago Castro-Gómez and Eduardo Mendieta, eds., *Teorías sin disciplina. Latinamericanismo, poscolonialidad y globalización en debate* (Mexico and San Francisco: Porrua and the University of San Francisco, 1998), 169–205.

7. On the notion of post-Occidentalism, see Fernando Coronil, "Beyond Occidentalism: Toward Nonimperial Geohistorical Categories," *Cultural Anthropology* 11, no. 1 (1996): 51–87.

8. See Walter Mignolo, "Dussel's Philosophy of Liberation: Ethics and the Geopolitics of Knowledge," in Linda Martín Alcoff and Eduardo Mendieta, eds., *Thinking from the Underside of History: Enrique Dussel's Philosophy of Liberation* (Lanham, Md.: Rowman & Littlefield, 2000), 27–50. See also his wonderful introduction to Walter Mignolo, ed., *Capitalismo y geopolítica del Conocimiento. El eurocentrismo y la filosofía de la liberación en del debate intellectual contemporáneo* (Buenos Aires and Durham, N.C.: Ediciones del Signo and Duke University Press, 2001), 9–53.

9. See Mario Sáenz, ed., *Latin American Philosophy and Globalization* (Lanham: Rowman & Littlefield, forthcoming), a collection of texts that further testify to this tradition within Latin American philosophy. See also Eduardo Mendieta, "From Modernity, through Postmodernity, to Globalization: Mapping Latin America," in Alfonso de Toro, Claudia Gatzemeir, and Cornelia Siber, eds., *Transversalidad y Transdisciplinaridad: Estrategias discursivas posmodernas y postcoloniales en Latinoamericana* (Frankfurt am Main: Verveurt Verlag. forthcoming).

10. Santiago Castro-Gómez, *Crítica de la razón latinoamericana* (Barcelona: Puvill Libros, 1996).

11. In addition to the texts by Coronil and Mignolo, see also the wonderful collection of texts in Alvaro Félix Bolaños and Gustavo Verdesio, eds., *Colonialism Past and Present: Reading and Writing about Colonial Latin America Today* (Albany: SUNY Press, 2001).

Part 1.
On the Historiography
of Latin American
Philosophy

1. Philosophy in Latin America in the Twentieth Century: Problems and Currents

ENRIQUE DUSSEL

This chapter is organized according to the most significant currents of Latin American philosophy in the twentieth century. I will analyze the central problems and main philosophers of each current, although I will have to leave out many names. At the end of the chapter is a minimal and indicative general bibliography, arranged by country—even though I did not treat the theme from a national perspective—and philosophical current. The chronology may be useful to readers who are new to the subject.

1. GENERAL PANORAMA[1]

In Latin America at the beginning of the twentieth century, a positivist philosophy (of Comtean inspiration, but subsequently Spencerian or Haeckelian) was dominant, articulated for hegemonic minorities of political society who had established the liberal state in the second half of the nineteenth century. The anti-positivist reactions (see section 2 of this chapter)—vitalist (inspired by Henry Bergson), anti-rationalist (departing from Schopenhauer or Pascal), historicist (José Ortega y Gasset), and traditional (Third Scholastic with influences from the universities of Louvain and Freiburg)—established Latin American university philosophy. These "founders," in the sense of Francisco Romero,[2] in some fashion identified themselves with the nascent national and industrial bourgeoisie (in countries such as Argentina, Mexico, Brazil, Peru, and Colombia) or with populist movements (such as the Mexican revolution of 1910 or Cárdenas's movement from 1934 on, Hipólito Irigoyen's radical party in Argentina in 1918, Perón's party from 1946 on, or Getulio Vargas's nationalism in Brazil from 1930 on).

The founders' consciousness was sundered by a "lack of focus," to use Miró Quesada's expression:[3] "Latin Americans who gave themselves to the activity of philosophizing could understand what they read. But they could not give a complete account *of what they did not comprehend*."[4] They lived in a non-European world, but they reflected a philosophy for which reality was European. This "lack of focus" made Latin American philosophical reflection ambiguous.[5]

The process evolved in what Miró Quesada called a "second generation,"[6] or "normalization," which began a "bifurcation" between a current (see section 3) inspired by Heideggerian ontology (e.g., Carlos Astrada, Wagner de Reyna) and one oriented by Husserlian phenomenology (e.g., Miguel Reale, Miguel Angel Virasoro, Luis Juan Guerrero). The latter had a certain impact and formed the basis for a school whose founders also included axiologists, personalist anthropologists, metaphysicians, and thinkers with other points of view.

In the early twentieth century, a current of philosophers followed neo-scholasticism (see section 4), through a revalorization of Thomas of Aquinas; in the thirties this current turned nationalistic in political philosophy. In the fifties, it was divided because of the personalist movement (inspired by Maritain or Mounier); some became earnest collaborators in military dictatorships, while others opened themselves up to new and creative Latin American philosophical currents.

After the nineteenth century, with the rise of anarcho-syndicalist movements and in contact with the First and Second Internationals, socialist and, later, Marxist thinking (see section 5) emerged with Juan B. Justo. José Carlos Mariátegui formulated the most creative version of Marxism in the twenties; shortly thereafter, Cesar Guardia Mayorga also became known as a Marxist; frontism and World War II weakened the movement. The Cuban revolution had an impact on all of Latin American philosophy in the sixties; Adolfo Sánchez Vázquez elevated it to the stature of problematic during a period in which Althusserianism reigned (in the seventies); and today it is embattled in the crisis produced by the events of 1989.

From within Husserlian phenomenological or ontological thinking (Leopoldo Zea) emerged a problematization of Latin America as a historical question to be reconstructed with meaning (Arturo Ardao, Arturo Roig) and as a problematic to be defined and developed (Abelardo Villegas). This led to the birth of a strong current that formulated "Latin America" as an object of philosophical reflection (see section 6). This "third generation," pressed to create and confirm an authentic Latin American identity, formed a school that was vigorously promulgated throughout the continent.

Facing the methodological difficulties of the Husserlian and Marxist currents after World War II and under Anglo-Saxon influence (Francisco Miró Quesada, Gregorio Klimoski, Mario Bunge), some thinkers (Luis Villoro, Fernando Salmerón, Alejandro Rossi) undertook epistemological studies and philosophical "analysis" in search of "strict rigor" (see section 7) . This current made new contributions in universal philosophical thinking and generally elevated the level of philosophical precision on the continent.

From diverse tributaries (phenomenological ontology, Latinamericanism, and the Frankfurt School), philosophy of liberation was born, coinciding with a triple diagnostic. First, there was a perception of a lack of "rigor" and "authenticity" (this was Augusto Salazar Bondy's position). Second, there was an awareness of the need for "militancy" (Osvaldo Ardiles) as an articulation of the theory-praxis dialectic. Finally, the misery of the great majority, as expressed in popular movements—student, political, social, ecological, anti-racist, and so on—was defined as a theme and context from the end of the sixties on, and before the military dictatorships—from 1964 on—in Brazil (see section 8). The movement elaborated its own discourse (Enrique Dussel, Juan C. Scannone), although it was divided into different points of view. Meanwhile, Latin American feminist philosophy produced its own discourse of liberation (e.g., Graciela Hierro).

2. ANTI-POSITIVIST PHILOSOPHIES: THE "FOUNDERS"[7]

In 1900, José Enrique Rodó published *Ariel*, a true symbol of the change of century.[8] This hermeneutic narrative demarcation of the cultural difference between Anglo-Saxon America (which a couple of years before, in 1898, had staged military occupations of Cuba and Puerto Rico) and Latin America was to traverse the entire century. "Ariel" is the spirit (the new philosophy, Latin America); "Caliban" is technology, instrumental rationality, and materiality (philosophical positivism, Anglo-Saxon America): "Thus, the vision of an America *de-Latinized* of its own will, without the extortion of the conquest, and later regenerated in the image of and with a resemblance to the archetype of the North, already floats in the dreams of many who are sincerely interested in our future."

Cuba seemed to be in a similar situation in the late nineteenth century as in the late twentieth century, as we can read in José Martí: "There is another, more sinister plan than any we have known up to now in our history, and it is the iniquity of precipitating the island into war, in order to have the pretext to intervene there. [. . .] Nothing more cowardly exists in the annals of free peoples."[9] The failure of the Latin American governments that had been peripherally integrated with the expansion of capitalism at the end of the nineteenth century (the Mexican Porfiriato, the Brazilian republic, Julio Roca's Argentina, criticized by the radical generation of the 1890s) was analogous to the failure of its militant ideology: philosophical positivism. The reaction to each was equally virulent. Among the philosophical figures were innovative thinkers and university professors with the pedagogical vocation of founders. All of them broke new ground. They intended to write not for philosophers, but for non-philosophers, propaedeutically, in order to invoke the vocation of thinking. In some cases, as in that of the Mexicans, their reaction to capitalism and positivism was a philosophical-political response that was a true articulation of the revolutionary movement of the moment. Nevertheless, their philosophies contained clear arguments against positivism.

Let us look at some central figures and philosophical positions of this "first generation" of the twentieth century. The first was Alejandro Deustua, who received his doctorate in 1872, although he occupied the chair of aesthetics at San Marcos University in Lima only in 1888. Prior to the advent of positivism, he was trained in its doctrine, though he was never tempted by its proposals. In reality, he was its first frontal attacker. At the beginning of the twentieth century he departed for

France (the Mecca of Latin American philosophy in the nineteenth century) and got to know Henry Bergson personally. He published his first work fairly late (when he was sixty), between 1919 and 1922, in two volumes: *Las ideas de orden y libertad en la historia del pensiamento humano* (The ideas of order and freedom in the history of human thought).[10] This work had a great influence on the new generation. Mariano Ibérico, decidedly a positivist, along with Deustua, brought about a definitive change by writing his thesis in 1916 on Bergson's philosophy.[11] Deustua went from an aesthetics of order and freedom to an ethics of value (the two-volume *Las sistemas de moral* [The systems of morality], published between 1938 and 1940). He knew the work of Krause, Wundt, Bergson, and Croce, and he was a true philosopher. Aesthetics is the contemplative moment; ethics, the actualizing moment (although inspired by *Les deux sources de la morale et de la religion* [The two sources of morality and religion]), he had his own theses: aesthetic freedom becomes practical solidarity, in the organic order of life, as a metaphysical realization of values. In the end, "In concordance with his attitude toward Peruvian politics and his social perspective, Deustua's pedagogical reflection culminates in aristocratism. Since his confidence in this selection of the spirit was complete, he believed that the salvific formula of national life was moralized education, radiating from the elite, and only the elite."[12]

Carlos Vaz Ferreira,[13] educated by Spencerian positivists, wrote in 1908, "Of Spencer's work, in itself, little remains. But today, can anyone be sure that he has not made use of it?"[14] The emancipated positivist retained a clear respect for science and practiced rigorous logic, but showed that it is impossible not to take recourse to metaphysics in his 1910 work, *Lógica viva* (Living logic). Following on from William James, Bergson, and even Stuart Mill, Vaz Ferreira related language to thought. His arguments against the positivism of the previous century *mutatis mutandis* served to show the limits of the analytic positivism of the twentieth century. In no way, however, does he fall into irrationalism: "Reason is not everything: reason [ought to be] complemented by feeling and imagination, but never forced, nor diminished, nor despised."[15] His was thus an anti-positivist vitalist rationalism of great currency,[16] powerful ethical structure, and rigorous argumentation, expressed by a strict thinker.

Alejandro Korn[17] (whose doctoral dissertation was titled *Crimen y Locura* [Crime and madness]) began as a professor of the history of philosophy in the philosophy faculty in Buenos Aires in 1906.[18] In *De San Agustín a Bergson* (From St. Augustine to Bergson), he dealt, on the one hand, with Augustine, Spinoza, Pascal (who enjoyed a great reputation with members of this generation), Keyserling, and Bergson, and, on the other, with Kant (he dedicated the course that he taught in 1924 to Kant and founded the Argentinean Kant Society), Hegel, and Croce. With the first group, in the voluntarist-vitalist current, he contrasted creative life with positivist mere matter; Kant and dialectical thinking allowed him to question the naively stated object of the empiricist, assuming the affirmation of science (Einstein delivered some lectures and gave some courses in Buenos Aires in 1925) and the freedom of the subject. Vitalist-transcendental thinking (very similar to that of Vaz Ferreira, although with less systematic penetration) constituted a categorical horizon that enabled development of a rigorous argument against the naive determinism of the positivists: "Economic freedom, domination over the objective world, ethical freedom, and self-control constitute, together, human freedom. [. . .] It is not the struggle for existence that is is the eminent principle, but the struggle for freedom."[19] This was Argentina before its identity crisis. Coriolano Alberini deserves mention here.

The Mexican revolution in 1910 was both a Latin American and a global event. Antonio Caso took a militant and destructive pickaxe to the positivism of Porfirio Díaz, the dictator of the "scientists"—the Mexican ideological current of the nineteenth century. Educated in positivism, Caso and other young philosophers founded *Ateneo de la Juventud* in 1909. In addition to the authors studied by other above-mentioned philosophers (especially Bergson and the North American pragmatists, but not Kant or Hegel), Antonio Caso read the vitalist works of Schopenhauer, Nietzsche, Tolstoy, and Driesch: "The mechanism of the universe maintains itself through *hunger and love*, as Schiller sang. . . . According to Bergson, instead of saying *homo sapiens*, one ought to say *homo faber*. Intelligence, an elegant solution to the problem of life, is the faculty of the creation of tools, instruments of action."[20] Existence as economy tends to the reproduction of life; existence as charity is the creative transcendental impulse, but in the final instance existence is an aesthetic creation: "In short, the scale of human value is this: the more one sacrifices and the more difficult it is to sacrifice the purely animal life [Porfirist positivism] with disinterested ends, until one arrives—from aesthetic contemplation and simple good actions—at heroic action, the more noble one is."[21] And inverting the Nietzschean meaning of the *Uebermensch*, Caso arrives at the opposite conclusion: "Nietzsche's superman, conceived in all of his magnitude of sacrifice [as was experienced daily during the Mexican revolution, in which more than one million died], in all of his desire for the elevation of life, has everything that is noble about being Christian."[22] As in all the above examples, this is an aesthetics that culminates in a creative, emancipatory ethics. It is no abstract philosophical reflection; it is a militant philosophy, like that of the late-in-life convert to Catholicism José Vasconcelos, who became the secretary of education during the national revolutionary government. Like previous philosophies, Vasconcelos joined the popular nationalist political movements—this is why the government called upon great Marxist artists, such as Rivera and Orozco, to paint ancestral Mexican motifs in public buildings. Inverting racist naturalism (which gave supremacy to the white race), Vasconcelos defends the mestizo identity in *La raza cósmica* (The cosmic race). Human life is action and ought to be organized through ethical behavior. From Schopenhauer to Hindu philosophy, Vasconcelos writes,

> Clearly seen and speaking truthfully, the European barely recognizes us, and we do not recognize ourselves in him. Neither would it be legitimate to talk of a return to the native . . . because we do

not recognize ourselves in the native nor does the Indian recognize us. By this fate, Spanish America is the new par excellence: newness not only of territory, but also of the soul.[23]

The disturbing Brazilian thinker Raimundo Farías Brito had no use for the critique of positivism. The Catholic Jackson de Figueiredo was part of the neoscholastic renaissance; he died too young.[24] Also worthy of mention are Enrique José Molina,[25] who introduced Bergson into Chile and published *Filósofos Americanos* (American philosophers) as early as 1913,[26] and Carlos Arturo Torres from Colombia.[27] There were many others.

This generation of "founders" has great relevance. They were philosophers who thought about their reality with conceptual tools that they forged, frequently autodidactically, and who ought to be rediscovered for contemporary reflection.

3. EXISTENTIAL ONTOLOGY OR PHENOMENOLOGY: THE "NORMALIZATION"

We now turn to a "second generation." These philosophers were professors of philosophy endowed with the formal exigencies of the academic vocation. They were inspired by phenomenology, in its diverse forms, and formulated the philosophy that predominated in Latin American thinking until the end of the sixties.

It must be underscored that there were two different styles of phenomenology. It is my opinion that these styles are the source of the "bifurcation." Carlos Astrada wrote about them, "Between phenomenological idealism (Husserl) and existential metaphysics (Heidegger), there lies a fundamental difference. Due to a radicalization of the notion of *existence*, Heidegger arrives at a conception of philosophy and its task that diverges from, and even opposes, those that Husserl considers fertilized rigorously by phenomenology."[28] Astrada showed that Husserl remained imprisoned within the horizon of the object of the consciousness-entity, while Heidegger was open to the totality of the "world" where entities confront us as phenomena. This "world" was to be discovered by those of my generation as "that which is Latin American."

One style, then, was more linked to Heideggerian ontology,[29] which gives primacy to being in the historical world, with practical relations that are national, and even popular (its inheritance[30] was to be Latinamericanist thinking [see section 6], and liberation philosophy [see section 8]). The other, more indebted to Husserlian phenomenology, which gives primacy to the subject before the object as eidos (e.g., F. Romero), of greater solipsistic inspiration (its inheritance was to be, among others, epistemological and analytic thinking [see section 7]). Both occurred simultaneously and in parallel, in mutual fertilization and communication.

In the first style, against Rodó's *Ariel*, Aníbal Ponce rose up in defense of Calibán, who now represented the Latin American people, the dominated classes (the humanist Ariel had failed).[31] In fact, the economic crisis of 1929 was echoed in major political changes from 1930 on throughout the continent (Roosevelt himself compromised the state with an active Keynesian-style intervention). Heideggerian thought had a profound impact on Latin America for reasons similar to those that determined its appearance in Germany: a telluric-historical interpretation was linked to the strengthening of the project of a national bourgeoisie[32] and to the simultaneous and massive emergence, in the more developed countries of Latin America, of a working class. Between 1930 and 1940, a group of thinkers[33] exalted nature, geography, and the Indian. Franz Tamayo wrote,

> [In Bolivia] the earth makes the man [. . .] colossal steep mountains that are like natural fortresses and also like natural prisons [. . .] the soul of the earth has gone through the country with all of its greatness, its solitude, that sometimes seem the cause of its desolation and its fundamental suffering. [. . .] Díaz, Melgarejos, Guzmán Blanco, Castro, Rosas, and others [. . .] all dominators, vanquishers, and hegemons, and all have the mestiza mark on the forehead, and the energy that they represent is of Indian origin—it is the blood of the Indian that surges up in adventurous and young blood.[34]

On the strictly philosophical plane, Latin American students who had studied in Germany or Switzerland (for the first time superseding the French horizon) between the two wars, with Heidegger (Carlos Astrada and Alberto Wagner de Reyna), with Cassirer (Nimio de Anquín), or in Zurich (Luis Juan Guerrero), began a Latin American ontological reflection. Some opted for an affirmative attitude, an assumptive, positive vision of that which is American, which was to have a long history. Carlos Astrada's *El mito gaucho* (The gaucho myth) was related to the nationalism of 1946—Astrada replaced Romero, who in turn replaced Astrada in 1956[35]—revives the figure of the "gaucho Martín Fierro" as an ancestral, authentic, proper phenomenon. It is not strange that he later turned to Marxism following an ontological progression from Heidegger to Hegel, in the fashion of the Frankfurt school—he demanded a return to history in order to subsume negations. In this way, the gaucho (cowboy)[36] became the proletariat as subject of history—in the Marxist tradition of José Aricó, as we will see.

Other ontologists analyzed with a tragic attitude the negation of that which is Latin American in many varied ways. Félix Schwartzmann, in Chile, wrote about that which is "bereft of history," the "savage lands," and the "ontological vacuum."[37] In Venezuela, Ernesto Mayz Vallenilla wrote about the merely turned toward the future as "expectation," before "the something that approximates" us, as "what is to come."[38] Nimio de Aquín in Córdoba pondered the pre-Socratic aural entity without past guilt, the "pure future."[39] And H. A. Murena wrote of the "original sin" of having been expelled from Europe: "For a time we inhabited a land fertilized by the spirit that is called Europe, and suddenly we were expelled from it and fell into another land, raw, empty of spirit, to which we gave the name

America."[40] The *criollo* (white child of immigrants) did not recognize the Amerindian, colonial world of the "inward land": he negated a millenary history. Thinking along the same lines were Edmundo O'Gorman, who spoke of the "discovery" of 1492 as the "invention of America" by Western culture, which did not notice the interpretation of the "discovery" by the indigenous peoples as an "invasion" of *Cemanahuac* ("the whole world" in Aztec);[41] and Alberto Caturelli,[42] for whom to be American was "to be a brute," without history, "immature."[43]

José Gaos, a Spaniard "trans-territorialized" to Mexico, similarly departed from Heidegger in order to situate the problem of the Latin American and Mexican. His translation into Spanish of *Being and Time* is more than a mere translation; it is in itself a historic philosophical work. Furthermore, from the ontological horizon he demonstrated the importance of thinking "*one's own* world," whence originated the Latinamericanist current (e.g., L. Zea)—a reconstruction carried out with such seriousness and extreme rigor that he passed this attitude on to his disciples, who carried his ideas forward into analytic philosophy (e.g., L. Villoro, F. Salmerón).

Alberto Wagner de Reyna[44] was educated in Lima, and he later studied with Hartmann, Spranger, and Heidegger in Germany. In 1937 he defended his doctoral dissertation, *La ontología fundamental de Heidegger* (The fundamental ontology of Heidegger). His mature work, *Analogía y evocación* (Analogy and evocation),[45] concerns Kierkegaardian and Christian interpretations of Heidegger's thought. His philosophical stature is such that he would have to be situated at the level of Carlos Astrada and José Gaos.

Danilo Cruz Vélez,[46] who studied with Heidegger in Freiburg in 1951, manifested a transition to Husserlian style in his main work, *Filosofía sin supuestos: De Husserl a Heidegger* (Philosophy without presuppositions: from Husserl to Heidegger) and *De Hegal a Marcuse* (From Hegel to Marcuse, an academic philosophical work. He did not reflect on the theme of the American.

Thinkers of the other style, phenomenological, axiological, more solipsistic (following closely, as mentioned above, Husserl, Scheler, or Hartmann), achieved a broad presence in the academic world as "professors of philosophy." Their most important representative was without question Francisco Romero;[47] if one also takes into account "his not written work"—his teaching and his influence on other philosophers—his importance becomes evident. In fact, thanks to his contacts, Romero launched, from Washington, D.C., a collection of publications on Latin American thought. He intended a project of rigorous philosophy in the continent, and his enthusiasm and initiative inspired a whole generation. His theoretical works[48] are closely inspired by Hartmann's ontology, by Scheler's position on the place of the human being in the cosmos, and by the distinction between individual and person unique to the personalists (especially Jacques Maritain). All of this stood out in his transcendentalism of the spirit and values.

In Argentina a group of great philosophers was working in this tradition. Luis Juan Guerrero, who wrote an important book on aesthetics,[49] with a decisive Heideggerian influence but also with sources in Husserl, Merleau-Ponty, and others, which makes his description of the operative constitution of the being of the work of art a philosophical example not superseded in the continent. Miguel Angel Virasoro, Vicente Fatone, Angel Vasallo, Risieri Frondizi, Arture García Astrada, Carlos Ceriotto, and, more recently, Ricardo Maliandi (influenced by Hartmann and later a student of Apel's transcendental pragmatics) are some of the other philosophers who should be mentioned.

In Brazil, Miguel Reale introduced the phenomenological movement, in the tradition of the philosophy of law, in an "axiological personalism" linked to the "tridimensionality of the doctrine of law." Vicente Ferreira da Silva analyzed phenomenologically the spheres of axiology, formal logic, metaphysics, and philosophy of religion. Emmanuel Carneiro Leão needs to be mentioned because of his creative ontological thinking.

It would be fitting to mention here, although his thinking supersedes phenomenology, the Mexican Eduardo Nicol, whose *Metafísica de la expresión* (Metaphysics of expression) is one of the most significant works of Latin American thought. Luis Villoro's *Estudios sobre Husserl* (Studies on Husserl) (1975), and Ramón Xirau's works similarly indicate the cultivation of phenomenology by an extensive number of professors.

Francisco Miró Quesada made his debut in 1941 with *Sentido del movimiento fenomenológico* (Meaning of the phenomenological movement).[50] He was never won over to the ontological style and remained at the phenomenological level of a rationalism self-conscious of its limits and of the need for a history of Latin American thought.

A phenomenological generation formed in Germany in the sixties. Guillermo Hoyos, a Colombian, strictly dominated the methodology (which passed from Husserl to Heidegger, and then to Habermas in the present day) and produced a critique of scientific positivism, subsuming it and attempting to transplant it within a more critical horizon.[51] In a more hermeneutic line, the notable Colombian philosopher Carlos Gutiérrez, elected in the nineties to the presidency of the Inter-American Society of Philosophy, must also be highlighted. The Venezuelan Alberto Rosales,[52] the Uruguayan Juan Llambias Acevedo, the Chilean Juan de Dios Vial Larraín, and the Colombian Daniel Herrera Restrepo, who was educated in Louvain, deserve a special place in this analysis.

4. PHILOSOPHY PRACTICED BY CHRISTIANS[53]

Since the sixteenth century, but especially since the end of the nineteenth century, Christians in Latin America have been cultivators of philosophy. I present briefly the complex and little-studied problematic of this tradition, which is relatively independent from the other currents due to its links to extended ecclesiastical institutions. It is a matter of philosophical thought practiced by Christians outside of the context of the church, which is one of the oldest institutions in the mestizo continent. Schools of philosophy were founded by the Dominicans in

Santo Domingo in 1538, and in Nichoacán, Mexico, in 1541. The first philosophical "normalization" (with master's and doctoral degrees in philosophy) took
place in the universities in Mexico City and Lima in 1553, and bachelor's degrees
were granted in dozens of centers, from Guadalajara and Durango to Santiago,
Mendoza, and Buenos Aires during the colonial period.[54] Similarly, in the twentieth century, dozens of Christian centers of learning cultivated philosophical studies—a tradition that dates back to the schools of Alexandria in the Roman empire,
the Muslims (from the rediscovery of Aristotle in the ninth century A.D.) or those
of the Latin medieval period, which maintained the autonomy of reason from
faith. Thousands of youths learned and appreciated philosophy through this path.
In general, European neo-scholasticism (in the style of Desiderio Mercier or Joseph
Gredt) by Italian, Belgian, and German authors was taught, repeated, and cri-
tiqued. Mercier's work *Programa analitico razonado de Metafísica* (Reasoned analytic
program of metaphysics) was translated in 1923 in Lima and had several editions.

The first stage was a frank anti-positivist struggle (as with the "founders" ana-
lyzed above in section 2). José Soriano de Souza, who received his doctorate from
Louvain, published, in Recife, Brazil, *Lições de filosofía elementar racional e moral*
(Lectures of elemental rational and moral philosophy), in which he opposed the
"Cartesian-Cusanian" philosophical position. In 1908 the Benedictines, following
Miguel Kruze, founded a faculty of philosophy in São Paulo,which grants degrees
recognized by Louvain. In Argentina, Mamerto Esquiú, in Córdoba, and Jacionto
Ríos made their arguments against positivism. In Colombia, the conservative
hegemony (1886–1930) made sure that Catholic thinking occupied the faculties
of philosophy during this period. In Uruguay, Mariano Soler, who had an acceptable European education, frontally attacked positivism.[55] The most distinguished
of this group was Rafael María Carrasquilla,[56] founder of the School of Rosario; he
seconded Leon XIII with respect to the movement to return to Thomas of Aquinas, and he published *Lecciones de metafísica y Ética* (Lectures of metaphysics and
ethics) in 1914.

Around 1920, faculties of philosophy began to be founded around the continent
(the Catholic university in Lima, in 1917; the Javeriana in Bogota, the faculty of
philosophy of the Benedictines in São Paulo, the Centreo Vital in Rio de Janeiro,
and the "Courses on Catholic Culture" in Buenos Aires, in 1922; San Miguel in
Buenos Aires, in 1931; and Medellin, in 1936). Journals (such as *Vozes*, founded
in Brazil in 1907; *Estudios*, Buenos Aires, 1911; *El Ensayo*, Bogota, 1916; *A Ordem*,
Rio, 1921; *Arx*, Córdoba, 1924; *Criterio*, Buenos Aires, 1928; *Revista Javeriana*, Bogotá, 1934; and *Stromata*, San Miguel, 1937) found an attentive reading public.

A critical moment was the Spanish crisis of 1936, which divided Christian democratic thinking (which was inspired first by Maritain and later by Emmanuel
Mounier), from which the Christian renovation evolved in the late sixties, from
the decidedly anti-Maritain thinking that supported Franquism, whose representatives ended up collaborating in the military dictatorships of the seventies.[57]

Thus there emerged Catholic thinkers such as Tomás Casares, César Pico, Luis
Guillermo Martínez Villada, Enrique Pita, Ismael Quiles, Raúl Echauri, and Diego

Pró in Argentina. The prototype of noncritical realist metaphysics was Octavio Derisi. In opposition, Juan Ramón Sepich stands out for his acuity and profundity, not soured with right-wing political attitudes, as does Guido Soaje Ramos, a specialist in ethics. Gonzalo Casas was a distinguished critical teacher of young philosophers. Alceu de Amorso Lima and Leonel France in Brazil; Víctor A. Belaúnde in Peru;[58] Ignacio Bravo Betancourt, José M. Gallegos Rocafull, and Antonio Gómez Robledo—noted translator of Aristotle—in Mexico; and Clarence Finlayson Elliot in Chile would join many of the above-mentioned thinkers, such as José Vasconcelos, Antonio Caso, Wagner de Reyna, and Nimio de Aquín, who declared themselves Christian. Together, they constitute a significant group of twentieth-century Latin American thinkers.

In the late twentieth century, Manuel Domínguez Camargo divided Christian thinkers in Latin America into three groups. First, those who are members of the Inter-American Society of Catholic Philosophers (A. Caturelli, Stanislaus Ladusans, O. Derisi) protect a true tradition and attempt to refute Marx, Nietzsche, Freud, Sartre, and others. Second are those who think that philosophy and faith do not mix with or negate each other (in the sense of Blondel's *The Philosophical Exigencies of Christianity*), who are the majority and who manifest an autonomous rationality. Finally, others start from the second position and "make an effort to find a new point of departure, elaborate a new language, or construct a new type of philosophical discourse that is at the level of contemporary rationality"[59] that is critical and Latin American.

5. MARXIST PHILOSOPHY[60]

Marxist thought had great relevance in Latin America, a continent featuring dependent capitalism, where extreme poverty (absolute and relative: there are more poor who are poorer) continued to grow throughout the twentieth century. Marx, as a philosopher-economist, is perceived to have formulated a critique of the reality of a suffering people. Marxist philosophy therefore has political, social, and ethical meaning.

In 1846, when Esteban Echevarría wrote *Dogma socialista* (Socialist dogma), there was no comprehension of what socialism was to mean to Latin America. Juan B. Justo, who translated *Capital* in 1895, had founded the magazine *La Vanguardia* the previous year. He organized the International Socialist Party in Argentina in 1896, and in 1909 he published *Teoría y práctica de la historia* (Theory and practice of history), in defense of a social-democratic thesis. Ricardo Flores Magón represented anarchist utopian thinking and, in the magazine *Regeneración* and the Liberal Fraternal Union of 1906, struggled against the Porfiriato in Mexico.

Among the first Marxists was Luis Emilio Recabarren, founder of the Socialist Worker's Party of Chile in 1912, and of the Communist Party in 1922. He wrote in 1910,

Where are my fatherland and my freedom? Did I have them in my childhood, when instead of going to school I had to go to the shop to sell my meager child's strength to the insatiable capitalist? Do I have them today, when the entire product of my work will be absorbed by capital without my enjoying an atom of my production? I aver that the fatherland is the fulfilled and complete home, and that freedom exists only when this home exists.[61]

Recabarren and Julio Antonio Mella, founder of the Communist Party of Cuba in 1925, who died very young in 1929, ought to be considered members of the generation of founders of Marxist critical thought in the continent. It is known that once the Third International was formed in 1919, the communist parties rapidly copied the Soviet formulations and fell into Eurocentrism in their diagnoses, and later, with Stalin, into an ideological ontological materialist dogmatism. This did not prevent the emergence of great philosophers who knew how to think in adverse situations. José Carlos Mariátegui was the most prominent, as he integrated Marx's ideas with theses extracted from the vitalism of Bergson and from the mythical-political thought of Sorel. He posited that the "Indian problem" was central to Peru and other Latin American peoples. He did not fear contradicting an ideology that had already begun to fossilize into a European-style unadulterated "classism." When, in 1928, his publishing company, Amauta, published *Siete Ensayos sobre la realidad peruvia* (Seven interpretive essays on Peruvian reality), he was greeted as the most original and least dogmatic Latin American Marxist of the first part of the twentieth century. He was harshly criticized during his lifetime, and after his death he was stigmatized as having been a "reformist populist" by the already triumphant Stalinist party in Peru. In a famous political-philosophical text, he wrote,

> The nationalism of the European nations—where nationalism and conservatism have been identified and co-substantiated—has imperialist goals. It is reactionary and anti-socialist. But the nationalism of the colonial peoples—yes, economically colonial, even if they boast of political autonomy—have a totally different origin and impulse. In these peoples, nationalism is revolutionary, and it therefore culminates in socialism. Among these peoples the idea of *nation* has not yet concluded its trajectory or exhausted its historical mission.[62]

His words are still valid in Latin America:

> Marxist critique concretely studies capitalist society. As long as capitalism has not been superseded definitively, the canon of Marx continues to be valid. Socialism—in other words, the struggle to

transform the capitalist social order into collectivism—keeps that critique alive; it continues, confirms, and corrects it. Any attempt to catalogue it as a simple scientific theory is in vain, as long as it is effective in history as a gospel and method of a mass movement.[63]

And he concludes, "Those phases of the economic process that Marx did not anticipate . . . do not affect in the least the foundations of Marxist economics."[64]

The frontist and Browderista crises prevented Marxism from being expressed with philosophical seriousness and rigor.[65] The great exception was Aníbal Ponce, whose works *Educación y lucha de clases* (Education and class struggle) (1937) and *Humanismo burgués y humanismo proletario* (Bourgeois humanism and proletariat humanism) (1935) are the most creative works after Mariátegui's writings. Ponce was born in Buenos Aires and died in exile in Michoacán, Mexico. In a lecture that he gave in 1930 at the faculty of economics, he said, "So great is the determination to separate intelligence from life that one might say that there is some hidden fear, some usurpation to defend, some great crime to hide. Societies have never esteemed the thinker. They have considered him, and with reason, a heretic."[66]

With the Cuban revolution of 1959, the impact of Marxist thinking extended throughout the continent, especially into faculties of philosophy. The ethical and voluntaristic focus of Ernesto Guevara and Fidel Castro won over the opinion of leftist youth for a time. Guevara expresses the same intuition that Antonio Caso had at the beginning of the century:

> *Latifundio* . . . results in low salaries, underemployment, and unemployment: *the hunger of the people*. All of these existed in Cuba. Here there was *hunger*. . . . The objective conditions for the struggle are given by the *hunger of the people*, the reaction to this *hunger*. . . . Our vanguard revolutionaries have to idealize this *love of the people*, make it into a sacred cause, and make it unique, indivisible. . . . Every day one must struggle because this living *love of humanity* is transformed into concrete events.[67]

This was a profound ethical sentiment rooted in physical suffering that opened altruistically to the other, the universal.

From a strictly theoretical point of view, Sergio Bagú's contribution was decisive: he demonstrated that the Latin American colonial system was not feudalism but dependent capitalism.[68] This insight enabled the question of dependency (André Gunder Frank, Theotonio dos Santos, etc.) and Immanuel Wallerstein's "world-system" to be formulated. All of this established Santiago as the intellectual center of the continent in 1970, with the triumph of Allende's Popular Unity party.

Meanwhile, Carlos Astrada turned from a Heideggerian to a Hegelian ontology, and he finally developed his Marxist thinking in Córdoba. During their Mexican exile, his students, among them José Aricó, launched a theoretical dispute within Latin American Marxism, publishing more than a hundred volumes in the "Past and Present" collection with Siglo XXI. In Mexico, Marxist philosophical thinking had flourished thanks to the presence of Alfonso Sánchez Vázquez, who wrote the classic *Filosofía de la praxis* (Philosophy of praxis) in 1967; he later criticized the Althusserian current which had a great influence in the seventies through the work of Martha Harnecker.

In 1979, the Nicaraguan revolution gave rise to a new theoretical impulse and a profound renovation of political philosophy, which took over popular nationalist positions and opposed Stalinist dogmatism, thus innovating at all levels of reflection. Orlando Nuñez wrote about the Nicaraguan revolution,

> Some reductively proclaim that there can be no revolution unless it is with the exclusive participation of the proletariat, and other reductivists state that the proletariat are no longer the ones making the revolution, but the people. . . . The myopia of the former resides in not seeing the *popular in the proletariat*, and that of the latter in not seeing *the proletariat in the popular*.[69]

The work of Bolivar Echeverría and Gabriel Vargas, director of the journal *Dialectics* (Puebla), in Mexico, Nuñez Tenorio in Venezuela, Antonio García and the Althusserianist Luis Enrique Orozco in Colombia,[70] as well as the three volumes of commentary of the four redactions of Marx's *Capital*,[71] ought to be mentioned. Raúl Fornet-Betancourt's work, published in German, fills an important vacuum.[72]

6. LATINAMERICANIST PHILOSOPHY: THE FIRST "BIFURCATION"[73]

If we return to an exposition of the historical evolution of Latin American philosophy, we discover that what Miró Quesada called the "bifurcation" deepened (it had begun with the prior generation; see section 3). Now there was a "third generation." In the thirties, a more detailed investigation of the history of Latin American philosophy began, corresponding to an ontological exigency in the surrounding historical world (from the philosophy of José Ortega y Gasset, Sartre, Dilthey, and Heidegger) and to the strengthening of industrial national bourgeoisies when the war began in 1939. It was conceived not only as historiography, but also with the philosophical intention of discovering the problematics that were formulated and resolved by the preceding currents. From these pioneering studies was born a philosophical-historical consciousness with a continental perspective.

In fact, in a speech he gave in Montevideo in 1842, Juan Bautista Alberdi had discussed an idea for a course on contemporary philosophy, twenty years before the first pragmatic formulations of Charles Sanders Peirce:

> The philosophy of each epoch and each country has commonly been the reason, the principle, or the most dominant and general sentiment that has governed its actions and conduct. And *this reason has emanated from the most imperious needs* of each epoch and country. Thus there have been Greek, Roman, German, English, and French philosophies, and it is necessary that there be an American philosophy. . . . There is, then, no philosophy in this century; there are only systems of philosophy, that is, more or less partial attempts, contradictory among themselves.[74]

In 1912, Alejandro Korn wrote, in his work on Argentinean philosophy,

> I can imagine the smile on the reader's face as he reads the following epigraph: Since when do we have Argentinean philosophy? Do we indeed have philosophy? . . . We Argentineans, the reader would say, belong to the realm of Western culture, and to this day we have assimilated only important ideas . . . [However,] our struggles were no mere brawls. Argentinean positivism is of autochthonous origin; only this fact explains its deep-rootedness. It was expression of a collective will . . .[75]

Even José Carlos Mariátegui wondered, years later, is there a Peruvian philosophy?

It was thus in the context of the pan-American organizations headquartered in Washington that Aníbal Sánchez Reulet published an article titled "Panorama de las ideas filosóficas en Hispanoamérica" (Panorama of ideas in Hispanic America) in 1936.[76] In 1940, Risieri Frondizi contributed a section on the history of ideas to the *Handbook of Latin American Studies*. In 1949, Leopoldo Zea, a student of José Gaos's, published a work in which he adopted a continental horizon: *Dos etapas del pensamiento en Hispanoamérica: del romanticismo al positivismo* (Two stages of Hispanic American thought: from romanticism to positivism). Francisco Romero himself, distanced from the faculty of philosophy in Argentina because of Peronism, published *Sobre la filosofía en América* (Concerning philosophy in America) in 1952. In Guayaquil, Ecuador, Ramón Insúa Rodríguez had also dealt with the theme in 1945. Shortly thereafter, in Washington, Sánchez Reulet, supported by Romero and Zea, edited a collection of the histories of thinking organized by country. Suddenly an unprecedented panorama began to emerge. Before the eyes of a new generation, there appeared the critical horizon that the philosophies practiced by the "normalizers" was alienating and "unauthentic," inasmuch as it had not taken account of the antecedent reality of Latin American philosophy.

The affirmation of a forgotten identity, the negation of the mere repetition of what is European, required a return to what is Latin American as object (what has to be thought) and as subject (knowing who is thinking and from where they think) of philosophical reflection. In this way, with the resources of the ontological current, the question of the "Latin American being" was problematized (see section 3). The philosophers that I will call "Latinamericanists" form part of this generation, but they specialized in historical investigations, with their own philosophical stamp—that is, doing history of Latin American philosophy does not mean stopping doing philosophy as such, even if only obliquely, and this is what the analytic philosophers criticized.

Leopoldo Zea began as a historian of ideas[77] of Mexico, and later he took on Hispanic America. His works were numerous and unprecedented.[78] Furthermore, he practiced what we could call a philosophy "as such" (*sin más*)[79] which he did not reconstitute from the perspective of the Latinamericanists' hypotheses. The third level of his work consisted in a "philosophy of the history" of Latin America,[80] at the beginning of which he attempted to answer the question "What is our being?" But as we have seen (in section 3), a concrete answer slipped through the fingers and little remained.[81] Zea then attempted to navigate through a positive reconstruction of Latin America in confrontation with the West. With the passing of the decades, Zea reformulated this discourse according to the advancing development of the continent's philosophy and history:

> A more intense and harder struggle because Western domination encounters allies in our peoples, in groups of oligarchical power who also speak of freedom but only to defend their interests, interests that coincide with those of the foreign dominators. . . . Zea moves from the philosophy of what is Mexican to what is [Latin] American, and then, in a stage of maturity, to the philosophy of the Third World. . . . This humanist integration of humanity and its history is, today, the horizon from which unfold the theories of cultures of dependence and in which the philosophy of liberation has many roots.[82]

If Zea's body of written work is immense, his "work not written" is even greater. Like no other Latin American philosopher of the twentieth century, he propelled the study of Latin American philosophy not only throughout the continent (and to the United States), but also to Europe and the world. From his center (CECYDEL) in Mexico, Zea has for decades radiated the Latinamericanist passion.

F. Miró Quesada, on the other hand, from his project of a historical rationality,[83] has drawn a suggestive interpretation of the recent Latin American philosophical transformation.

Arturo Ardao is the prototype of the historian of ideas, with his own philosophical style. Similarly, Arturo Roig reflects creatively, departing from Hegel, to discern what he calls the "anthropological *a priori*,"[84] "to want to hold oneself as valid (*für sich gelten will*)" from the perspective of a universal horizon and with reference to "the concrete figure of a people" (*die konkrete Gestalt eines Volkes*). The subject that is affirmed is an "us" (Latin America) before the "ours" (not only a territory) that has as a "legacy" the cultural inheritance of tradition, in the dialectic between civilization and barbarity. Thus, when we think about the "beginning" (*Anfang*)—which is not merely a "point of departure" (*Ausgang*)—of American philosophy, we must think of it as "self-consciousness," as a thinking about ourselves, but in reality as constantly starting again. In turn, the "philosophies of accusation"[85] are not to be left unexplored.

Abelardo Villegas published notorious works in his time.[86] With a very purified dialectical methodology, relating the philosophical text to historical economic, political, and social structures, Villegas diagnosed that the central problem of the Latin American conflict is the contradiction between traditional and modern society. Revolution reveals the answer, which is simultaneously (in the case of the Mexican revolution, Batlista in Uruguay, and the Cuban revolution) anti-traditional and anti-imperialist. The reformist movements (radical Argentineans or Peronists, Vargistas in Brazil, etc.) are included. Unfortunately, Villegas's project has not received new contributions in recent years. I ought to mention here a whole group of Latinamericanists, such as Weinberg, Horacio Cerutti, Carlos Paladines, Germán Marquínez Argote (who organized the International Congresses of Latin American Philosophy at the Universidad Santo Thomas Aquino in Bogotá without interruption every year since 1982), Hugo Biaggini, and many others.

7. PHILOSOPHY OF SCIENCE AND ANALYTIC PHILOSOPHY: THE SECOND "BIFURCATION"[87]

As I have mentioned, the "bifurcation" is accentuated in this "third generation." Some started from the position of the preceding phenomenological current (this being the path of evolution of Miró Quesada and Mario Bunge; see section 3). Others, with greater rigor in the use of resources, employed linguistic analysis,[88] and they therefore distanced themselves from the Latinamericanist tradition (e.g., L. Villoro and F. Salmerón). All were influenced by the "linguistic turn" in postwar Anglo-Saxon thought. Philosophy in Latin America took a clear forward step—although the project of quasi-perfect rigor of mathematical formalization or analysis meant an exaggerated skepticism regarding the other currents, and by the eighties, the limits of its internal and external consistency, especially with respect to practical philosophy, had been discovered. In any event, Latin American philosophy became conscious of its own methodological-linguistic mediations.

First, V. Ferreira da Silva, proceeding from phenomenology in Brazil, published *Elementos de lógica matemática* (Elements of mathematical logic) in 1940. Similarly, Miró Quesada[89] went from phenomenology to the cultivation of logic and mathematical logic (*Lógica* [Logic], 1946); *Filosofía de las Matemáticas* [Philosophy of mathematics], 1954), and later supported the axiomatization of juridical philosophy (*Problemas Fondamentales de lógica juridica* [Fundamental problems of juridical logic], 1956); he wrote his most important philosophical work, *Apuntes para una teoría de la razón* (Notes towards a theory of reason), in 1962. Miró Quesada's particular position in twentieth-century Latin American thought consists in his definition of reason, which allowed him to ascend to the level of logical, mathematical, formalizing knowledge without disdain for the knowledge that he termed ideological, metaphysical, or ethical; even if these forms could not achieve the formal rigor of the former, they still did not lose their rational validity. The broad rational spectrum (from the formal to the Latin American historical) corresponded, for Miró Quesada, to a strict, albeit broad, vision of historical reason.[90]

In 1944, W. V. O. Quine and Hans Lindemann, who was from the Vienna circle and lived in Buenos Aires, visited Brazil, where interest in Bertrand Russell's work was starting to grow. Through Russell, the mathematician Julio Rey Pastor and Gregorio Klimoski began their path. In Canada, a colleague of Romero's in Buenos Aires, Mario Bunge (who published *Causality* in 1959), attempted the most ambitious work of this current, the seven-volume *Treatise on Basic Philosophy*, (1974–85); he added an eighth volume on ethics.[91] In the prologue to the last volume Bunge writes, "The ultimate goal of theoretical research, be it in philosophy, science, or mathematics, is the construction of systems, i.e., theories . . . because the world itself is systemic, because no idea can become fully clear unless it is embedded in some system or other, and because sawdust philosophy is rather boring."[92] Therein lies its value and its limitation: formalizing theoretical rationalism. Leaving aside logic and mathematics, Bunge began with semantics[93] and continued through ontology[94] and epistemology.[95] Finally, his ethics were developed from an axiological, Aristotelian teleological model—"values" as the evaluative horizon that takes over the utilitarian position; morality as the set of moral norms; ethics as the theories on values, morality, and action; the theory of action as a praxiology: "The morality advocated in this book is based on a value theory according to which anything that promotes welfare is good. Our morality can be summed up in the norm *Enjoy life and help live*."[96]

Héctor-Neri Castañeda, born in Guatemala (his first publication in the United States was *Morality and the Language of Conduct*, 1963), is the best known of the Latin American analytic philosophers.[97] Castañeda has devoted himself to the development of an analysis of ethical language in a creative, rigorous, and personal manner.[98] He concluded one of his first works presenting his position: "Thus Morality builds, upon the connection between the moral value of sets of actions and happiness, the basis of a special complex and pervasive network of duties (obligations, oughts, or requirements)."[99] Ontologically, as with Moore and Bunge, Castañeda's point of departure is an axiology, from out of which moral principles are determined with reference to an ethos. The "elements of practical thinking," unities (*noema*), are analytically sought and formulated in "propositions" that can constituted as "imperatives," with intentions, until deontic judgments are arrived at. Little by little, the "logical structure of practical thinking," the justification of prescriptions and intentions, imperatives and duties, is discovered, until "the structure of morality" is analytically reached.

Thomas M. Simpson (*Formas lógicas, realidad y significado* [Logical forms, reality and meaning], 1964), in Buenos Aires, and Roberto Torreti, in Chile, also pioneered work in the analytic tradition. Eduardo Rabossi wrote *Análisis filosófico, lenguaje y metafísica* (Philosophical Analysis, language and metaphysics) in 1977.

Meanwhile, in 1967, Alejandro Rossi, who had returned from Oxford, Luis Villoro, and Fernando Salmerón founded the journal *Crítica*, which became the organ of the analytic movement in Latin America. Carlos U. Moulines, a Venezuelan doctor living in Munich (1975), and in fact with a degree in epistemology from that city's university, published *La estructura del mundo sensible* (The Structure of the Sensible World)—departing from Stegmüller's position—in 1973. At the University of Campinas, near São Paulo, Zeljko Loparic promoted a center for logic, epistemology, and the history of science, where the journal *Manuscrito* was published in 1977.

In *Creer, saber, conocer* (Belief, knowledge, learning), Luis Villoro wondered, "How has human reason operated throughout history? Has it repeated situations of domination or, on the contrary, liberated us from our subjection?"[100] And he concluded, "If intolerance is an indispensable part of a philosophy of domination, then critical activity is the first step toward a philosophy of liberation."[101] Critique starts from beliefs.[102] Every rational being has reasons for his or her beliefs; when these reasons are sufficient they are enough; when they are insufficient, causes for their insufficiency and better reasons must be sought. When sufficient reasons are objectively justified as valid, it can be said that S has knowledge of p.[103] To learn adds to knowledge "personal experience,"[104] which is judged specifically in discoveries, empirical application, and wisdom. Vehemently criticizing the skepticism of scientism, which measures everything according to the disproportionately rigorous degree of justification of some sciences, Villoro concludes,

> Contemporary scientism is akin to the scornful arrogance with which the civilized contemplate the beliefs of human groups that have not ascended to a specific level of technical development. . . . The West, with its colonial expansion, has despotically ruled entire peoples, destroying their cultures, with the supposed justification of introducing them to science and modern technology.[105]

The clear defense of "wisdom," as knowledge extracted from lived experiences, which is different from scientific knowledge, allows Villoro to be precise without delegitimating the narrative of a Shakyamuni, a "wise man of the Shakya tribe."[106]

Putting aside the critiques that were made of them, and that they themselves formulated,[107] proponents of this current contributed greatly to raising the level of philosophical reflection. Born with the vocation of rigor, it achieved its objective.

8. PHILOSOPHY OF LIBERATION[108]

Members of a new generation[109] (of those born after 1930, although it was anticipated by some), began their reflection at the end of the sixties, not without
some relation to the events of 1968, with respect to a philosophy of liberation,
which was thus linked to Latinamericanist philosophy. Salazar Bondy belonged to
this current, and he responded negatively to the question, Is there a philosophy of
our America? He saw the need for the birth of a new philosophy that would be
more rigorous and engaged in the struggle against the culture of domination. For
Salazar Bondy, only one who understands "domination" can, without illusion,
hope for an exit: "The insufficiencies and weaknesses of our philosophy, which
subsist despite the present efforts and progress, are not, then, negative characteristics of philosophy taken separately and as such, but symptomatic of a deeper and
more fundamental failure that affects both our culture and our society."[110] With extreme lucidity, Salazar Bondy concludes, "Philosophical thinking ought to become, as far as the human energies that are empowered by it, an instrument of
radical critique with the goal of achieving, through analysis and rational illumination, a fully realistic consciousness of our situation."[111] He gives a clear diagno-
sis on the need for a new philosophy:

> Outside of the philosophies linked with the great contemporary
> blocs or the immediate future, it is necessary, then, to forge a think-
> ing that both takes root in the socio-historical reality of our com-
> munities and conveys their needs and goals, and also serves to wipe
> out the underdevelopment and domination that typify our histor-
> ical situation. Within the general framework of the Third World,
> the Hispanic American countries must be challenged to construct
> their development and achieve their independence with the sup-
> port of a philosophical reflection conscious of the historical cross-
> roads and determined to construct itself as a rigorous, realist, and
> transforming thinking.[112]

He concludes, "But there is still no possibility of liberation, and, to the extent that
there is, we are obliged to opt decidedly for a line of action that materializes this
possibility and avoids its frustration. Hispanic American philosophy also has before itself the option that *its own constitution* depends on its being an authentic reflection."[113] Salazar Bondy explained in 1973 in Buenos Aires, during the dialogue
that I helped to organize at that time:

> When philosophy set out historically to liberate itself, it did not
> achieve even the liberation of the philosopher, because no one who
> dominates another can be liberated. Thus, in truth, the only possi-
> bility of liberation is occurring *for the first time in history with the*

Third World, the world of the oppressed and underdeveloped, who are liberating themselves and at the same time liberating the other, the dominator. Thus, *for the first time can there be a philosophy of liberation.* In the concrete case of the struggle of classes, groups, and nations, there is another who is the dominator, who unfortunately I have to remove from the structure of domination: I have to dismantle their machinery of oppression. And philosophy has to be in this struggle, because if it is not, it becomes abstract thought with which, although we intend to liberate others, as philosophers, not even we are liberated.[114]

Salazar Bondy indicated that this new philosophy ought to respond diachronically to three criteria: to be "[a] a critical work to the extent that historical reality allows it, [b] a work of *reformulation* to the extent that we emerge towards a new optic, and [c] a *reconstruction* of philosophy to the extent that this optic gives us a way to produce a thinking already oriented in the sense of the philosophy of liberation."[115]

Leopoldo Zea's reaction[116] was not so much to negate Salazar Bondy's historiographical position—or my own—but instead to defend "Latinamericanist philosophy" in the sense that it already responded to the exigencies of the new philosophy that Salazar Bondy was looking for. This was the debate: Latinamericanist philosophy with a long existing tradition or a nascent liberation philosophy? Zea wanted to demonstrate that there had always been Latin American thought, and even a philosophy of liberation, authentic insofar as it responded to the Latin American reality.[117] These philosophies responded to the reality of their time, especially the political reality. Salazar Bondy and I perfectly accepted this hypothesis, and Salazar Bondy had in fact written numerous historiographical works along these lines. We were in agreement with Zea that to a large extent "academic" or "normalized" philosophy, the philosophy of the "community of hegemonic European and North American philosophers" propounded among ourselves, was not authentic;[118] it was imitative, Eurocentric—and the analytic philosophers of the sixties added, with validity, that it was not sufficiently rigorous. We admitted that for philosophy to be rigorous, it ought to depart from concrete (or particular) reality and elevate itself to universality—and in this there was concordance with the analytic and epistemological current. All philosophy departs from the concrete (Aristotle's departed from a political reality of slavery, while Hegel's global-historical philosophy was Germanocentric) and is raised to universality. Each philosophy is originally particular (and because of that each has deserved the label of Greek, Roman, Muslim, Medieval, German, Anglo-Saxon, and even North American, since Charles S. Peirce), as a point of departure, and at the same time each is "philosophy as such" (*filosofía sin más*), as a point of arrival—since they can learn/teach something "universal" from/to all others.[119] The discussion does not reside here, but is located elsewhere: Zea thinks that "Latinamericanist philosophy" suffices; Salazar Bondy advocates a *new philosophy* that is more rigorous, illuminating with respect to the question of "negativity," and more linked to praxis in the question of social "transformation." To achieve this, the social sciences, the political economy of dependence (today we would say the horizon of the "world-system"), must be assimilated. The original group identified with the philosophy of liberation, in my opinion, was in agreement with Salazar Bondy on this issue. I believe that there are four possible positions for facing this problem: first, that which admits the validity of historiographical "Latinamericanist philosophy," even as a hermeneutics of the "life world"; second, that which discovers the degree of prostration of Latin American academic-normalized philosophy; third, that which indicates the possibility of a Latin American philosophy as historiography, and that dialogues with the best of the hegemonic Euro-American philosophical community; and fourth, that which attempts to develop a philosophy of liberation as differentiated from prior projects, although it ought to be articulated in conjunction with them—that is, supporting itself in historiography, in epistemological rigor, and in dialogue or clarifying debates with the other recognized and hegemonic philosophical positions.

Salazar Bondy's project, and that of a philosophy of liberation in a strict sense,[120] is distinguished from the first type of Latinamericanist philosophy (see section 4), although the former can be considered a movement that emerged from "Latinamericanist philosophy." But, since it is not only a particular process (although it set out from this particularity), it is also a "universal philosophy"—that is, it opens itself to globality (but in the sense of linking up with the philosophical movements of liberation in the periphery in general—of underdeveloped nations, dominated social classes, ethnicities, the marginal, women, homosexuals, children, youths, popular culture, discriminated-against races, and on behalf of the future generations in advocating the ecological question, etc.). The *new philosophy*, whose agenda was opened by Salazar Bondy from a negative moment (as "philosophy of domination"), has evolved in recent decades.[121]

Some, such as Osvaldo Ardiles in the seventies, who belonged to the Latinamericanist ontological current developed this philosophy with a political consciousness, from an analysis of continental reality as it was practiced by nascent Latin American critical social science (think here of Fals Borda, *Sociología de la liberación* (Sociology of liberation), published in 1969), and arising from militant engagement with popular groups in action against the military dictatorships.[122] The "late" Heidegger was criticized with and through Emmanuel Levinas (thanks to the contribution of J. C. Scannone), allowing for the emergence of a Latin American thought which discovered that the domination of the exploited Latin American people originated with the beginning of the "world-system" itself in 1492. The reality of Latin American oppression, criticized by Bartolomé de las Casas in the sixteenth century (in the first counter-discourse of modernity), was the point of departure for this uniquely Latin American philosophy in terms of theme, method, and awareness of a different discourse. Immediately, positivity, the dignity of the cultural alterity of the Latin American historical subject, was affirmed from the perspective of a project of liberation.

Perhaps the philosophy of liberation (which emerged in late 1969 in Argentina) began with my work *Para una ética de la liberación latinoamericana* (Towards an ethics of Latin American liberation) (five volumes written between 1970 and 1975).[123] A group of philosophers emerged at the Second National Congress of Philosophy (Cordoba, 1972), whose discourse had as its point of departure the massive poverty of the underdeveloped and dependent Latin American continent. It was a reflection by those oppressed by and/or excluded from the system (politically, economically, erotically, pedagogically, etc.)—in the way that pragmatists did from the perspective of the process of *verification;* it was a practical process not of freedom, but of *liberation*, which departed from another process—not that of the modern consciousness, but that of becoming aware (*concientización*), which required the outlining of an alternative project to the one constructed by the "principle of hope."

This current has followed several paths. Some thinkers were included because of their ethical analysis, with links to Levinas or Marx (an ethics of liberation), others returned to an indigenous hermeneutics of long tradition (Rodolfo Kusch), while others set out from popular wisdom (J. C. Scannone[124] Carlos Cullén[125]). Still others dealt with ideological deconstruction (Hugo Assmann) or with the critique of utopian reason (Franz Hinkelammert[126]). Some turned frankly nationalist or populist (Mario Casalla[127]); others inserted themselves within the study of tradition (L. Zea[128]); or emerged from an ideological practical project of rationality as emancipation and solidarity (F. Miró Quesada[129]), or as a philosophy of intercultural dialogue (R. Fornet-Betancourt); or they emerged from concrete situations, such as Cuban Marxist humanism (Guadarrama[130]). Because of the thematic of the philosophy, there are also a pedagogy of liberation (Paulo Freire since his famous *Pedagogy of the Oppressed*, 1968) and a philosophy of erotic liberation (begun by Vaz Ferreira and continued with a strictly philosophical conceptual horizon, not without its own ambiguities due to the social context of the period, begun by me in the seventies,[131] and adopted into feminism by Graciela Hierro, among many others).

The debate established by Karl-Otto Apel and representatives of the philosophy of liberation began to give this current greater significance, with the possibility of incorporating the achievements of the "linguistic turn." From the popular culture of the oppressed and excluded (the majority of humanity living in the Southern Hemisphere), a strictly Latin American philosophy was formulated. The challenge was launched.

9. SITUATION AT THE END OF THE TWENTIETH CENTURY

As could be observed at the 19th World Congress of Philosophy in Moscow (1993), and the 13th Inter-American Congress of Philosophy in Bogotá (1994), the "bifurcation" of the sixties and eighties (between epistemological and analytic philosophy and Latin American historical-political philosophy) is beginning to be transformed into a possibility for dialogue. This is a result of two factors. First is the weakening of dogmatism, which affirmed its own discourse without sufficient critique and ignored other discourses (such as pre-pragmatic analytic philosophy, reductive and one-dimensional mathematizing epistemology, Marxism and Stalinism, historicisms that expected too much from mere reflection on the past, crises of political and social alternatives, etc.). Second, there is a healthy skepticism (that does not require arguments that exceed reasonable exigencies in order to validate rational consensus, and that therefore also opposes the skepticism of extreme rigor), which today allows a more tolerant discussion with other positions, that is, a fertile dialogue between the different currents in the late twentieth century.[132] Perhaps a rational exchange between Latin American philosophers, aware of their own limits, the hegemonic European-North American philosophical community, and Afro-Asiatic philosophers[133] will allow a "world" philosophy to emerge for the first time. Should not the constitution of this first *global dialogue* (West/East, North/South) between continental philosophical communities be one of the initial and central tasks of the twenty-first century?

Translated by Eduardo Mendieta

NOTES

General note: All quotations in this chapter were translated by Eduardo Mendieta.

  1. See the bibliography, section 1.
  2. See F. Romero, *Teoría del hombre* (Buenos Aires: Losada, 1952). The full name, nationality, dates of birth and death (if it has taken place), and principal works of the Latin American philosophers named in the text can be found in the chronology and/or in the bibliography at the end of this chapter.
  3. Francisco Miró Quesada, *Despertar y proyecto del filosofar latinoamericano* (Mexico City: FCE, 1974), 30ff.
  4. Ibid., p. 33.
  5. With respect to the "professorial style" of this concrete generation, Salazar Bondy indicated (as did I) that its philosophy was "imitative or inauthentic," and not with respect to the totality of Latin American thought that affirmed itself as existing and as historical reflection (which in no way is negated). See Enrique Dussel, "Leopoldo Zea's Project of a Philosophy of Latin American History," in Amaryll Chanady, ed., *Latin American Identity and Constructions of Difference* (Minneapolis: University of Minnesota Press, 1994), 26–42.
  6. Miró Quesada, *Despertar y proyecto*. This was the second institutionalization ("normalization") of university philosophy; the first "normalization" began in 1553 with the foundation of the first universities in Mexico City and Lima and philosophical studies within the renovated second Scholastic cultivated with precision by some great creative Latin American philosophers.
  7. See the bibliography, section 3.1.

8. José Rodó, "Ariel," in *Obras Completas* (Buenos Aires: Ed. Antonio Zamora, 1956), 190–191.

9. José Martí, "Carta a Gonzalo de Quesada" [December 14, 1889, New York], in Martí, *Obras completas*, vol. 2, 197–198.

10. Alejandro Deustua, *Las ideas de orden y de libertad en la historia del pensamiento humano* (Lima: E. R. Villaran, 1919); see A. Salazar Bondy, *Historia de las ideas en el Perú contemporáneo* (Lima: Moncloa, 1967), vol. 1, 149ff.

11. See D. Sobrevilla, *Repensando la tradición nacional I* (Lima: Editorial Hipatia, 1989), vol. 1, 8ff.

12. Salazar Bondy, *Historia de las ideas*, vol. 1, 189.

13. See Arturo Ardao, *La filosofía en el Uruguay en el Siglo XX* (Mexico City: FCE, 1956), 45ff; and A. Roig, *Teoría y crítica del pensamiento latinoamericano* (Mexico City: FCE, 1981), 115ff.

14. See Carlos Vaz Ferreira, *Conocimiento y acción* (Montevideo: Mariño y Caballero, Impresores, 1908), 100.

15. Vaz Ferreira, "El pragmatismo," in *Conocimiento y Acción*, 168–169.

16. In *Lógica viva* (Montevideo: Impresora Uruguaya, 1957), in the chapter on "false precision," Vaz Ferreira writes, "There are scientific systems, whole theories [. . .] that can be considered illustrations of this fallacy—for instance, Herbart's psychology. This author attempts to explain psychology through mathematics [. . .] Such explications are deceptive: they claim that psychology has acquired precision. [. . .] This precision is false and illegitimate" (110).

17. It ought to be recalled that Korn was mayor of his town, Ranchos, when he was a field doctor; municipal manager of La Plata; dismissed during the coup of 1893; and a representative of the Radical Party (early populism, before Peronism). As part of the university reform of 1919 he was appointed dean of the faculty of philosophy at the University of Buenos Aires. In the thirties, when the socialist Alfredo Palacios won the election in Buenos Aires (similar to Hamburg, Germany, where the door was opened to the triumph of Nazism), Korn entered the socialist party to oppose the military coup of 1930, which allowed Captain Francisco Romero, who supported the coup, to occupy an undisputably preeminent position in the philosophy faculty until 1946.

18. He called himself an "autodidact," when speaking of those who admired Ortega y Gasset's exposition in Buenos Aires in 1916.

19. Alejandro Korn, *La libertad creadora* (Buenos Aires: Editorial Losada, 1944).

20. Antonio Caso, *La existencia como economía y como caridad. Ensayo sobre la esencia del cristianismo*, in *Obras Completas* (Mexico City: UNAM, 1972), vol. 3, 9.

21. Ibid., 16.

22. Ibid., 17.

23. Cited in M. Kempff Mercado, *Historia de la filosofía en Latinoamérica* (Santiago: Zig-Zag, 1958), 153.

24. See Antonio Paim, *Historia das Idéias filosóficas no Brasil* (São Paulo: Editora Convivio, 1984), 417ff.

25. See Roberto Escobar, *La filosofía en Chile* (Santiago: Universidad Técnica del Estado, 1976), 63ff.

26. See Germán Marquínez Argote, *La Filosofía en Colombia* (Bogotá: Editorial el Búho, 1988), 343ff.

27. See the bibliography, section 3.2.

28. Carlos Astrada, *Idealismo fenomenológico y metafísica existencial* (Buenos Aires: Imprenta de la Universidad, 1936) p. 6. The bibliography in this chapter calls attention to the fact that Astrada achieved a high technical level in the use of sources by the range of canonical issues he wrote about.

29. On Latin American "contemporary ontologies," see Roig, *Teoría y crítica*, 138ff.

30. This distinction, however, should not be seen as immutable, since J. Gaos, republican and anti-Francista, was Heideggerian and advocated the study of that which is Mexican. Carlos Astrada himself ended up adhering to Marxism after the fall of Peronism.

31. Aníbal Ponce, "*Ariel* o la agonía de una obstinada ilusión" (*Ariel* or the agony of an obstinate illusion), in idem, *Humanismo y revolución* (Mexico City: Siglo XXI, 1970), 94ff.

32. In Latin America the peripheral bourgeoisie in countries with populist governments searched for national emancipation; the German or Japanese bourgeoisie sought, instead, global hegemony, in competition with Anglo-Saxon domination of the global market.

33. See Franz Tamayo, *Creación de la pedagogia nacional* (La Paz, 1910); Ezequiel Martínez Estrada, *Radiografía de la Pampa* (Buenos Aires: Losada, 1961); Gilberto Freyre, *Casa-grande y senzala* (Buenos Aires: Biblioteca de Autores Brasileños, 1942); Samuel Ramos, *El perfil del hombre y la cultura en México* (Mexico City: Imprenta Mundial, 1934).

34. Quoted in Guillermo Francovich, *El pensamiento boliviano en el Siglo XX* (Mexico City: FCE, 1966), 229. See A. Villegas, *Panorama de la filosofía iberoamericana actual* (Buenos Aires: EUDEBA, 1963), 74–92. Rodolfo Kusch was a late member of this generation.

35. Only if the history of Europe and its change of "meaning" in the periphery of capitalism are taken into account can the division between Romero and Astrada be understood. In 1930, with the anti-nationalist "military coup," Captain Romero took over the chair of philosophy in Buenos Aires; in 1946 it was taken over by Astrada, during the military coup that later gave rise to Peronism. In 1956 Romero returned with the "liberating revolution" that brought independence from North American expansion. In 1966, with Onganía's military coup, some went into exile; in 1976, with the neoliberal military coup, others went into exile. One has to be extremely careful not to confuse the "sense" of each one of these divisions and situate them in the periphery. Hitler was not the same thing as Adenauer, but Getulio Vargas and Cárdenas were not simply Hitler, and Frondizi and Chilean Christian democracy were not simply Adenauer. Therefore, Astrada was not Heidegger (although he had much in common with him), and he and Romero did not have philosophical-political analogues in Europe.

36. The Argentinian gaucho, like the Colombian or Venezuelan *llanero*, was the prototype for Sarmiento's "barbarian." Astrada recuperated the positivity of this prototype.

37. Félix Schwartzmann, *El sentimiento de lo humano en América* (Santiago: Universidad de Chile, 1950).

38. Ernesto Mayz Vallenilla, *El problema de América* (Caracas: Universidad Central., 1959).

39. Nimio de Anquín, "Lugones y el ser americano," in *Arkhé* (Córdoba, 1964): 29–48.

40. H. A. Murena, *El pecado original de América* (Buenos Aires: Grupo Sur, 1954), 39.

41. Edmundo O'Gorman, *La invención de América: el universalismo de la culture de Occidente* (Mexico City: FCE, 1958). See my critique in Enrique Dussel, *1492: El encubrimiento del Otro* (Madrid: Nueva Utopía, 1992), 31–47.

42. Alberto Caturelli, *América Bifronte. Ensayo de ontología y de filosofía de la historia* (Buenos Aires: Troquel, 1961).

43. I believe that Caturelli does not realize that he has used the same expression that Kant used in his definition of *Aufklärung:* "Unmundigkeit" (see Dussel, *1492: El encubrimiento del Otro,* 19–30.

44. See Sobrevilla, *Repensando la tradición nacional I,* vol. 1, 203ff; F. Miró Quesada, *Proyecto y realización del filosofar latinoamericano* (Mexico City: FCE, 1981), 52 ff; Salazar Bondy, *Historia de las ideas,* vol. 2, 413ff.

45. Alberto Wagner de la Reyna, *Analogía y evocación* (Madrid:Editorial Gredos, 1976).

46. See Daniel Herrera Restrepo, "La filosofía en Colombia contemporánea (1930–1988)," in Germán Marquínez Argote, ed., *La Filosofía en América Latina* (Bogotá: El Buho, 1993), 381ff.

47. See Solomon Lipp, "Francisco Romero," in Solomon Lipp, *Three Argentine Thinkers* (New York: Philosophical Library, 1969), 113–167.

48. See Francisco Romero, *Filosofía de la persona* (Buenos Aires: Losada, 1944) and Romero, *Teoría del Hombre.*

49. See Luis Juan Guerrero, *Estética operatoria,* 3 vols. (Buenos Aires: Losada, 1956–67), in three carefully thought-through volumes.

50. See Salazar Bondy, *Historia de las ideas,* vol. 2, 394ff; and Sobrevilla, *Repensando la tradición nacional I,* vol. 2, 607–854.

51. See Restrepo, "La filosofía en Colombia contemporánea," 389ff.

52. See his dissertation, Alberto Rosales, *Transzendenz und Differenz: ein Beitrag zum Problem der ontologischen Differenz beim frühen Heidegger* (The Hague: Nijhoff, 1971).

53. See the bibliography, section 3.3.

54. See Walter Redmond, *Bibliography of the Philosophy in the Iberian Colonies of America* (The Hague: Nijhoff, 1972).

55. See Arturo Ardao, *La filosofía en el Uruguay en el Siglo XX* (Mexico City: FCE, 1956), 163ff. In his work *La iglesia y la civilización* (1905), Ardao demonstrates an open, liberal, anti-positivist spirit. Enrique Legrand, an astronomer, in *Divagaciones filosóficas* (1906), showed the ability of a believing scientist to maintain the mutual autonomy of science and faith.

56. See Leonardo Tovar González, "Tradicionalismo y neoescolástica," in Marquínez Argote, *La Filosofía en Colombia,* 320ff.

57. The 1st World Congress of Christian Philosophy of 1979, held in Córdoba, published three volumes entitled *La filosofía cristiana, hoy* [Universidad Nacional de Córdoba, 1980. It was chaired by the dictator General Videla, who made a speech written by Alberto Caturelli that was the extreme expression of this attitude.

58. See Victor A. Belaúnde, *La realidad nacional* (Lima: El Mercurio Peruano, 1945).

59. Manuel Dominguez Camargo, "La neoescolástica de los siglos XIX y XX," in Marquínez Argote, *La Filosofía en Colombia,* 262.

60. See the bibliography, section 3.4.

61. Luis Emilio Recabarren, "Ricos y pobres," in L.E. Recabarren, *Obras* (Havana: Casa de las Américas in Recabarren, 1976), 74–75.

62. José Carlos Mariátegui, "El problema indígena," in J. C. Mariátegui, *Obra política* (Mexico City: Era, 1978), 232.

63. José Carlos Mariátegui, *Defensa del marxismo* (Santiago: Ed. Nacionales y Extranjeras, 1934), 40–41.

64. Ibid., p. 75.

65. See Enrique Dussel, *El último Marx (1863–1882) y la liberación latinoamericana* (Mexico City: Siglo XXI, 1990), 275–293.

66. Ponce, *Humanismo y revolución*, 55.

67. E. Guevara, *Obra revolucionaria* (Mexico City: Era, 1974), 520, 637.

68. The most important works dealing with this debate were Sergio Bagú, *Economía de la sociedad colonial* (Buenos Aires: El Ateneo, 1949); Caio Prado Júnior, *Historia econômica do Brasil* (São Paulo: Circulo do Livro, 1982); and Silvio Frondizi, *La realidad argentina, ensayo de interpretación sociológica* (Buenos Aires: Praxis, 1960 [1957]).

69. Orlando Nuñez, "Las condiciones políticas de la transición," in José Luis Coraggio et al., *Transición difícil. La autodeterminación de los pequeños países periféricos* (Mexico City: Siglo XXI, 1986), 60.

70. See Orlando Fals Borda et al., *El marxismo en Colombia* (Bogota: Universidad Nacional, 1983).

71. Marx wrote his magnus opus *four times*: in 1857–58, in 1861–63, in 1863–65, and from 1866 to 1867. See Enrique Dussel, *La producción teórica de Marx* (Mexico City: Siglo XXI, 1985); idem, *El último Marx*; idem, *Hacia un Marx desconocido* (Mexico City: Siglo XXI, 1988).

72. See R. Fornet-Betancourt, *Ein anderer Marxismus? Die philosophische Rezeption des Marxismus in Lateinamerika* (Mainz: Gruenewald, 1994). This is the first work that studies the development of Marxism in the continent in a philosophically strict manner.

73. See the bibliography, section 3.5.

74. See G. Marquinez Argote, *Filosofía latinoamericana?* (Bogotá: El Búho, 1981), 12–13.

75. Alejandro Korn, *El pensamiento argentino* (Buenos Aires: Nova, 1961), 233–234.

76. See the bibliography, section 1.

77. See Miró Quesada, *Despertar y proyecto*, 208ff; idem, *Proyecto y realización*, 136–180.

78. See Leopoldo Zea, *Dos etapas del pensamiento en Hispanoamérica: del romanticismo al positivismo* (Mexico City: Colegio de México, 1949); idem, *La filosofía en México* (Mexico City: Libro Mexicano 1955); idem, *The Latin American Mind* (Norman: University of Oklahoma Press, 1963).

79. Enrique Dussel, "El proyecto de una *Filosofía de la historia latinoamericana* de Leopoldo Zea," *Cuadernos Americanos* (Mexico City) 35 (Sept.–Oct. 1992): 203–218.

80. See L. Zea, *La filosofía latinoamericana como filosofía sin más* (Mexico City: Siglos XXI, 1969), and *Filosofía de la Historia Americana* (Mexico City: FCE, 1978).

81. To a certain extent, Emilio Uranga in *Análisis del ser del mexicano* (Mexico: Porrúa, 1952), in which he defined Mexican being by its "radical ontological insufficiency," had already closed the path toward ontological analysis of the American being. In turn, Luis Villoro, in *Los grandes momentos del indigenismo en México* (Mexico City: Colegio de México, 1950), following the negative tradition, showed that given that the Indian was "the other," the only way of overcoming discrimination was by intregating him into the Mexican as such, and he thus disappeared as an Indian.

82. Miró Quesada, *Proyecto y realización*, 149, 183.

83. To Sobrevilla, in *Repensando la tradición nacional I*, vol. 2, 835, Miró Quesada's project appears to be a contradiction between his formal conception of rationality (in his works on logic, mathematical logic, formalization of a juridical philosophy, and the theory of rationality) and what he is trying to achieve in his works on the history of Latin American ideas. We will return to this theme, but here it is necessary to take into consideration that Miró Quesada's theory of rationality is flexible and that he is aware of its limits. Fur-

thermore, with reference to ethics, or the experience of having to formulate an ideology for a Peruvian political party, he understood the difficulty of axiomatization and the need of a "broad" concept of rationality (which I think would not be accepted by Mario Bunge, for instance, who is far more reductivist with reference to these questions).

84. See Roig, *Teoría y crítica*, 9ff. It is a matter of a historical "reconstruction" of subjectivity, a fertile method for a history of Latin American philosophy.

85. Ibid., 100ff. On the concept of "recognition," see 106.

86. See Villegas, *Panorama de la filosofía*; Miró Quesada, *Proyecto y realización*, 184ff.

87. See the bibliography, section 3.6, especially Jorge Gracia, ed., *El análisis filosófico en América Latina* (Mexico City: FCE, 1985).

88. Note that rigor is desired in the linguistic apparatus but not in the socio-historical apparatus (which is another epistemological horizon that these philosophers do not attempt to broaden).

89. See Sobrevilla, *Repensando la tradición nacional I*, 607–854.

90. See Francisco Miró Quesada, "Outline of My Philosophical Position," *Southern Philosopher* 2 (1953): 1–5; idem, "La filosofía como actividad racional," *Philosophische Selbstdarstellunge* (1986): 195–203.

91. See also M. Bunge, *The Mind-Body Problem* (New York: Pergamon Press, 1980), in which he makes note of a theme of great importance.

92. M. Bunge, *Treatise on Basic Philosophy* (Boston: Reidel Bunge, 1974–1989), vol. 8, v–vi.

93. Vol. 1 deals with designation, reference, representation, intention, content; vol. 2, with interpretation, meaning, truth, precision, contiguous fields. It is to be noted that this is all a pre-pragmatic reflection.

94. Vol. 3 deals with substance, form, thing, world (only as the totality of real things), possibility, change, time-space; vol. 4, with system, life, mind, society, a systematic vision of the world. This work deserves special study. For Bunge, ontology is the formal reflection of systems as systems (formal systematizability). It would be interesting to compare this position with Niklas Luhmann's, which is, in synthesis, "Everything interacts with other things, so that all things cohere forming systems" (vol. 4, 245). This is neither atomistic, nor holistic, nor scientistic. The "systematicity" of things is diverse (insofar as they are heterogeneous systems). Lastly, since the universe is the sum of all systems, "it endures eternally although no part of it does" (246).

95. Vol. 5 deals with cognition, knowledge, investigation, communication; perception, conception, inference, exploration, conjecture, systematization; vol. 6, with understanding, production of evidence, evaluation, epistemological change, types of knowledge, results; vol. 7, with formal science and physical science.

96. Bunge, *Treatise on Basic Philosophy*, vol. 8, 398. But this is precisely where the difficulties *begin*. How can the majority of humanity, in misery, in the peripheral world, accomplish this philosophical objective? Bunge indicates that this would be more concrete levels of reflection on application that depart from what has been presented.

97. Castañeda's students included Ricardo Gómez, an excellent Argentinian epistemologist living in Los Angeles, and Jorge Gracia, a Hispanic-American living in Buffalo, who has produced extremely relevant work since he is a true "intercultural bridge" between the United States and Latin America.

98. See H.-N. Castañeda, *The Structure of Morality* (Springfield: Thomas, 1974); idem, *Action, Knowledge and Reality* (Indianapolis: Bobbs-Merrill, 1975); idem, *Thinking, Language and Experience* (Minneapolis: University of Minnesota Press, 1989).

99. Castañeda, *The Structure of Morality*, 175.

100. Villoro, *Creer, saber, conocer* (Mexico City: Siglo XXI, 1982), 9.

101. Ibid., 292.

102. "In an acquired dispositional state which causes a coherent set of responses and which is determined by an object or apprehended objective situation" (ibid., 71).

103. Ibid., 175.

104. Ibid., 220.

105. Ibid., 294–295. And he adds, "Skepticism toward every possibility of innovation and profound change accommodates very well to conformism with the existing situation and its structures of domination. It is not without reason that technocratic and conservative focuses on social life often attempt to disguise themselves with a scientistic posture" (ibid., 296).

106. Ibid., 227. Here the "second" Villoro follows the "first" (the phenomenological and historian of ideology Villoro), and encounters the "third" (his present political philosophy).

107. From within the current, Gracia writes, "A more serious weakness from the philosophical standpoint that I see in the work of Latin American analysts is their lack of interest and competence in the history of philosophy in general and particularly in the history of Latin American thought. [. . .] At a time when the analytic tradition in the Anglo-American world is opening up to other philosophical traditions and trying to engage in dialogue with them, some Latin American analysts seem to be going in exactly the opposite direction" ("Impact of Philosophical Analysis," 138–139).

108. See the bibliography, section 3.7.

109. This is Miró Quesada's "fourth" generation (*Proyecto y realización*, 184). The term "generation" is not meant here as a category, but as an approximate indication of membership both in a certain problematic and in a certain time (where the age of the philosopher is an ambiguous term, which nevertheless indicates a certain historicity).

110. A. Salazar Bondy, *La filosofía en el Perú. Panorama histórico* (Washington, DC: Unión Panamericana, 1954), 118.

111. Ibid.

112. Ibid., 127.

113. Ibid., 133.

114. A. Salazar Bondy, "Diálogo con los expositores," *Stromata* (Buenos Aires) 29 (Oct.–Dec. 1973): 441–442. I must mention here that Salazar Bondy was pleasantly surprised to encounter a philosophical movement, with publications, a presence in the universities, and interdisciplinary congresses, that had been developing for several years, called "philosophy of liberation," whose existence he had not known of. He inmediately felt himself a member and entered into the constructive discussion. It was as if it were a project of his own that he had not been able to develop. He honored us greatly when he said, "I find it very interesting what you are doing, [since] you are in fact attempting a *reformulation* of the traditional problematic of a *new optic*" ("Filosofía de la dominación y filosofía de la liberación," *Stromata*, 29 [Oct.–Dec. 1973]: 397).

115. Salazar Bondy, "Filosofía de la dominación," 397.

116. Both in Zea, *La filosofía americana*, and in his critique of Salazar Bondy (and me) in San Miguel (see Zea, "La filosofía latinoamericana como filosofía de la liberación," *Stromata*, 29 [Oct.–Dec. 1973]: 406: "Enrique Dussel, in turn, has formulated a similar need and, with Salazar Bondy, he has asked: is an authentic philosophy possible in our underdeveloped, dependent, and oppressed continent, even culturally and philosophically?").

117. See L. Zea, "La filosofía latinoamericana como filosofía de la liberación," in idem, *Dependencia y liberación en la cultura latinoamericana* (Mexico City: Joaquín Mortiz, 1974).

118. Zea himself wrote, "Not to want to become aware of our own situation explains partly why we have not been able to have *our philosophy*" ("La filosofía como compromiso," in Leopoldo Zea, *La filosofía como compromiso y otros ensayos* [Mexico: Fondo de cultura Económica, 1952], p. 33). Note that here Zea agrees with Bondy and me.

119. See Antonio Sidekum, ed., *Ética do Discurso e Filosofia da Libertaçâo. Modelos Complementares* (São Leopoldo, RS: Editora Unisinos, 1994). This volume emerged from a meeting at which the question "Is there a Latin American philosophy?" was discussed.

120. Salazar Bondy advanced to the first position, called attention to the second position, and attempted the third position, which we had held independently in Argentina since 1969–1970. On the fourth position we agreed personally in 1973. Salazar Bondy experienced the entire process of development of the philosophy of liberation, which he had not known about, but which he recognized inmediately.

121. For an overview, see Enrique Dussel, "Filosofía de la liberación desde la praxis de los oprimidos," in E. Dussel, *Apel, Ricoeur, Rorty y la Filosofía de la Liberación* (Guadalajara: Universidad de Guadalajara, 1993), 13–31.

122. I refer to the military dictatorships of dependence, which began with Castello Branco in Brazil (1964) and Onganía in Argentina (1966), and that were later generalized (Banzer in Bolivia, Pinochet in Chile in 1973, Videla in Argentina in 1976, etc.). These historical "ruptures," until there was a return to formal democracy in Argentina in 1983, produced deep fissures in philosophical development, as we have seen. The European "fissures" (the irruption of Nazism and fascism in the late twenties, and the return to democracy in 1945) were equally acute and produced important "philosophical" effects. One has to know how to analyze them analogically with Latin America, where those dictatorships have not yet ended. In Latin America there were many expulsions of philosophers, similar to those from the Frankfurt school, many analogous to Walter Benjamin (think of the philosopher Mauricio Lopez, tortured and assassinated in Argentina in 1976), many Marcuses (more than ten professors, including me, shared a commitment to the philosophy of liberation and were expelled from the university and the country), and many collaborationist Heideggers (although they remained philosophers). The historical analysis of the global periphery is more complex than is that of Europe or the United States.

123. See Luis Sánchez, "Dussel, Enrique," in F. Maffé, ed., *Dictionnaire des Oeuvres Philosophiques* (Paris: PUF, 1992), vol. 2, 3196.

124. See J. C. Scannone, *Nuevo punto de partida de la Filosofía Latinoamericana* (Buenos Aires: Editorial Guadalupe, 1990), in which he announces a new beginning.

125. See Carlos Cullén, *Reflexiones desde América*, 3 vols. (Buenos Aires: Ross, 1986). This work has to be taken into account from the perspective of Rodolfo Kusch.

126. Hinkelammert's work is of great interest, particularly in view of the debate with K.-O. Apel in September of 1993 in São Leopoldo, Brazil.

127. In *Razón y Liberación: notas para una filosofía latinoamericana* (Buenos Aires: Siglo Veintiuno Argentina Editores, 1973), Casalla does not overcome the horizon of the totality. The alterity of the oppressed class, the poor, and the marginalized (different levels) are not clarified: the national is identified as the popular.

128. For Zea, in *Filosofía de la Historia Americana*, the "assumptive moment" supersedes and subsumes the emancipatory project of independence, whether liberal or conservative,

but, as with Vasconcelos's *cosmic race*, only a *national* liberation, which is not the same as popular liberation, is proposed.

129. Miró Quesada's commitment to philosophy of liberation did not come from the level of what he called "pure philosophy," but from the "ideological character" of certain rational discourses. His *Humanismo y Revolución* (Lima: Casa de la Cultura del Perú, 1969) is not a work of philosophy of liberation, but it indicates how he formulated the political problem. For him, "ideology"—theoretical justification at the practical level—can be formulated rationally departing from teleological principles: "Political problems can be faced through theoretical principles, through rational rules that allow the achievement of objective and valid conclusions for all humans" (*Humanismo y Revolución*, 21). Throughout his analysis, Miró Quesada follows the rationalist Aristotelian model. Here, he has not formulated the difference between theoretical and practical rationality. He thinks that the first operates in ideology with the same rules as practical reason (a problem which, posed in a different manner, has not been solved by the rationalism of Apel and Habermas). Compare Miró Quesada's *Humanismo y Revolución* and my *Para una ética de la liberación latinoamericana*, vol. 4, *Politics* (Bogotá: USTA, 1980). When Miró Quesada learned of the existence of liberation philosophy, in the seventies, he understood its importance, since it allowed him to formulate the theoretical-ideological principle that he needed. I think that the question is far more complex, as I show in my *Ethics of Liberation* (Madrid: Trotta 1998). For me, practical reason is the first reason (and not simply ideological reason), just as ethics is *prima philosophia*.

130. The very worthy analysis by the Cuban team, like that by H. Cerutti, tends to confuse the planes, since it claims to analyze everything through the criteria of a universalist, humanist "Engelsian materialist" Marxism (see Pablo Guadarrama, *Humanismo y Filosofía de la Liberación en América Latina* [Bogotá: El Buho, 1993]), or from the perspective of a "classism" in which the category of "people" is populist (see Horacio Cerutti, *Filosofía de la Liberación Latinoamericana* [Mexico City: FCE, 1983]; there is a response to his objections in Dussel, *La producción teórica de Marx*, 400–413, and *El último Marx*, 243–293).

131. See, for instance, Enrique Dussel, *Liberación de la mujer y erótica latinoamericana* (Bogotá: Nueva América, 1980), with retractions and clarifications in idem, "Liberation Philosophy from the Praxis of the Oppressed," *The Underside of Modernity*, trans. and ed. Eduardo Mendieta (New York: Humanities Press, 1995), 2–18.

132. These currents, or philosophical styles, in the nineties are an epistemological and pragmatic philosophy (that subsumes analytic thinking), from out of the brain-mind problematic; a "continental" philosophy (especially from Kant to Habermas), as history of contemporary philosophy, including the modernity-postmodernity debate; a Latin American philosophy, philosophy of liberation, and political philosophy (this last one in expansion, through positions such as that of Carlos Pereyra in Mexico, which has as tributary some Marxism, and with debates on the question of "democracy" drawing on political science), with works such as those by Guillermo O'Donell, "Apuntes para una teoría del Estado," *Revista Mexicana de Sociología* 40, no. 4 (1978): 1157–1199; and with philosophical works such as Enrique Serrano, *Legitimación y racionalización. Weber y Habermas: la dimensión normativa de un orden secularizado* (Barcelona and Mexico City: Anthropos-UAM, 1994).

133. On December 5–9, 1994, Latin American philosophers participated in the 2nd Congress of the Afro-Asiatic Association of Philosophy in Cairo, Egypt. This was the beginning of a dialogue between the philosophers of the peripheral world (the so-called Third World).

INDICATIVE BIBLIOGRAPHY

A bibliography on this theme, on its own, could be hundreds of pages long. I wish only to indicate some works in order to inform colleagues of other cultural horizons. This is a minimal, but reasoned, bibliography.

1. General Bibliography

These works concern the entire Latin American continent and not countries or currents.

Abellán, José Luis. *Filosofía española en América (1936–1966)*. Madrid: Guadarrama, 1967.

Baggini, Hugo. *Filosofía americana e identidad*. Buenos Aire: EUDEBA, 1989.

Crawford, W. R. *A Century of Latin American Thought*. Cambridge, Mass.: Harvard University Press, 1961.

David, H. E. *Latin American Thought: A Historical Introduction*. New York: Free Press, 1972.

Dussel, E. "Hipótesis para una Historia de la Filosofía en América Latina." In E. Dussel, *Historia de la Filosofía Latinoamericana y Filosofía de la Liberación*, pp. 13–54. Bogotá: Nueva América, 1994.

Fornet-Betancourt, Raúl. *Kommentierte Bibliographie zur Philosophie in Lateinamerika*. Frankfurt: Peter Lang, 1985.

———. *Problemas actuales de la filosofía en Hispanoamérica*. Buenos Aires: FEPAI, 1985.

Gaos, José. *El pensamiento hispanoamericano*. Mexico City: Colegio de México, 1944.

Gracia, Jorge. *Latin American Philosophy in the Twentieth Century: Man, Values and the Search for Philosophical Identity*. Buffalo: Prometheus Books, 1986.

———. *Directory of Latin American Philosophers*. Buffalo: State University of New York, and Buenos Aires: CISP, 1988.

Gracia, Jorge, ed. *El hombre y los valores en la filosofía latinboamericana en el Siglo XX*. Mexico City: FCE, 1975.

———. 1988. "Latin American Philosophy Today." *The Philosophical Forum* 20, no. 1–2: 1988–1989.

Insúa Rodríguez, Ramón. *Historia de la filosofía en Hispanoamérica*. Guayaquil: Editorial Universitaria, 1945.

Kempff Mercado, Manfredo. *Historia de la filosofía en Latinoamérica*. Santiago: Zig-Zag, 1958.

Krumpel, Heinz. *Philosophie in Lateinamerika. Grundzüge ihrer Entwicklung*. Berlin: Akademie Verlag, 1992.

Larroyo, Francisco. *La filosofía latinoamericana*. Mexico City: UNAM, 1958.

Marquínez Argote, Germán, ed. *La Filosofía en América Latina*. Bogotá: El Buho, 1993.

Miró Quesada, Francisco. *Despertar y proyecto del filosofar latinoamericano*. Mexico City: FCE, 1974.

———. *Proyecto y realización del filosofar latinoamericano*. Mexico City: FCE, 1981.

Roig, Arturo. *Teoría y crítica del pensamiento latinoamericano*. Mexico City: FCE, 1981.

———. *Rostro y filosofía de América Latina*. Mendoza: EDIUNC, 1993.

Romero, Francisco. *Sobre la filosofía en América*. Buenos Aires: Raigal, 1952.

Saarti, Sergio. *Panorama della filosofía ispanomaericana contemporanea*. Milan: Cisalpino-Goliardica, 1976.

Sánchez Reulet, Aníbal. *Contemporary Latin American Philosophy*. Albuquerque: University of New Mexico Press, 1954. A prior publication by Sánchez Reulet is "Panorama de las ideas filosóficas en Hispanoamérica," *Tierra Firme* 2 (1936): 181–209.
Stabb, M. *In Quest of Identity*. Chapel Hill: University of North Carolina Press, 1967.
Villegas, Abelardo. *Panorama de la filosofía iberoamericana actual*. Buenos Aires: EUDEBA, 1963.
Wagner de Reyna, Alberto. *La filosofía en Iberoamérica*. Lima: Sociedad Peruana de Filosofía, 1949.
Zea, Leopoldo. *Dos etapas del pensamiento en Hispanoamérica: del romanticismo al positivismo*. Mexico City: Colegio de México, 1949.
———. *The Latin American Mind*. Norman: University of Oklahoma Press, 1963.

2. Bibliography by Country

In this section are works that touch on nations as a whole, although they study authors who belong to particular currents.

2.1. Argentina

Alberini, Coriolano. *Die deutsche Philosophie in Argentinien*. Berlin: H. W. Hendriock, 1930.
———. *Problemas de la historia de las ideas filosóficas en la Argentina*. La Plata: Universidad de La Plata, 1966.
Biaggini, Hugo. *Panorama filosófico argentino*. Buenos Aires: EUDEBA, 1985.
Caturelli, Alberto. *La filosofía en la Argentina actual*. Córdoba: Universidad de Córdoba, 1962.
Farré, Luis. *Cincuenta años de filosofía en Argentina*. Buenos Aires: Peuser, 1958.
Ingeniero, J. *La evolución de las ideas argentinas*. Buenos Aires: Futuro, 1961.
Korn, Alejandro. *El pensamiento argentino*. Buenos Aires: Nova, 1961.
Pro, Diego. *Historia del pensamiento argentino*. Mendoza: Universidad Nacional de Cuyo, 1973.
Roig, Arturo. *La Argentina del 80 al 80. Balance social y cultural*. Mexico City: UNAM, 1993.
Romero, Francisco. *El desarrollo de las ideas en la sociedad argentina del Siglo XX*. Mexico City: FCE, 1965.
Torchia Estrada, Juan C. *La Filosofía en Argentina*. Washington, DC: Unión Panamericana, 1961.

2.2. Mexico

Córdoba, Arnaldo. *La ideología de la revolución mexicana*. Mexico City: UNAM, 1974.
Cueva, Mariano de la. *Major Trends in Mexican Philosophy*. South Bend: University of Notre Dame Press, 1966.
Gaos, José. *En torno a la filosofía mexicana*. Mexico City: Porrua, 1952.
Salmerón, Fernando. "Los filósofos mexicanos del siglo XX." In F. Salmerón, *Cuestiones educativas y páginas sobre México*, 138–181. Zalapa: Universidad Veracruzana, 1980.
Vargas Lozano, Gabriel. "Notas sobre la función actual de la filosofía en México. La década de los setenta." *Dialéctica* 5, no. 9 (1980): 81–102.
Villega, Abelardo. *La Filosofía de lo mexicano*. Mexico City: FCE, 1960.
Villega, A., et al. *La filosofía en México Siglo XX*. Tlaxcala: Universidad Autónoma de Tlaxcala, 1988.

Zea, Leopoldo. *La filosofía en México*. Mexico City: Libro Mexicano, 1955.

2.3. Brazil

Costa, Cruz. *Contribuçâo à história das idéias no Brasil*. Rio di Janeiro: José Olimpio, 1956. (English trans., *History of Ideas in Brazil*, Berkeley and Los Angeles: University of California Press, 1964).

Gómez Robledo, Antonio. *La filosofía en Brasil*. Mexico City: Imprenta Universitaria, 1946.

Lima Vaz, Henrique Cláudio. "O Pensamento filosófico no Brasil de hoje." *Revista Portuguêsa de Filosofía* (1961): 267–285.

Paim, Antonio. *Historia das Idéias filosóficas no Brasil*. São Paulo: Editora Convivio, 1984.

2.4. Peru

Salazar Bondy, Augusto. *La filosofía en el Perú. Panorama histórico*. Washington, DC: Unión Panamericana, 1954.

———. *Historia de las ideas en el Perú contemporáneo*. 2 vols. Lima: Moncloa, 1967.

Sobrevilla, David. *Repensando la tradición nacional I*. 2 vols. Lima: Editorial Hipatia, 1989.

2.5. Uruguay, Bolivia, Chile, Ecuador

Ardao, Arturo. *La filosofía en el Uruguay en el Siglo XX*. Mexico City: FCE, 1956.

Barcelo Larraín, Joaquín. "La actividad filosófica en Chile en la segunda mitad del siglo XX." In Fernando Astorquiza, ed., *Bio-Bibliografía de la filosofía en Chile desde el siglo XVI hasta 1980*, 56–80. Santiago: Universidad de Chile, 1982.

Escobar, Roberto. *La filosofía en Chile*. Santiago: Universidad Técnica del Estado, 1976.

Francovich, Guillermo. *La filosofía en Bolivia*. Buenos Aires: Losada, 1945.

———. *El pensamiento boliviano en el siglo XX*. Mexico City: FCE, 1956.

Lipp, Solomon. *Three Chilean Thinkers*. Waterloo, ON: McGill University, 1975.

Molina, Enrique. *La filosofía en Chile en la primera mitad del Siglo XX*. Santiago: Nacimiento, 1951.

Roig, Arturo. *Esquemas para una historia de la filosofía ecuatoriana*. Quito: EDUC, 1982.

2.6. Venezuela, Colombia, Central America

García Bacca, Juan. *Antología del Pensamiento venezolano*. 3 vols. Caracas: Ministerio de Educación, 1964.

Jaramillo Uribe, Jaime. *El pensamiento colombiano en el siglo XIX*. Bogotá: Temis, 1974.

Lascaris Conneno, Constantino. *Desarrollo de las ideas filosóficas en Costa Rica*. San José: Ed. Studium, 1983.

Marquínez Argote, Germán, ed. *La Filosofía en Colombia*. Bogotá: Editorial el Búho, 1988.

Sierra Mejía, Rubén. "Temas y corrientes de la filosofía colombiana en el siglo XX." In Rubén Sierra Mejía, *Ensayos filosóficos*, 91–126. Bogotá: Colcultura, 1978.

Valle, Rafael. *Historia de las ideas contemporáneas en Centroamérica*. Mexico City: FCE, 1960.

2.7. The Caribbean

Cordero, Armando. *Estudios para la historia de la filosofía en Santo Domingo*. 2 vols. Santo Domingo: Arte y Cine, 1962.

Lizaso, Félix. *Panorama de la cultura cubana*. Mexico City: FCE., 1949

Piñera Llera, Humberto. *La enseñanza de la filosofía en Cuba*. Havana: Hércules, 1954.
———. *Panorama de la filosofía cubana*. Washington, DC: Unión Panamericana, 1960.
Vitier, Medardo. *Las ideas en Cuba*. Havana: Trópico, 1938.
———. *La filosofía en Cuba*. Mexico City: FCE, 1948.

3. Bibliography of Philosophical Currents

I include in this section some representative philosophers of the respective philosophical currents.

3.1. Anti-Positivist, Vitalist, Spiritualist

Ardao, Arturo. *Espiritualismo y positivismo en el Uruguay*. Montevideo: Universidad de la República, 1968.
Caso, Antonio. *La existencia como economía y como caridad. Ensayo sobre la esencia del cristianismo*. Vol. 3 of Antonio Caso, *Obras Completas*. Mexico City: UNAM, 1972.
Deustua, Alejandro. *Estética general*. Lima: Imprenta E. Rávago, 1923.
———. *Los sistemas eticos*. 2 vols. Lima: El Callao, 1938.
Gonidec, Bernard Le. *Aspects de la pensée hispano-américaine, 1898–1930*. Rennes: Centre d'Études Hispaniques, 1974.
Korn, Alejandro. *La libertad creadora*. Buenos Aires: Claridad, 1963.
———. *De San Agustin a Bergson*. Buenos Aires: Nova, 1959.
Martí, José. *Obras Completas*. 2 vols. Havana: Editorial Lex, 1953.
Rodó, José E. *Ariel*. In José E. Rodó, *Obras Completas*. Buenos Aires: Ed. Antonio Zamora, 1956.
Vasconcelos, José. *Estética*. Mexico City: Ed. Botas, 1945.
———. *La raza cósmica*. In José Vasconcelos, *Obras Completas*. Mexico City: Libreros Mexicanos Unidos, 1958.
Vaz Ferreira, Carlos. *Conocimiento y acción*. Montevideo: Mariño y Caballero, Impresores, 1908.
———. *La pragmatisme: exposition et critique*. Montevideo: Tall. Graf. A. Barreiero y Ramos, 1914 [1908].
———. *Sobre Feminismo*. Montevideo: Ediciones de la Sociedad Amigos del Libro Rioplatense, 1933.
———. *Lógica viva*. Montevideo: Impresora Uruguaya, 1957.
Woodward, R. L. *Positivism in Latin America, 1850–1900*. Lexington, MA: Heath and Co., 1971.
Zea, L. *Positivism in Mexico*. Austin: University of Texas Press, 1976.

3.2. Existential and Phenomenlogical Ontology

Anquín, Nimio de. "Lugones y el ser americano." *Arkhé* (Córdoba) (1964).
Astrada, Carlos. *Idealismo fenomenológico y metafísica existencial*. Buenos Aires: Imprenta de la Universidad, 1936.
———. *El mito gaucho*. Buenos Aires: Cruz del Sur. 1948.
———. *Dialéctica e historia*. Buenos Aires: Juárez Editor, 1969.
Caturelli, Alberto. *América Bifronte. Ensayo de ontología y de filosofía de la historia*. Buenos Aires: Troquel, 1961.
Cruz Vélez, Danilo. *Filosofía sin supuestos: De Husserl a Heidegger*. Buenos Aires: Sudamericana, 1970.

Guerrero, Luis Juan. *Estética operatoria*. 2 vols. Buenos Aires: Losada, 1956–67.

Mayz Vallenilla, Ernesto. *El problema de América*. Caracas: Universidad Central, 1959.

———. *Ontología del conocimiento*. Caracas: Facultad de Humanidades, 1960.

———. *El problema de la nada en Kant*. Madrid: Revista de Occidente, 1965.

Murena, H. A. *El pecado original de América*. Buenos Aires: Grupo Sur, 1954.

Nicol, Eduardo. *Metafísica de la expresión*. Mexico City: FCE, 1957.

Ramos, Samuel. *El perfil del hombre y la cultura de México*. Mexico City: Imprenta Mundial, 1934.

Romero, Francisco. *Filosofía de la persona*. Buenos Aires: Losada, 1944.

———. *Teoría del hombre*. Buenos Aires: Losada, 1952. (Translated into English as *Theory of Man* [Berkeley: University of California Press, 1964].)

Schwartzmann, Félix. *El sentimiento de lo humano en América*. Santiago: Universidad de Chile, 1950.

Sobrevilla, David. "Phenomenology and Existentialism in Latin America." In Jorge Gracia, ed., *Directory of Latin American Philosophers*, 85–113. Buffalo: State University of New York, and Buenos Aires: CISP, 1988.

Wagner de Reyna, Alberto. *La ontología fundamental de y Heidegger*. Buenos Aires: Losada, 1939.

Xirau, Joaquín. *La filosofía de Husserl*. Buenos Aires: Losada, 1941.

3.3. Philosophy Practiced by Christians

Amoroso Lima, Alceu. "Maritain et l'Amérique Latine." *Revue Thomiste* 1 (1948): 12–48.

———. *Obras completas*. 35 vols. Rio: Agir, 1960.

Arruba Campos, Fernando. *Tomismo e neotomismo no Brasil*. São Paulo: Grijalbo, 1968.

De Anquín, Nimio. *Ente y ser*. Madrid: Gredos, 1972.

Derisi, Octavio. *Los fundamentos metafísicos del orden moral*. Buenos Aires: Imprenta López, 1941.

Dominguez Camargo, Manuel. "La neoescolástica de los siglos XIX y XX." In Germán Marquínez Argote, ed., *La Filosofía en América Latina*, 227–265. Bogotá: El Buho, 1993.

Echauri, Raúl. *Heidegger y la metafísica tomista*. Buenos Aires: Editorial Universitaria de Buenos Aires, 1971.

Gonzalo Casas, Manuel. *Introducción a la filosofía*. Buenos Aires, 1954.

Perdomo Garcia, José. "El maritenismo en Hispanoamérica." *Estudios americanos* (Seville) 11 (Oct. 1951): 567–592.

Robles, Oswaldo. "El movimiento filosófico neoescolástico en México." *Filosofía y Letras* (UNAM) (July–Sept. 1946): 178ff.

Sepich, Juan Ramón. *La filosofía de Ser y Tiempo de M. Heidegger*. Buenos Aires: Editorial Nuestro Tiempo, 1954.

Villaça, Antonio. *O pensamiento católico no Brasil*. Rio di Janeiro: Zahar, 1975.

3.4. Marxist Philosophy

Aricó, José. *Marx y América Latina*. Mexico City: Alianza, 1982.

Aricó, José, ed. *Mariátegui y los orígenes del marxismo latinoamericano*. Mexico City: Siglo XXI, 1978.

Astrada, Carlos. *Marx y Hegel: Trabajo y alienación en la Fenomenología y en los Manuscritos*. Buenos Aires: Siglo Veinte, 1958.

Bagú, Sergio. *Economía de la sociedad colonial*. Buenos Aires: El Ateneo, 1949.

48   Enrique Dussel

Dussel, Enrique. *La producción teórica de Marx*. Mexico City: Siglo XXI, 1985.
———. *El último Marx (1863–1882) y la liberación latinoamericana*. Mexico City: Siglo XXI. 1990.
Fornet-Betancourt, R. *Ein anderer Marxismus? Die philosophische Rezeption des Marxismus in Lateinamerika*. Mainz: Gruenewald, 1994. (This is the most important work on the theme.)
Guevara, Ernesto. *Obra revolucionaria*. Mexico City: Era, 1974.
Justo, Juan B. *Teoría y práctica de la historia*. Buenos Aires: Ed. Libera, 1969.
Liss, Sheldon B. *Marxist Thought in Latin America*. Berkeley: University of California Press, 1984.
Löwy, Michael. *El marxismo en America Latina (de 1909 a nuestros días)*. Mexico City: Era, 1980.
Mariátegui, José Carlos. *Defensa del marxismo*. Santiago: Ed. Nacionales y Extranjeras, 1934.
———. *Siete Ensayos sobre la relidad peruana*. In J. C. Mariátegui, *Obras completas*, vol. 2. Lima: Amauta, 1959. (There are translations into English and other languages.)
———. *Obra política*. Mexico City: Era, 1978.
Nuñez, Orlando. "Las condiciones políticas de la transición." In José Luis Coraggio et al., eds., *Transición difícil. La autodeterminación de los pequeños países periféricos*. Mexico City: Siglo XXI, 1986.
Ponce, Aníbal. *Humanismo y revolución*. Mexico City: Siglo XXI, 1970.
Posada Zárate, Francisco. *Los orígenes del pensamiento marxista en Latinoamérica*. Bogotá: Nuevas Ediciones, 1977.
Recabarren, Luis Emilio. *Obras*. Havana: Casa de las Américas, 1976.
Sánchez Vázquez, Adolfo. *Filosofía de la praxis*. Mexico City: Grijalbo, 1967.
———. "Marxism in Latin America." In Jorge Gracia, ed., *Directory of Latin American Philosophers*, 114–128. Buffalo: State University of New York, and Buenos Aires: CISP, 1988.

3.5. Latinamericanist Philosophy

Ardao, Arturo. *Estudios latinoamericanos*. Caracas: Monte Avila Editores, 1978.
Dussel, Enrique. *1492: El encubrimiento del Otro*. Madrid: Nueva Utopía, 1992. (Trans. into English, *The Inventory of the Americas: Eclipse of "the Other" and the Myth of Modernity*. New York: Continuum, 1995).
Marquínez Argote, G. *Filosofía latinoamericana?* Bogotá: El Búho, 1981.
Miró Quesada, Francisco. *Despertar y proyecto del filosofar latinoamericano*. Mexico City: FCE, 1974.
———. *Proyecto y realización del filosofar latino-americano*. Mexico City: FCE, 1981.
Roig, Arturo. *Teoría y crítica del pensamiento latinoamericano*. Mexico City: FCE, 1982.
Villoro, Luis. *Los grandes momentos del indigenismo en México*. Mexico City: El Colegio de México, 1950.
Zea, L. *La filosofía latinoamericana como filosofía sin más*. Mexico City: Siglos XXI, 1969.
———. *Filosofía de la Historia Americana*. Mexico City: FCE, 1978.

3.6. Analytic Philosophy and Philosophy of Science

Bunge, Mario. *Causality*. Cambridge, Mass.: Harvard University Press, 1959.
———. *Treatise on Basic Philosophy*. 8 vols. Boston: Reidel, 1974–1989.

———. *The Mind-Body Problem*. New York: Pergamon Press, 1980.

Castañeda, Héctor-Neri. *Morality and the Language of Conduct*. Detroit: Wayne State University Press, 1963.

———. *The Structure of Morality*. Springfield: Thomas, 1974.

———. *Action, Knowledge and Reality*. Indianapolis: Bobbs-Merrill, 1975.

———. *Thinking, Language and Experience*. Minneapolis: University of Minnesota Press, 1989.

Gracia, Jorge. "The Impact of Philosophical Analysis in Latin America?" In Jorge Gracia, ed., *Directory of Latin American Philosophers*, 129–140. Buffalo: State University of New York, and Buenos Aires: CISP, 1988–89.

Gracia, Jorge, ed. *El análisis filosófico en América Latina*. Mexico City: FCE, 1985. (A very complete and excellent study. There is a partial translation into English: Dordrecht: Reidel, 1984.)

Moulines, Carlos U. *La estructura del mundo sensible*. Barcelona: Ariel, 1973.

Villoro, Luis. *Creer, saber, conocer*. Mexico City: Siglo XXI, 1982.

3.7. Philosophy of Liberation

Ardiles, O., et al. *Hacia una filosofía de la liberación latinoamericana*. Buenos Aires: Bonum, 1974.

Cerutti, Horacio. *Filosofía de la Liberación Latinoamericana*. Mexico City: FCE, 1983.

Cullen, Carlos. *Reflexiones desde América*. 3 vols. Buenos Aires: Ross, 1986.

Demenchonok, Eduard. *Filosofía latinoamericana*. Bogotá: El Búho, 1992.

Dussel, Enrique. *Para una ética de la liberación latinoamericana*. Vols. 1–2, Buenos Aires: Siglo XXI, 1973; vol. 3, Mexico City: Edicol, 1977; Vols. 4–5, Bogotá: USTA, 1979–80.

———. *Método para una filosofía de la liberación*. Salamanca: Sígueme, 1974.

———. *Filosofía de la Liberacion*. Mexico City: Edicol, 1977. (Trans. into English, *Philosophy of Liberation*. New York: Orbis Books, 1985.)

———. *Apel, Ricoeur, Rorty y la Filosofía de la Liberación*. Guadalajara: Universidad de Guadalajara, 1993.

Fornet-Betancourt, R. "Filosofía y liberación, o el problema de la constitución de una Filosofía de la Liberación." In R. Fornet-Betancourt, *Problemas actuales de la filosofía en Hispanoamérica*, 117–142. Buenos Aires: FEPAI, 1985.

———. *Diskursethik oder Befreiungsethik*. Aachen: Augustinus, 1992.

Guadarrama, Pablo. *Humanismo y Filosofía de la Liberación en América Latina*. Bogotá: El Buho, 1993.

———. "La filosofía latinoamericana de la liberación." In Germán Marquínez Argote, ed., *La Filosofía en América Latina*, 309–361. Bogotá: El Buho, 1993.

Hierro, Graciela. *La naturaleza femenina*. Mexico City: UNAM, 1985.

———. *Etica y feminismo*. Mexico City: UNAM, 1985.

Hinkelammert, Franz. *Crítica a la razón utópica*. San José: DEI, 1984.

Miró Quesada, Francisco. *Humanismo y Revolución*. Lima: Casa de la Cultura del Perú, 1969.

———. "Filosofía de la liberación: convergencias y divergencias." Paper presented at the 4th National Congress of Philosophy (Toluca, Mexico), 1987.

Salazar Bondy, Augusto. *Existe una filosofía en nuestra América?* Mexico City: Siglo XXI, 1968.

Scannone, Juan Carlos. *Sein und Inkarnation: zum ontologischen Hintergrund der Frühschriften Maurice Blondels*. Freiburg: Karl Alber, 1968.

———. *Nuevo punto de partida de la Filosofía Latinoamericana*. Buenos Aires: Editorial Guadalupe, 1990.

Schelkshorn, Hans. *Ethik der Befreiung*. Freiburg/Vienna: Herder, 1992.

Schutte, Ofelia. "Philosophy and Feminism in Latin America." In Jorge Gracia, ed., *Directory of Latin American Philosophers*, 62–84. Buffalo: State University of New York, and Buenos Aires: CISP, 1988.

Sidekum, Antonio, ed. *Ética do Discurso e Filosofica da Libertaçâo. Modelos Complementares*. São Leopoldo: Editora Unisinos, 1994.

Zea, Leopoldo. "La filosofía latinoamericana como filosofía de la liberación." In Leopoldo Zea, *Dependencia y liberación en la cultura latinoamericana*. Mexico City: Joaquín Mortiz, 1974.

———. "La filosofía como dominación y como liberación." In Leopoldo Zea, *El pensamiento latinoamericano*, 513–540. Barcelona: Ariel, 1976.

Zimmermann, Roque. *América Latina. O nâo ser*. Petropolis: Vozes, 1987.

MINIMAL CHRONOLOGY

The country in parentheses indicates where the person was born.

1810	Juan Bautista Alberdi born (Argentina; died 1884)
1826	Mamerto Esquiú born (Argentina; died 1883)
1842	Jacinto Ríos born (Argentina; died 1892)
1849	Alejandro Deustua born (Peru; died 1945)
1853	José Martí born (Cuba; died 1895)
1857	Rafael Carrasquilla born (Colombia; died 1930)
1860	Alejandro Korn born (Argentina; died 1936)
1862	Raimundo Farias Brito born (Brazil; died 1917)
1865	Juan B. Justo born (Argentina; died 1928)
1867	Carlos Arturo Torres born (Colombia; died 1911)
1871	José Enrique Rodó born (Uruguay; died 1917)
	Enrique Molina born (Chile; died 1964)
1872	Carlos Vaz Ferreira born (Uruguay; died 1958)
1873	Ricardo Flores Magón born (Mexico; died 1922)
1876	Luis Emilio Recabarren born (Chile; died 1924)
1882	José Vasconcelos born (Mexico; died 1959)
1883	Antonio Caso born (Mexico; died 1946)
1886	Coriolano Alberini born (Argentina; died 1960)
	Luis Guillermo Martínez Villada born (Argentina; died 1956)
1891	Francisco Romero born (Argentina; died 1962)
	Jackson de Figueiredo born (Brazil; died 1928)
1893	Mariano Ibérico born (Peru; died 1974)
	Alceu Amoroso Lima born (Brazil; died 1983)
1894	Carlos Astrada born (Argentina; died 1970)

1895	José Carlos Mariátegui born (Peru; died 1930)
	J. B. Justo translates Marx's *Capital*.
	Farías Brito
1896	Nimio de Aquín born (Argentina)
1897	Samuel Ramos born (Mexico; died 1959)
1898	Aníbal Ponce born (Argentina; died 1938)
1899	Luis Juan Guerrero born (Argentina; died 1957)
1900	J. E. Rodó, *Ariel*
	Miguel Angel Virasoro born (Argentina; died 1966)
1901	Juan García Bacca born (Spain–Venezuela)
1903	Cesar Guardia Mayorga born (Peru; died 1983)
1906	Juan Ramón Sepich born (Argentina; died 1979)
	Ismael Quiles (Argentina; died 1993)
1907	Eduardo Nicol born (Spain–Mexico; died 1990)
	Octavio Derisi born (Argentina;)
1909	J. B. Justo, *Teoría y práctica de la historia*
1910	C. Vaz Ferreira, *Lógica viva*
	A. Caso, "Conferencia del Ateneo" (Mexico)
	Miguel Reale born (Brazil)
	José Gaos born (Spain–Mexico; died 1959)
	Aníbal Sánchez Reulet born (Argentina; died 1997)
	Risieri Frondizi (Argentina–United States; died 1982)
1912	A. Korn, *El pensamiento argentino*
	R. M. Carrasquilla, *Lecciones de Metafísica y Ética.*
	Leopoldo Zea born (Mexico)
	Arturo Ardao born (Uruguay–Venezuela)
	Francisco Larroyo born (Mexico)
1915	Alberto Wagner de Reyna born (Peru)
	Adolfo Sánchez Vázquez born (Mexico)
1916	A. Caso, *La existencia como economía y caridad*
	Vicente Ferreira da Silva born (Brazil; died 1963)
	Ortega y Gasset's first visit to Argentina
1918	Francisco Miró Quesada born (Peru)
1919	Mario Bunge born (Argentina–Canada)
1920	Danilo Cruz Vélez born (Colombia)
1921	Paulo Freire born (Brazil; died 1999)
1922	A. Korn, *La libertad creadora*
	Jackson de Figueiredo, *Pascal e a Inquietaçâo Moderna*
	Gregorio Klimoski born (Argentina)
	Arturo Andrés Roig born (Argentina)
	Luis Villoro born (Mexico)
1923	A. Deustua, *Estética general*
1924	Héctor-Neri Castañeda born (Guatamala–United States; died 1991)
1925	Augusto Salazar Bondy born (Peru; died 1974)
	Ernesto Mayz Vallenilla born (Venezuela)
	Fernando Salmerón born (Mexico)
	Einstein's visit to Argentina

1928	J. C. Mariátegui, *Siete ensayos de la realidad peruana*
	Ernesto Guevara born (Argentina–Cuba; died 1967)
1929	J. C. Mariátegui, *En defensa del marxismo*
	Thomas Moro Simpson born (Argentina)
1930	Eduardo Rabossi born (Argentina)
1931	Juan Carlos Scannone born (Argentina)
	Rodolfo Kusch born (Argentina; died 1979)
1932	E. Martínez Estrada, *Radiografía de la Pampa*
	Alejandro Rossi born (Venezuela–Mexico)
1933	Hugo Assmann born (Brazil)
1934	S. Ramos, *El Perfil del Hombre y la Cultura en México*
	Abelardo Villegas born (Mexico; died 2001)
	Enrique Dussel born (Argentina–Mexico)
1935	Guillermo Hoyos born (Colombia)
1936	C. Astrada, *Idealismo fenomenológico y metafísica existencial*
1937	A. Ponce, *Educación y lucha de clases*
1939	A. Wagner de Reyna, *La ontología fundamental de Heidegger*
1940	J. Vasconcelos, *La raza cósmica*
	V. Ferreira da Silva, *Elementos de lógica matemática*
1941	O. Derisi, *Fundamentos metafísicos del orden moral*
1942	Jorge Gracia born (Cuba–United States)
1943	L. Zea, *El Positivismo en México*
	Carlos Cullen born (Argentina)
1944	W. V. Quine gives lectures in Brazil: *O sentido da nova lógica*
1946	D. Cruz Vélez, *Nueva imagen del hombre y de la cultura*
	Carlos Ulises Moulines born (Venezuela–Germany)
1948	C. Astrada, *El mito gaucho*
1949	S. Bagú, *Economía de la sociedad colonial*
1952	F. Romero, *Teoría del Hombre*
	J. Gaos, *En torno a la filosofía mexicana*
1955	F. Miró Quesada, *Filosofía de las Matemáticas*
1956	L. J. Guerrero, *Estética operatoria en sus tres dimensiones*, Vols. 1–3 (third volume unpublished, *Lo mejor de la ontología latinoamericana*)
1957	L. Zea, *América en la historia*
1961	M. Bunge, *Causalidad*
1962	F. Miró Quesada, *Apuntes para una teoría de la razón*
1963	XIII Congreso Mundial de Filosofía (Mexico City)
1967	A. Sánchez Vázquez, *Filosofía de la praxis*
1968	A. Salazar Bondy, *¿Existe una filosofía en nuestra América?*
1972	II Congreso Nacional de Filosofía (Argentina)
1973	E. Dussel, *Para una ética de la liberación latinoamericana*, Vols. 1–5 (1980)
1974	F. Miró Quesada, *Despertar y proyecto del filosofar latinoamericano*
	M. León Portilla, *La filosofía náhuatl*
	H.-N. Castañeda, *The Structure of Morality*
	M. Bunge, *Treatise of Basic Philosophy*, Vols 1–8 (1989)
1975	I Coloquio Nacional de Filosofía (Mexico): Declaración de Morelia: "Filosofía e Independencia"

1977   G. Marquínez Argote, *Metafísica desde América Latina*
             E. Dussel, *Filosofía de la Liberación*
             E. Rabossi, *Análisis filosófico, lenguaje y metafísica*
1978   G. Hoyos, *Fenomenología como Epistemología*
1980   F. Miró Quesada, *Proyecto y realización del filosofar latinoamericano*
             M. Bunge, *The Mind-Body Problem*
1981   C. U. Moulines, *Exploraciones en filosofía de la ciencia*
1982   L. Villoro, *Creer, saber, conocer*
1988   D. Sobrevilla, *Repensando la tradición nacional* I–II (1989)
1993   XIX Congreso Mundial de Filosofía (Moscow)
1994   XIII Congreso Interamericano de Filosofía (Bogotá)
             III Congreso Nacional de Filosofía (Lima, Peru)
             R. Fornet-Betancourt, *Otro marxismo? La recepción filosófica del marxismo en America Latina*

Part 2.
Can or Should There Be a Latin American Philosophy?

2. Ethnic Labels and Philosophy: The Case of Latin American Philosophy

JORGE J. E. GRACIA

Many histories of philosophy are arranged according to categories that appear to be national. In a library, it does not take very long to find histories of French philosophy which claim to deal with the philosophies produced by the French nation, and it is similar for histories of Spanish philosophy, German philosophy, American philosophy, and so on. Indeed, there are societies, such as the Society for the Advancement of American Philosophy in the United States, which purport to be devoted to the study of some of these philosophies. Of course, many histories of philosophy concentrate on periods and cut across national boundaries, such as histories of ancient, Renaissance, and medieval philosophy. Likewise, there are histories of problems, themes, and schools, which also do not seem to pay much attention to nationalities. Nonetheless, a favorite way of organizing histories of philosophy is along boundaries which are taken to be national.

When one looks at these histories more carefully, however, it becomes clear that what is included in them often has little to do with nations as we generally understand them today—as groups of people organized politically and living in particular territories.[1] Much more than the work of French citizens is included within French philosophy, and the same could be said about other "national" philosophies. Consider, for example, that histories of Spanish philosophy routinely include references to Seneca and Averroes, philosophers who lived long before the Spanish nation was constituted as a political reality, and whose relationship to this nation, as we have known it since the sixteenth century, is less than tenuous. Indeed, it appears that other considerations, such as language, culture, and history, play important roles in inclusion within these categories.

This suggests that the use of these categories as reflecting national identities is inaccurate, and that they should, rather, be understood in other ways. One possibility is to take them to reflect ethnic, rather than national, identities. Thus, "Spanish philosophy" and "French philosophy" become ethnic labels, which name and include the philosophical work of persons who do not necessarily belong to the same nation even though they belong to the same ethnic group.

The notion of an ethnic philosophy poses all sorts of philosophically interesting questions. Some of these are related to the notion of ethnicity itself, which is

receiving considerable attention these days, but which remains quite murky. I
have dealt with ethnicity elsewhere in some detail, so I shall not take up this issue
here.[2] Instead, I shall examine the question of inclusion: What counts as part of
an ethnic philosophy? Unfortunately, posing the question in this way does not
take us very far. In order to make some progress we need to pose the question in
concrete terms, and so I have chosen the case of Latin American philosophy for
this purpose. There are several reasons for the choice. First, it is a clear case of ethnic philosophy in the sense that I understand it here, insofar as there is no Latin
American nation; second, there has been much discussion about the nature, and
even existence, of Latin American philosophy; and third, I am well acquainted
with the topic.[3] In addition, I need to clarify some points of confusion. The first of
these has to do with the notion of history. This notion is important because when
one speaks of an ethnic philosophy, often what is meant is the history of that philosophy, but "history" itself is frequently used ambiguously.

My overall thesis is that ethnic philosophies are historical realities enmeshed
in webs of complicated relations, and that a proper understanding of them must
reflect this reality. Moreover, it is a mistake to think of these philosophies as
classes whose members satisfy necessary and sufficient conditions. The conditions
of membership vary, as history itself does, allowing for different groupings and ways
of looking at them.

I. HISTORY

The term "history" has several meanings that give rise to various ambiguities. I
see at least three whose distinction may be useful to us.[4] First, "history" refers to
certain events from the past. The history of Mexico, for example, includes past
events that had something to do with Mexico: the Revolution of 1910, the struggle for independence from Spain, Maximilian's debacle, and so on. In philosophy,
the pertinent events are primarily ideas expressed in texts—say, Scotus's notion of
haecceitas or Wittgenstein's concept of "fact." Even though history understood in
this way also includes references to events that are not ideas, such as the birth of
an author and the publication of a book, the key events are ideas.

In a second sense, we understand by "history" an account of history considered
in the first sense. In this case, we speak of the history of Mexico as an account,
composed by a historian, of events related to Mexico, such as the ones mentioned
above. Conceived in this way, history is an oral, written, or even mental text that
describes what happened in, or to, Mexico. For many, this is the primary and fundamental sense of history, even though the truth of history in this sense depends
on history conceived in the first sense—that is, on history conceived as past
events. A history of philosophy in this second sense is an account of certain philosophical ideas from the past.

Finally, we speak of history as a discipline of learning. Taken thus, "history" consists in a series of human actions guided by certain methodological principles with

the aim of composing an account of the past. Still, this allows for two possibilities: on the one hand, we can speak of a historian's actions in themselves as history. The work of the historian is part of the discipline; what historians do in archives to determine the date of a birth is history. On the other hand, history as a discipline can be constituted of the methodological rules and principles by which the historian is guided. In this sense, the principle "Primary sources have more authority than do secondary ones" is part of history.

II. HISTORY OF AN ETHNIC PHILOSOPHY

The history of an ethnic philosophy, then, can be conceived in at least three different ways. First, it can be conceived as certain past ideas; second, as an account of those past ideas; and third, as either the actions taken in order to produce such an account or the methodological rules that govern such actions. In the particular case of Latin American philosophy, for example, the first sense consists of certain ideas from the past, such as José Vasconcelos's notion of cosmic race or Risieri Frondizi's concept of the self as a structural quality. In the second sense, it is an account composed by a historian, such as *Historia de la filosofía en Latino-américa* by Manfredo Kempff Mercado. Finally, it can be taken as a series of actions taken by a historian, such as Kempff Mercado, to compose his history in the second sense, or as the historiographical rules governing such actions.

Some may think that these clarifications are sufficient, or perhaps too many and too trivial—but further reflection shows that even with them in mind, the issue under consideration is not quite clear. The problem originates with the notion of an ethnic philosophy, such as "Latin American philosophy." We have been speaking of ethnic philosophies as if the subject matter were well understood, but what happens with it is what happened to Augustine with regard to time: according to what he tells us, he knew what it was until he asked about it. Once we ask what ethnic philosophy is in general, or what a specific ethnic philosophy, such as Latin American philosophy, is in particular, we get into a muddle from which it is difficult to emerge.

The difficulties begin insofar as "ethnic philosophy" can refer to the concept of "ethnic philosophy" itself, to the concepts of particular ethnic philosophies such as "Latin American philosophy" or "German philosophy," or to the realities behind these concepts. And it can also refer to a certain discipline (actions, principles, or both) concerning these concepts.

III. HISTORY OF THE CONCEPTS OF ETHNIC PHILOSOPHY AND PARTICULAR ETHNIC PHILOSOPHIES

Histories of the concepts of specific ethnic philosophies are generally quite new. Indeed, if we were to dig a bit in the historical record, I am sure we would find that labels such as "French philosophy" and "Spanish philosophy" did not come to be used until fairly recently in the West. In some cases the record is quite clear. For example, the concept of "Latin America" does not predate the period of independence, if it goes that far back, even though the concept of "America" is much older. The concept of "Latin American philosophy" seems to have made its debut with Juan Bautista Alberdi in the second half of the nineteenth century,[5] and even then, as first used, it was fairly rudimentary, giving rise to questions about its identity by some historians. A full development of the notion of Latin American philosophy had to wait until the second quarter of the twentieth century.[6] Since then, however, it has maintained the interest of Latin American philosophers, so there is no dearth of detailed analyses of it.[7] The history of Latin American philosophy as a discipline, however, has received only scant attention.[8] So much for histories of the concepts of particular ethnic philosophies. The history of the concept of "ethnic philosophy" itself has yet to take place and be written for the simple reason that the concept of ethnicity, let alone the concept of an ethnic philosophy, is quite a new development.[9] Indeed, the words "ethnicity" and "ethnic" did not appear in English dictionaries until relatively recently.

Up to this point, I have been speaking about the history of the concept of "ethnic philosophy" and of the concepts of particular ethnic philosophies, but this is the easy part of our project. The difficult part concerns the history of the realities that we know as ethnic philosophies, such as Latin American or German. Here, the problem has to do with ethnic philosophy itself. Although much has been said about particular ethnic philosophies, including Latin American philosophy, the main historiographical issues of interest to the philosopher seem to have been largely ignored.

IV. HISTORY OF THE REALITY OF PARTICULAR ETHNIC PHILOSOPHIES

It is worth repeating that whereas the concepts of particular ethnic philosophies did not develop until fairly recently, this does not mean, contrary to what many think today, that the realities did not exist before. When I hit my head on an open window that I did not see, it would be difficult to hold that the event did not happen unless I grasp the concepts of "hit" and "window." The reality of an ethnic philosophy, such as Latin American philosophy, may antecede the concept of that philosophy, although in order to decide whether there is such a reality we need to develop an appropriate concept of it—a concept that is not only consistent but also adequate. To establish this concept is not at all easy. In fact, the scant attention that the concepts of particular ethnic philosophies, and especially that of Latin American philosophy, have received indicates that the proposals made in this direction have failed.

My thesis is that the failure of these proposals rests on a common mistake. They ignore the reality that ethnic philosophies exist, and because of this they try to understand them in inadequate ways. They misunderstand the nature of ethnic philosophies insofar as they do not realize that the realities about which they speak are historical and relational and that the concepts we need to understand them are subject to historical and relational conditions that go beyond the conditions that establish the realities in question. I shall explain this more clearly later. For the moment, to illustrate the usual deficiencies that occur when historiographers deal with ethnic philosophies let me cite three examples of the approaches that have failed to produce an understanding of Latin American philosophy. I call these approaches, respectively, nativist, originalist, and culturalist.

V. THREE MISTAKEN CONCEPTIONS OF LATIN AMERICAN PHILOSOPHY

The nativist conception postulates its native origin as the necessary and sufficient condition of Latin American philosophy. Latin American philosophy must consist of ideas born in Latin America, and being born in Latin America is a sufficient condition to make an idea be part of Latin American philosophy. Obviously, the problems with this position begin with the notion of Latin America itself, a notion much disputed these days. But, leaving these problems aside, there are still others that cannot be avoided easily. One of these is that very few of the ideas that could form part of a Latin American philosophy originate in Latin America, and the few that do originate there are mixed with many others that have no Latin American origin. If we were to adopt this criterion strictly, we would be left with little or nothing. On the other hand, there is the problem of origin. If we were to take this proposal seriously, we would have to determine more clearly the criterion of origin. For example, should an idea of a Latin American thinker who lives outside Latin America be considered Latin American or not?

The originalist position posits as a necessary condition of Latin American philosophy that it be composed of original ideas.[10] Here the problem we encounter is similar to the one that we faced with the nativist position, because the number of original philosophical ideas that have been produced in Latin America is extremely small. In fact, the idea that Latin American philosophy must be composed of original ideas, and only original ideas, is absurd. There is no other ethnic philosophy on which this requirement is imposed, and with good reason, for the thought of every thinker is the product of many ideas borrowed from many different sources.

The culturalist position posits as the necessary and sufficient condition of Latin American philosophy that the ideas of which it is composed be the product of Latin American culture.[11] This position encounters many problems, but let me mention just two: first, that of establishing a clear distinction between Latin American culture and other cultures; second, that of finding philosophical ideas that have a direct and demonstrable connection to Latin American culture. The first problem is difficult to solve insofar as, to date, no one has been able to establish something which can be identified as the Latin American culture. The second problem is serious because philosophy aspires to truths that transcend what is culturally specific, and the problems it addresses affect human beings in general and not exclusively members of certain cultures.

A common and fundamental problem with these three positions is that they include an essentialist element. The ideas that constitute Latin American philosophy are supposed to satisfy one or more necessary and sufficient conditions, but this would reduce the number of ideas in question to a laughable number. The essentialist requirement indicates that ethnic entities such as Latin American philosophy are not well understood. The moral of the story is that ethnic philosophies cannot be conceived in essentialist terms, as having necessary and sufficient conditions that apply to all that counts as part of the ethnic philosophy in question.

VI. A PROPOSAL FOR THE CONCEPT
OF ETHNIC PHILOSOPHY

The proposal I want to make for conceiving ethnic philosophies can best be understood in the context of a particular ethnic philosophy, such as Latin American philosophy. Let me begin, then, with a description, more or less neutral and brief, of some things that are included when one speaks of Latin American philosophy. We speak generally of texts that express ideas; that is, we speak of books, articles, declarations, and so on. The book *What Is Value?*, by Risieri Frondizi, is part of Latin American philosophy, and so are *Psychology*, by Enrique José Varona, and *Todology*, by José Vasconcelos. All these texts were composed by authors born in Latin America. In addition, they are written in Spanish and of recent origin, produced after the period of independence. But not all the authors of texts of philosophy considered Latin American were born in Latin America. Alonso de la Vera Cruz was born and educated in Spain, and yet his works are considered to be among the first works of Latin American philosophy. It is curious that these texts are written in Latin and that their topics and approach are not only scholastic, but Iberian scholastic. There is nothing in them that could be characterized as idiosyncratically Latin American, but neither is there anything of this sort in the works of Frondizi or Varona mentioned earlier.

From the inclusion of the works of de la Vera Cruz, it follows that being written in Spanish or, for that matter, Portuguese cannot be a necessary condition of Latin American philosophy. In fact, a text in English or French written by a Latin American is also considered Latin American. But who is to count as a Latin American philosopher? Someone born in Latin America? This would exclude such well-known Latin American philosophers as Francisco Romero, Alonso de la Vera Cruz, and Ignacio Angelelli. Or becoming a citizen of a Latin American country? But this would still exclude de la Vera Cruz and many like him who lived during the colonial period. Does someone born in Latin America but taken to the

United States by adoptive parents at an early age count as a Latin American philosopher if this person does not show any interest in Latin America or its philosophy?

These and other cases that could be mentioned indicate that it is not possible to establish a list of necessary and sufficient conditions for what might be called Latin American philosophy. It is clear that a particular language is neither a necessary nor a sufficient condition: there is Latin American philosophy written in languages other than Spanish and Portuguese, and there is philosophy which is not Latin American written in these languages.

Geographical origin cannot be a necessary condition because there is Latin American philosophy written outside of Latin America, and being written in Latin America does not make something Latin American philosophy. Otherwise, any philosophy produced by a philosopher from elsewhere in the world vacationing in Latin America would be part of Latin American philosophy.

Nor can one take very seriously recent proposals by postmodernists, philosophers of liberation, and others who claim that what is peculiar to Latin American philosophy is the experience of so-called coloniality, or even perhaps marginality.[12] In the first place, Latin America is not the only part of the world that has suffered colonialism, so it can hardly be claimed that this experience and its results are what characterizes Latin American philosophy as such and separates it from all other philosophies and philosophical traditions. But, even if one were to accept that coloniality is in fact something that characterizes Latin American philosophy, this would help to separate it only from philosophy which is a product of the First World, not from the philosophy of other parts of the world that have also suffered colonial exploitation.

Second, I am very skeptical even of the more modest claim that Latin American philosophy shares the effects of colonialism with other philosophies, but not with philosophies from Europe and the United States—for what exactly does this mean? The claim has a wonderful rhetorical ring to it, but how does it translate into concrete observations about the philosophy of Latin America? How has "coloniality" affected the thought of de la Vera Cruz, Romero, and Mario Bunge, for example? Until this is actually shown *in concreto*, the claim remains empty. And there is another factor that should be considered: not everyone in Latin America can really be said to have suffered from the consequences of colonialism. Indeed, the upper classes can hardly be said to have suffered at all! And, let us not forget that philosophy in most cases has been the province of these classes—the educated, the powerful, the ones who have access to books and other resources that seem so closely tied to philosophical productivity. So, again, I am skeptical about these claims in spite of their rhetorical appeal.

Particular topics cannot be posited as necessary and sufficient conditions of Latin American philosophy either. Indeed, even a brief inspection of the most common texts regarded as part of Latin American philosophy shows an extraordinary variety in the philosophical topics discussed. I doubt that there are many topics discussed outside of Latin America that have not been discussed in Latin America, and vice versa. Perhaps there have been some themes for which there has been a certain predilection in certain periods or at certain times, but it is not possible to establish the identity of Latin American philosophy based on particular topics or even certain philosophical perspectives.[13] This lack of unity and perspective naturally undermines every attempt to establish a certain cultural orientation as a necessary and sufficient condition of Latin American philosophy.

Finally, there is the genetic or racial possibility. Someone with little knowledge of the composition of our countries could argue that it is a particular genetic or racial line in those who practice philosophy in Latin America that identifies Latin American philosophy. But this position is too absurd to be taken seriously. The genetic and racial variety of Latin America is extraordinary.[14]

What can we do, then? Obviously we have a category without strict boundaries, and for inclusion in which there are no definite parameters. Does this mean, then, that the notion of Latin American philosophy is incoherent? Or that there is no way of identifying what Latin American philosophy is? And if this is so, does it also apply to other ethnic philosophies?

The notion of Latin American philosophy would be incoherent if only essentialist concepts—ones that tolerate necessary and sufficient conditions—are coherent. But many of our concepts are not of this sort. For example, it has not yet been possible to establish necessary and sufficient conditions for concepts such as "game" and "funny," as disciples of Wittgenstein never tire of pointing out.[15] But this does not prevent us from identifying members of the categories that correspond to these concepts.[16] Any English speaker can, without a great deal of difficulty, determine whether something is a game or not, or whether something is funny or not, even when the reasons for the identification in each case are different and depend on particular contexts. This last factor, context, appears to allow us to choose the condition whose satisfaction helps us to identify something as belonging to the category.

For example, in a context composed of philosophical texts in English, the language of a text in Spanish which uses Mexican idiomatic expressions could serve to identify it as Latin American. In a context in which all texts are in English and have American authors except for one, who is Uruguayan, the origin of the author could be sufficient to identify the text as belonging to Latin American philosophy. In a situation in which we have a series of Latin texts published in Spain, but one of which was written by an author who spent the greatest part of his life in Mexico, we could identify this text as Latin American.

Naturally, someone will object that these criteria are not strict enough. In the first case, it is always possible that the author of the text in Spanish is a Spaniard or Englishman who has learned Mexican idiom and is trying to pass himself off as Latin American. Forgeries are common. It could be that the Uruguayan was born in Uruguay but has spent his life in the United States and does not know, or want to know, anything about Uruguay and its philosophy. In the last example, it could be that the text in question was written before the author went to Latin America and therefore it has little to do with our continent.

These are important objections not because they undermine the foundation of my thesis, but because they make it possible to understand more clearly the nature of, and problems posed by, concepts, like that of Latin American philosophy, which include ethnic labels. Three points seem to be particularly important.

First, with respect to ethnic categories such as Latin American philosophy, we can never be completely certain of the identity of all the members. Membership in the category is not a matter of apodictic certainty. A geometrical figure is or is not a triangle, and we can be absolutely certain of this because there are necessary and sufficient conditions of triangularity. With ethnic categories such as Latin American philosophy, on the other hand, there are many situations in which membership in the category is a question of more or less, not of yes or no. In a certain sense, even the work of the author who spent so much time in Latin America, but which was produced in Spain before he arrived at our shores, belongs to Latin American philosophy insofar as it is related to the author and Latin America. But this relationship is weaker than that of the work that the author produced and published in Latin America after having spent many years there. And even more clearly a part of Latin American philosophy is the work of an author who has lived her whole life in Latin America. It is, as I said, a question of degree with respect to the epistemic perception or certainty of the membership.

This brings us to a second important point that has to do not with certainty or perception, but with ontological reality. We are speaking of texts which find themselves in a web of relations to many other things: the author who produced them, the place where they were produced, the language in which they are presented, the ideas of the culture in which they were developed, and so on. These texts are historical entities, the product of historical beings in particular times and places whose identities are linked to the contexts in which they were produced and which, for that reason, depend on them.

This in turn brings us to the third point: because of their historical nature and multiple contextual relations, it is possible to categorize these texts in different ways that, though apparently incompatible, are not necessarily in fact so. Let us use an example taken from art for the sake of illustration. Is Picasso's art Spanish or French? The Spaniards would like to say that it is exclusively Spanish, and the French would like to say that it is exclusively French. And, indeed, one finds histories of Spanish art that include Picasso, and histories of French art that also include him. Who is right? Both and neither, because Picasso's art is both Spanish and French, and therefore neither exclusively. There are reasons why it is Spanish, and there are reasons why it is French, and these reasons are not the invention of nationalist zealots. They are based on real relations of Picasso's work with Spain and the Spanish ethos, and with France and the French ethos. To categorize Picasso's work as Spanish is to leave out much of this work, and the same thing happens when we try to conceive of it as exclusively French. Similarly, something can be Latin American philosophy and Spanish philosophy, or Anglo-American philosophy and Latin American philosophy. There is no cause for dispute, because our categorizations try only to reflect reality, and the historical reality of what we categorize as Latin American philosophy is complex and multirelational. The error lies in failing to recognize Latin American philosophy, or any other ethnic philosophy, for what it is.

Let me finish this section with an illustration of how what has been said can help us diffuse some historiographical problems. One of the most heated topics of discussion among Latin American philosophers for the past fifty years has been whether there is such a thing as a Latin American philosophy. Let us consider two possibilities: (1) Latin American philosophy does not exist; (2) Latin American philosophy exists. If we adopt a particular selective point of view with respect to certain philosophical texts, we can easily conclude that there is no Latin American philosophy, or very little of it. And if we take a different selective point of view with respect to the same texts we can conclude that there is Latin American philosopy—and, furthermore, that there is much of it. It all depends on the measurement we use. And the measurement depends on many other things. Without doubt, ideologies play an important part, as do nationalism, structures of power, and economic interests. Apart from the measurements, however, there is the reality: the texts, with their multiple and complex relations to their historical context. The matter does not concern just perspective, but also reality. Understanding this should help move the discussion from the barren assertions of opinion to the peculiarities of the concepts of ethnic philosophies such as Latin American philosophy. And this, it seems to me, is a more profitable enterprise, philosophically speaking, even if it really has little to do with particular ethnic philosophies themselves.

VII. CONCLUSION

In sum, let us go back and generalize from the particular case of Latin American philosophy to ethnic philosophies. Ethnic philosophies, understood as past ideas expressed in texts, are historical entities enmeshed in a variety of relations which make possible their classification in various ways. The concept of a particular ethnic philosophy, then, must reflect this reality by allowing flexibility within identity. It is useless to try to search for strict necessary and sufficient conditions for what counts as a particular ethnic philosophy. The conditions are themselves historical and subject to change, and they depend in part on the perspective that is used to establish them. It is essential, therefore, that historians, or anyone speaking about particular ethnic philosophies, make explicit the perspective from which they are speaking in order to avoid confusions about their claims as well as useless controversies about the subject matter. This is only the tip of the iceberg, of course. There is much more that needs to be done and said with respect to the concept of an ethnic philosophy, but it will have to wait for another occasion.

NOTES

1. Not everyone understands nations in this way, however. In Europe, for example, nationality is frequently understood as ethnicity. Thus, some speak of the Slavic or Germanic nations irrespective of political boundaries.

2. See Jorge J. E. Gracia, "The Nature of Ethnicity," *Public Affairs Quarterly* 13, no. 1 (1999): 25–42, and the discussion of Hispanic/Latino ethnicity in idem, *Hispanic/Latino Identity: A Philosophical Perspective* (Malden, Mass.: Blackwell Publishers, 2000). I am now working on a more general and thorough discussion of these issues in *Race, Ethnicity, and Nationality*, which is in progress.

3. For a bibliography on this topic, see chapter 5 of Gracia, *Hispanic/Latino Identity*.

4. I elaborate on this distinction in Jorge J. E. Gracia, *Philosophy and Its History: Issues in Philosophical Historiography* (New York: State University of New York Press, 1992), 42–55.

5. Juan Bautista Alberdi, "Ideas," in *Escritos póstumos de J. B. Alberdi* (Buenos Aires: Imprenta europea, 1900), vol. 25, 603–619.

6. It took off with Leopoldo Zea's "En torno a una filosofía americana," in idem, *Ensayos sobre filosofía en la historia* (Mexico City: Stylo, 1948), 165–177.

7. See the texts gathered in Jorge J. E. Gracia and Iván Jaksi, eds., *Filosofía e identidad cultural en América Latina* (Caracas: Monte Avila Editores, 1983).

8. See, for example, Diego Pró, *Historia del pensamiento filosófico argentino* (Mendoza: Universidad de Cuyo, 1973), and Horacio Cerutti-Guldberg, *Hacia una metodología de la historia de las ideas (filosóficas) en América Latina* (Guadalajara: Universidad de Guadalajara, 1986).

9. See the introduction to Nathan Glazer and Daniel P. Moynihan, eds., *Ethnicity: Theory and Experience* (Cambridge, Mass.: Harvard University Press, 1975).

10. Many of the things that Augusto Salazar Bondy says seem to take this view for granted. See his *Existe una filosofía de nuestra América?* (Mexico City: Siglo XXI, 1968), 112–133.

11. The classic expression of this position is found in Leopoldo Zea. See Zea, "En torno a una filosofía americana."

12. I have heard claims to this effect made by such different authors as Walter Mignolo and Enrique Dussel.

13. So far, any attempts in this direction have failed. This is why it has been difficult to develop a notion of Latin American philosophy.

14. For the racial composition and variety in Latin America, see Magnus Mörner, *Race Mixture in the History of Latin America* (Boston: Little, Brown, 1967).

15. See *Ludwig Wittgenstein, Philosophical Investigations*, trans. G. E. M. Anscombe (New York: Macmillan, 1965), 75, 35.

16. Some philosophers identify categories with concepts, but I do not. See Jorge J. E. Gracia, *Metaphysics and Its Task: The Search for the Categorial Foundation of Knowledge* (Albany: State University of New York Press, 1999), chapter 9.

3. Latin American Philosophy as Critical Ontology of the Present: Themes and Motifs for a "Critique of Latin American Reason"

SANTIAGO CASTRO-GÓMEZ

For Myriam Zapata, *compañera*

"The safari through the unknown, still-to-be-discovered world in which we live can now begin."
—Ulrich Beck

When Max Horkheimer and Theodor Adorno published *The Dialectics of Enlightenment* in 1947, few imagined the decisive influence that this book would have on the form of theorizing the world in times of globalization. In this work, the philosophers from Frankfurt posit that the processes of rationalization project an image of dominion and control over the world that, by virtue of its own dynamic, ends up producing the perverse effect of self-destruction.[1] The increase in rationalization advanced by modernity, instead of eliminating incertitude, fear, and contingencies, ends up *producing* them. This means that the "project of modernity," in the process of the intensification of its structures, culminates in suppressing itself, in undermining its own normative principles. Behind the backs of social actors—that is, independent of what they might or might not want—modernity has generated the globalization (*mundialización*) of its *undesired consequences*: risk, unknowability of the world, the loss of ontological security, the return to myth, individuation, and hedonism. The disintegration of the project of modernity and the exhaustion of its technologies of control over the social world are not imputable to external enemies of the project itself. For it is not because of a *lack* of social, economic, scientific, and political "development" that the promises of modernity could not be fulfilled, but, on the contrary, *because* of such development.[2]

According to Ulrich Beck, we live in a *Risikogesellschaft*, a global society of risk in which the properly "modern" categories with which we thought about the world have ceased to be operative.[3] When modernity was not yet a "project," it was still possible to conceptualize the social world in a normative manner, as if we could impose on it our taxonomic imperatives of control, rational organization,

and prevention of eventualities. But the globalization of modernity implies, para-
doxically, its cancellation as a project of control over social life and the tempestuous apparition of *contingency* as its engine.[4] It is not teleological rationality but
the collateral and "unforeseen" effects of modernity that have become the engine
of politics, economics, and society in an era of globalization. This requires, as Beck
shows, that we abandon the binary codes with which modern rationality worked
(this *or* that) in order to advance toward a thought of the interstices, where it
would be possible to conceptualize the coexistence of apparently incommensurable times, spaces, and situations (this *and* the other).[5] Zygmut Bauman speaks in
this sense of a *thinking of ambivalence,* in which it is assumed that contemporary
social life is traversed by plurivalence, dichotomy, perspectivism, and a mix of an-
tithetical elements that do not resolve into a "synthesis."[6]

In Latin America, cultural studies in the nineties echoed the hybridity and ambivalence of thought. The challenge to think of Latin America from the perspective of a *non-normativistic* vision has led to results that surely seem scandalous to
purists of both the right and the left: the great majority of the population in Latin
America have acceded to modernity—not through education or the lettered (*letrados*) and ideological programs of the intellectual vanguards, but instead through
the new information technologies.[7] In contrast to what transpired in Europe, the
consolidation of cultural modernity in Latin America did not produce films, radio,
and television, but instead is precisely *due to them.* In this sense, it would be fitting
to talk of a "peripheral modernity" in which different times and logics intermix.
The "non-simultaneity of the simultaneous" (Carlos Rincón) that characterizes
modernity in Latin America challenges, then, the theoretical frameworks generated by the "project of modernity," with its accent on social evolution, historical
teleology, epistemological humanism, pre-established harmony, and lettered rationality. At the center of socio-cultural analysis now appear identitarian fragmentation, historical discontinuity, cultural heterogeneity, consumption of
symbolic commodities, and a proliferation of divergent meanings—that is, all that
the modern project had attempted to domesticate and neutralize.

With respect to philosophy, specifically the current that is concerned with reflecting on this slippery object of knowledge called "Latin America," a similar development is observed. Although in the seventies and eighties Latin American
philosophy was presented as a species of "critical conscience" of emancipation
(Augusto Salazar Bondy and Enrique Dussel), an axiology of utopian imaginaries
(Horacio Cerutti Guldberg and Franz Hinkelammert), a "philosophy of history"
oriented to the rational reconstruction of historical memory (Leopoldo Zea and
Arturo Roig), or even a hermeneutics of a "collective identity" born of soil and
blood (Kusch and Scannone), in the nineties another type of philosophical reflection on "Latin America" began to be sketched out that I will name, following
Foucault, *critical ontology of the present.* Here, as in the United States, an anti-nor-
mativist position is expressed in the face of present Latin American societies, and
in the face of the new contingencies that constitute them. The theoretical adventure is, in any event, similar to that already undertaken by Joaquín Brunner,

Garcia Canclini, Martín-Barbero, Renato Ortiz, Santos, Walter Mignolo, and many others: to formulate the lines of escape from the monopolizing thought model of modernity is equivalent to beginning a safari through the terra incognita of the present that constitutes us as citizens of contemporary times.

To show what this philosophical program consists of, I will proceed in the following manner: starting from the characterization made by Michel Foucault, I will distinguish between two lines of thought and exemplify them with the works of two contemporary Latin American thinkers: the Colombian Roberto Salazar Ramos and the Venezuelan Beatriz González Stephan. My objective is to show how the "critical ontology of the present" has become fruitful for a philosophical reconceptualization of the "Latin American" in times of globalization.

1. WHAT IS "CRITICAL ONTOLOGY OF THE PRESENT"?

In the 1983 essay "What Is Enlightenment?" Michel Foucault describes his philosophical project as an "ontology of the present." As has been well shown by Richard Bernstein, Foucault's reflection on his own philosophical investigation, linking it directly to Kant's thought, constitutes, in reality, an apologia, a response to the critiques he had been receiving to the effect that his project suffered from "fundamental inconsistencies" or lacked any defined philosophical status.[8] Some years later, the German philosopher Jürgen Habermas summarized some of these critiques when he stated that Foucault's thinking lacked reflection on the "normative grounding" of his own writings, which had led him to fall into "methodological aporias" that Habermas subsumed under the concrete formula of "performative self-contradiction."[9] Following, then, Bernstein's reading, what Foucault was seeking in his text was to respond to objections such as these by showing that his project should be understood as a *critical theory of society*, while at the same time distinguishing himself from the way that the "philosophical discourse of modernity" had been defining what "theory" and "critique" mean.

What, then, is the model of the "critique of society" outlined by Foucault? First of all, it no longer attempts to see the *present* under the aspect of its universal validity and rationality; rather, it considers its radical particularity and dependence on historical factors. In this sense, then, what Foucault seeks is to advance toward a "history of the present" that no longer departs from a normative model of "humanity"—that is, from a *particular* (modern) idea of what it means to be "human," abstracted from the historical contingencies that gave rise to it. It is a matter, then, of examining the ontological status of the present, foregrounding precisely the historical contingencies and the strategies of power that configured its humanistic claims to universal validity. Foucault recognizes here a new form of approaching philosophically the problem of modernity in which, before discovering the "truth" of its inherent promises (freedom, equality, fraternity), what is sought is to reveal the technologies of domination that aided in its fabrication, as well as the different forms in which such a truth constitutes our contemporary subjectivity.

I will now distinguish two lines of work in this philosophical agenda, and then show how these lines have been developed in Latin America by the thinkers named above. The program of the "critical ontology of the present" entails at least two different tasks:

a) To contemplate the present as a product of historical contingencies— that is, as a tempestuous configuration in which different social practices are combined. In this context, philosophy should be questioned because of the role played by "truth" in the legitimating of all those practices. For truth does not function solely in its metaphysical and epistemological dimension, but instead is articulated by social *dispositifs* that produce, administer, and distribute it and link it up to cultural or moral ends, or that theatricalize it through academic rituals. To think of risk and contingency as preconditions for globalization entails, then, that the purpose of philosophy no longer be to seek truth as such, but to seek the *political economy of truth*, according to how the rules that configure its discourses appear and disappear.

b) If "truth is of this world," then philosophy should question the network of *institutions* that modernity generates so that social agents "appropriate" it normatively. For the socialization of knowledge comes linked to *dispositifs* that tend to form profiles of subjectivity, a specific type of human being who can function according to the objectives defined by this "project of modernity." Such *dispositifs* of subjectification control behavior, model bodies, increase productivity, and strengthen the character of citizens. But at the same time, the disciplinary regimentation of what it means to be a "good citizen" clearly establishes a frontier between those "within" and those "outside of" modernity.

2. THE TRUTH REGIMES ON "LO LATINOAMERICANO"

Let us take, then, the first point in the agenda and look at how the ontology of the present has been put in play by a critique of Latin American society in times of globalization. It is necessary to begin by saying that broaching present Latin American society as a tempestuous configuration is a program that is extremely different from that formulated in the seventies by philosophers such as the Mexican Leopoldo Zea, for whom the history of our continent has followed a type of immanent "logic," which he characterized as the incremental "becoming conscious" of its own humanity. For Zea, today's Latin America is the result of a series of historical continuities that can be reconstructed through thought and, concretely, by a "philosophy of history." The mission of this philosophy would be, then, to indicate the way in which Latin Americans have been becoming conscious of their own cultural identity, their own specificity as human beings.[10]

But, from the point of view of the ontology of the present, an investigation of the history of Latin American societies acquires an entirely different profile. Here, it is not a question of discovering the way in which "Latin American reason," expressed in the work of its best intellectuals, has "unfolded" historically, but of showing which social mechanisms of discipline have produced both that reason and those intellectuals. That is, it is not a matter of delineating the "logic" of a supposed "Latin American reason," but of highlighting the technologies of social control that generated the psychological profile of an intellectual who feels compelled to unearth the mystery of the "Latin American being," and that have been the *dispositifs* of the power-knowledge from which an object of knowledge called "Latin America" was discursively produced. Before we reflect on the history of discourses in Latin American identity, taken as humanistic objectifications of the lettered conscience, I should mention that the ontology of the present intends to describe the *discontinuous history of production of these discourses*, showing their anchoring in certain *dispositifs* of organization, selection, agency [*agenciamiento*], hierarchization, and legitimation of knowledge. Inasmuch as it investigates genealogically the conditions of possibility of the theoretical discourses on Latin America, the ontology of the present becomes something like a *critique of Latin American reason*.

In his book *Posmodernidad y verdad* [Postmodernity and truth], the Colombian philosopher Roberto Salazar Ramos reflects on the social function of knowledge and, more precisely, the *dispositifs* through which the knowledge of the social world becomes "second nature." Social life would be impossible without the ordering of experience, without the horizon of meaning from which the world is clarified, typified, and explained.[11] This means that the *sense* depends not on the cognitive activity of the "subject" but on a series of socially constructed codes that change according to the mode in which the interweaving of relations between social actors is configured or dis-configured. Knowledge is not, then, something "natural" —although our compulsive tendency to seek ontological and epistemological security leads us to believe it is—but something historical that is therefore at the mercy of transgressions, disequilibriums, changes, and mutations. It is from this historically modeled set of norms and social relations, in which we all come into play, that results impossible to interpret nevertheless give sense to our quotidian experience. To speak, think, indicate, perceive, and understand are not activities anchored in a transparent consciousness, but are social constructions, collective sedimentations that explode and fragment with time. In Salazar Ramos's words, "The 'reason for being' of things and their relations are established through a determined system of ordering, a specific series of organizations, and a certain network that weaves and configures their sense and significance. Outside this system, things and their relations would lose sense and significance."[12]

The question asked by Salazar Ramos, then, is the following: How has a specific order of words and things been constructed from which we have been able to generate knowledge on the "what is one's own" and what is "foreign" in Latin America? This concerns, certainly, a question that provokes a certain discomfort in some parts of the Latin American intellectual community. We have become accustomed to thinking of Latin America as a place of utopia and magical realism, as the site of a project that is autochthonous and presents an alternative project to Western modernity, or as a space of lacks and concealments that have prevented us from reaching the "true modernity" that was achieved by Europe and the United States. But Salazar Ramos's question is directed not at the "being" of Latin America, or at the "normative grounds" of modernity, but at the epistemological-social ordering that has made possible the construction of objects of knowledge such as "Latin America," "the West," "Europe," and "modernity." The question establishes, then, a line of escape with respect to the *episteme* from which some have been formulating the problem: both sides insisted on questioning Latin American's access to modernity, without acknowledging that both categories denote *absolutely nothing* outside the symbolic order from which they were constructed.

This exemplifies the critical function of an ontology of the present: the transparency of an order of knowing, its invisibility and legitimacy, remain destabilized to the extent that they are thrown into question by the way in which they have appeared historically and by the juridical procedures that constitute them. In fact, it is possible to observe or question an order of knowledge only because a displacement has *already* taken place in the structure of social relations that undergirds it. It is the *present* of Latin American societies, marked by the de(re)-territorialization of the local, that has shattered the entire system of ontological and epistemological security from which is articulated the question about Latin American's "entry" into Western modernity.[13] The philosophical question that is imposed on us by the present is no longer, then, what we should do in order to enter or exit from modernity, but through which practices we have been *invented* as collective agents (Latin Americans, Colombians, Mexicans, Brazilians, etc.) who "enter" or "exit from" something called "modernity."

Salazar Ramos suspects that the essay-like philosophical and sociological meta-narratives on "Latin American identity" in relation with modernity played as key-words so that the groups and individuals functioned and recognized themselves in their social practices, their forms of perception and interaction.[14] These keywords should have made possible a fixed point of reference, a historical memory, a sense of telluric belonging, a "cultural identity" that would serve as support for the great project that the Criollo elites have attempted to impose since the nineteenth century: the construction of the nation. As "imagined communities," Latin American nationalities were produced through a series of social *dispositifs* that organized experiences, thinking, and learning with the goal of preventing uncertainty and ensuring "progress." There thus emerged *Latinamericanismo*, the set of knowledge on "what is one's own," as a cognitive technology used to reorganize social reality. *Latinamericanismo* fulfills the same function as do Pilar Ternera's cards in the story by Garcia Márquez or José Arcadio Buendias's memory machine: to establish an order of meanings that ensures the continuity and regularity of history, which would re-establish the correspondence between words and things. The centennial project of the nation demanded the construction of a world in which all of its officials—politicians, soldiers, intellectuals [*letrados*]—could feel comfortable and secure; a world in which all signs would have their referents, all words their meaning, and all actions a justification. Theoretical discourses on the "national" and the "Latin American" played precisely in accordance with this intent: to transmit to citizens the feeling that they recognized themselves in a fictitious "common history" that synthesized the contradictions of race, gender, class, age, and sexual orientation.

3. THE DISCIPLINARY FORMATION OF THE "NATIONAL SUBJECT"

The critical ontology of the present certainly operates as an archaeology that unearths historical contingencies. Salazar Ramos wonders if the soil of contemporary Latin American societies is formed of the same rocks, reliefs, heights, valleys, and landscapes that modeled the habitat of disciplinary society in the nineteenth century. The stubborn persistence of certain policies of truth on the "national" or "the Latin American" in some academic institutions or the collective imagination would seem to indicate that we still resist the assimilation of globalization as a condition of our present.[15] It is useless to cry and to place flowers on the tomb of historical projects, such as "autochthonism" and "modernization," that have been superseded by the processes of economic and cultural transnationalization.[16]

The Venezuelan thinker Beatriz González Stephan also investigates the archaeological layers that sustain and configure the present of Latin American societies in order to curtail the temptation to flee from that present. But, in contrast to Salazar Ramos, González Stephan emphasizes not the political economy of truth that generates theoretical discourses about the "Latin American," but the mechanisms of discipline that modeled a specific type of "national citizen." We arrive, then, at the second item in the theoretical agenda for a critical ontology of the present: to examine the historical *dispositifs* of subjectification that made possible the production of docile and useful bodies for the centennial project of the nation. The creation of Latin American nationalities presupposes the forging of actors—"subjects"—that are the base on which the structures of post-independence modern society are erected. In this context, disciplinary practices, with their techniques of codification of behavior and the programming of quotidian life, play an important role.

González Stephan identifies three disciplinary practices that contributed to the making of Latin American citizens in the nineteenth century: *constitutions*, *manuals of urbanity*, and *grammars of language*. Following the Uruguayan theoretician Angel Rama, Beatriz González verifies that these technologies of subjectification had a common denominator: their legitimacy rested on *writing*. In the nineteenth century, to write was a skill that responded to the necessity to order and establish the logic of "civilization" and that anticipated the modernizing dream of the Criollo elites. The written word inscribed national laws and identities, designed modernizing programs, and organized an understanding of the world in terms of inclusions and exclusions. For this reason, the foundational project of the nation was carried out through the implementation of institutions legitimated by the word [*letra*] (schools, orphanages, factories, prisons) and of hegemonic discourses (maps, grammars, constitutions, manuals, treatises of hygiene) that regimented the behavior of social actors, established frontiers between some and others, and transmitted to them the certitude of existing within or outside the limits defined by that writerly [*escrituraria*] legality. "Writing," states González Stephan, "was the decisive exercise of the civilizing practices on which rested the power to domesticate the barbaric and ameliorate custom; under the letter (law, norms, books, manuals, catechism), passions would recoil and violence would be contained."[17]

The formation of the citizen as a "subject of right" was possible only within the framework of a disciplinary writing—in this case, within the space of legality defined by the constitution. The juridical-political function of the constitution was, precisely, to *invent citizenship*—that is, to create a field of homogeneous identities that made viable the modern project of governmentality. The Venezuelan constitution of 1839 states, for instance, that only married males who are over twenty-five years of age, can read and write, own real state, and exercise a profession that generates an annual income of not less than four hundred pesos can be citizens.[18] Thus, acquisition of citizenship was a litmus test (*tamiz*) which only persons whose profile fit the type of subject required by the project of modernity could pass: male, white, head of a household, Catholic, property owner, literate, and heterosexual. Individuals who did not fit these requirements (women, servants, madmen, illiterates, blacks, heretics, slaves, *indios*, homosexuals, dissidents) were left outside the "lettered city" (*ciudad letrada*), relegated to the sphere of illegality, submitted to the punishment and therapy of the very law that excluded them.

If the constitution formally defined a desirable type of modern subjectivity, pedagogy was the great artifice of its materialization. The school became a space of internment where the type of subject that the "regulative ideals" of the constitution clamored for was formed. What was sought was to interject a discipline on the mind and body that enabled the person to be "useful to the fatherland." Children's behavior was to be regulated and watched over, submitted to the acquisition of knowledge, capacities, habits, values, cultural models and styles of life that would allow them to take a "productive" role in society. But it is not toward the school as an "institution of sequestering" that Beatriz González directs her reflections, but toward the disciplinary function of certain pedagogical technologies, such as the manuals of urbanity, and in particular the famous one by Carreño published in 1854. The manual functioned within the sphere of authority revealed by the book as an attempt to regulate and constrict instincts, control the movements of the body, and domesticate every type of sensibility deemed "barbarous."[19] No manuals were written on how to be a good farmer, Indian, black man, or gaucho, since all of these types of human beings were seen as belonging to the sphere of the barbarian. The manuals were written to form a "good citizen" who would be part of the *civitas*, the legal space wherein dwelt the epistemological, moral, and aesthetic subjects that needed modernity. For this reason, Carreño's manual notes that "without more or less perfect observance of these rules, according to the degree of *civilization* of each country . . . there would be no way to cultivate sociality, which is the principle of the conservation and the *progress* of peoples [*pueblos*] and the existence of every *well-ordered* society."[20]

The manuals of urbanity became the new bible that indicated to the citizen what his behavior ought to be in the different situations of life, for on faithful obedience to such norms would depend his greater or lesser success in the *civitas terrena*, the material kingdom of civilization. The entrance to the banquet of modernity demanded the fulfillment of a normative cookbook that distinguished the members of a new urban class that began to emerge in all of Latin America during the second half of the nineteenth century. The "we" to whom the manual makes reference is, then, the bourgeois citizen, the same one at whom the republican constitutions were aimed;[21] the one who knew how to speak, eat, use cutlery, blow his nose, deal with servants, and behave in society. He was the subject who knew perfectly "the theater of etiquette, the rigidity of presentation, the mask of contention."[22] In this sense, the observations of González Stephan coincide with those of Max Weber and Norbert Elias, for whom the constitution of the modern subject went hand in hand with the demand for self-control and repression of the instincts, with the goal of making social difference more visible. The "process of civilization" dragged in its wake a rise in the threshold of shame, because it was necessary to differentiate clearly between all the social strata that did not belong to the sphere of the urban, the *civitas* that Latin American intellectuals such as Sarmiento had identified as the paradigm of modernity.[23] "Urbanity" and "civic education" played, then, as pedagogical taxonomies that separated the vest from the poncho, the elegant from shoddiness, the capital from the provinces, the republic from the colony, civilization from barbarism.

The grammars of language also played a fundamental role in this taxonomic process. González Stephan mentions in particular *Gramática de la Lenguage Castellana destinada al uso de los americanos* (Grammar of the Castilian language for the use of Americans) published by Andrés Bello in 1847. The project of construction of the nation required linguistic stabilization for the adequate implementation of laws and also to facilitate commercial transactions. There existed, then, a direct relationship between language and citizenship, between grammars and manuals of urbanity. In any event, the project concerned the creation of a *homo economicus*, the patriarchal subject in charge of fomenting and carrying out the modernization of the republic. From the normativity of the letter, grammars sought to generate a culture of "speaking well" (*buen decir*) to the end of preventing "the vicious practices of popular speech" and the grotesque barbarisms of the plebe.[24] Thus, we have a disciplinary practice in which were reflected contradictions that ended up sundering the project of modernity: to establish the conditions for "freedom" and "order" entailed submission of the instincts, suppression of spontaneity, control of differences. In order to be civilized, to become part of modernity, to be Colombian, Brazilian, or Venezuelan citizens, individuals not only had to behave correctly and know how to read and write, but also had to make their language conform to a whole series of norms. Submission to order and norm led the individual to substitute the heterogeneous and spontaneous flow of the vital with adoption of a *continuum* arbitrarily constituted through the letter.

To examine how the mechanisms of "ontological security" proper to modernity are established in our midst: this is the intent of a critical ontology of the present as exemplified by Roberto Salazar Ramos and Beatriz González Stephan. Both have shown that the projects of modernization of Latin American societies in the nineteenth and twentieth centuries led to a series of *dispositifs* oriented to the rational control of human life. If social control of contingencies, without submission of the body and mind to the discipline of work and an education in the customs were impossible, it would be impossible to reach the level of development, prosperity, humanization, and progress that seem so evident in industrialized nations. As it was in Europe, the project of modernity in Latin America was directly linked to the juridical-political construction of national states. As much here as there, modernity was a "project" because the rational control of contingencies had to be exercised under a central authority, which was in fact the nation-state.

But this type of deconstructive critique is not simply a historiographical exercise. It is, rather, an attempt to answer the question, Who are we Latin Americans *today*, in times of globalization? If Salazar Ramos and González Stephan direct their gaze toward the archaeological layers of the nineteenth century, it is because they know that the properly *modern dispositifs* of social control have been overtaken by their own dynamics and given rise to a phenomenon that we call "globalization." If the project of modernity requires the formation of structures that social actors *reproduce*, globalization opens the bars of the "iron cage" and projects the image of structures that the actors themselves *transform*. The modern dialectics between subject and structure loses thrust and begins to "weaken"—as Vattimo would put it—in such a way that structures become the object of processes of action and social change. There is a simple reason for this: globalization is not a homogeneous structure, nor is it a "project"; it is the tempestuous result of the crisis of modernity as the project of structuring social subjects. Modernity ceases to be operative as a "project" when the political, social, and cultural life of human beings is uncoupled from the nation-state and begins to be configured by transnational processes.[25] Thus, all those elements that in the period of modernity formed a "project" coordinated by the state are now subject to dispersion, or *globalization*. We are witness, then, to the transition from modernity's rational project to the global disorder of world-modernity, with all of its risks and possibilities. To give an account of these risks and possibilities, to think in the interstices opened up by the crisis of the modern project—such is the task of a critical ontology of the present.

TRANSLATED BY EDUARDO MENDIETA

NOTES

1. Max Horkheimer and Theodor W. Adorno, *Dialectic of Enlightenment* (London: Verso, 1979 [1947]).

2. See Anthony Giddens, "Living in a Post-Traditional Society," in Ulrich Beck, Anthony Giddens, and Scott Lash, *Reflexive Modernization: Politics, Tradition and Aesthetics in the Modern Social Order* (Stanford, Calif.: Stanford University Press, 1994), 56–109.

3. See Ulrich Beck, *Risikogesellschaft. Auf dem Weg in eine andere Moderne* (Frankfurt: Suhrkamp, 1986). See also Niklas Luhmann, *Risk: A Sociological Theory* (New York: Walter de Gruyter, 1993).

4. On the end of modernity as a "project," see Santiago Castro-Gómez, "The World Is No Longer Wide but Continues Being Alien: The End of Modernity and Transformations of Cultures in Times of Globalization," in Mario Saenz, ed., *Globalization and Latin American Thought* (Lanham, Md.: Rowman and Littlefield, forthcoming).

5. See U. Beck, "Teoría de la modernización reflexiva," in J. Beriain, ed., *Las consecuencias perversas de la modernidad. Modernidad, riesgo y contingencia* (Barcelona: Anthropos, 1996), 223ff; see also Martin Albrow, *Abschied vom Nationalstaat. Staat und Gesellschaft im globalen Zeitalter* (Frankfurt: Suhrkamp, 1998).

6. Zygmut Bauman, *Modernity and Ambivalence* (London: Polity, 1991); see also idem, *Intimations of Postmodernity* (London: Routledge, 1992).

7. See J. Martín-Barbero, *De los medios a las mediaciones. Comunicación, cultural y hegemonia* (Barcelona: Ediciones Gili, 1991); see also J. J. Brunner, *América Latina: cultura y modernidad* (Mexico City: Grijaldo, 1996).

8. Richard Bernstein, "Foucault: Critique as a Philosophical Ethos," in Michael Kelly, ed., *Critique and Power. Recasting the Foucault/Habermas Debate* (Cambridge, Mass.: MIT Press, 1994), 211–241.

9. Jürgen Habermas, "The Critique of Reason as an Unmasking of the Human Sciences: Michel Foucualt," in J. Habermas, *The Philosophical Discourse of Modernity: Twelve Lectures* (Cambridge, Mass.: MIT Press, 1987), 238–265.

10. I have amply dealt with the exposition and critique of Latin American philosophy of history in chapter 4 of my book *Crítica de la razón latinoamericana* (Barcelona: Puvill libros, 1996).

11. Roberto Salazar Ramos, *Posmodernidad y verdad. Algunos metarelatos en la constitución del saber* (Bogotá: Ediciones USTA, 1994), 65ff.

12. Ibid., 70.

13. On the problem of de(re)territorialization in Latin America see Santiago Castro-Gómez and Eduardo Mendieta, "La translocalización discursiva de 'Latinoamérica,' en tiempos de globalización," in S. Castro-Gómez and Eduardo Mendieta, eds., *Teorías sin disciplina. Latinoamericanismo, poscolonialidad y globalización en debate* (Mexico City: Porrua, 1998), 5–30.

14. R. Salazar Ramos, "Los grandes meta-relatos en la interpretación de la historia latinoamericana," in *Ponencias VII Congreso Internacional de Filosofía Latinoaméricana* (Bogotá: Universidad Santo Tomás, 1993), 63–93.

15. Concerning how this "metaphysics of the Latin American" still constitutes us today, see Santiago Castro-Gómez, "Latinamericanismo, modernidad, globalización. Prolegómenons a una crítica poscolonial de la razón," in S. Castro-Gómez and E. Mendieta, *Teorías sin disciplina*, 169–205.

16. See R. Salazar Ramos, "Notas para una postfilosofía latinoamericana" (forthcoming).

17. Beatriz González Stephan, "Economías fundacionales. Diseño del cuerpo ciudadano," in B. González Stephan, ed., *Cultura y tercer mundo. Nuevas identidades y ciudadanias* (Caracas: Editorial Nueva Sociedad, 1996), 20.

18. Ibid., 31.

19. Beatriz González Stephan, "Modernización y disciplinamiento. La formación del ciudadano: del espacio público y privado," in B. González Stephan, J. Lasarte, G. Montaldo, and M. J. Daroqui, eds., *Esplendores y miserias del siglo XIX. Cultura y sociedad en América Latina* (Caracas: Monte Avila Editores, 1995), 431–455.

20. Ibid., 436.

21. It is not a coincidence that in 1855 the national congress of Venezuela agreed to the use of Carreño's manual in schools.

22. Stephan, "Modernización," 439.

23. See D. F. Sarmiento, *Facundo o civilización* (Caracas: Biblioteca Ayacucho, 1985).

24. B. González Stephan, "Economias fundacionales," 29.

25. See Martin Albrow, *Abschied vom Nationalstaat*, 87ff.

4. Philosophy and the Colonial Difference

WALTER D. MIGNOLO

In the fifties, the distinguished ethno-historian and expert on ancient Mexico Miguel León-Portilla published his classic book, *La filosofía Nahuatl* (Nahuatl philosophy).[1] He did not have to wait long for criticism, and one of the major attacks concerned his "imprudent" use of the term "philosophy" to designate something that the Aztecs or Nahuatl-speaking people could have been engaged in. But the criticisms were ambiguous. The "lack" of philosophical discourse among the Aztecs could have meant that they were "barbarians," uncivilized, or undeveloped. On the other hand, it could have meant just that they were "different." In this case, Nahuatl-speaking people may not have had "philosophy," but the "difference" should not be considered a lack but an assertion that they had or did something else. Europeans, in turn, did not have whatever that "something" else could have been. In another study, León-Portilla reflected on the social role of the *tlamatini*. He did not translate this social role as "philosopher" but described it as "those who have the power of the word."[2] León-Portilla, like others, had difficulties in defining what philosophy is so that he could then show that the Aztec or Nahuatl-speaking people indeed had it. He managed, however, to give an acceptable picture of what philosophy was for the Greeks and then matched it with the remains of Aztec documentation from the early sixteenth century, before Cortes's arrival in Mexico-Tenochtitlan.

León-Portilla overlooked the fact that philosophy, in Greece, went together with the emergence of what is today considered the Western alphabet and Western literacy. Indeed, if I had to define what philosophy is (following the Greek legacy), I would begin by saying that it is something that is linked to writing and to alphabetic writing. I would add that it was alphabetic writing, linked to the concept of philosophy, that allowed Western men of letters, from the sixteenth century on, to establish the difference between philosophy and other forms of knowledge. There is a caveat in this argument, however: the Arabic language and the Arabic early contact with and translation of philosophical texts from Greek to Arabic. I will not pursue this point, since I am concentrating on Latin America, but it is indeed an issue to keep in mind for an understanding of the emergence of the colonial difference.

Beyond overlooking the complicity of alphabetic writing in the Western self-description of philosophy, León-Portilla accepted without further question (and here he is not alone) that philosophy is a Greek invention and the natural point of reference for deciding whether something is or is not philosophy. We could certainly extend this argument to other practices. But let us stay with philosophy. So, the argument goes, philosophy did not exist before the Greeks invented it. Therefore, communities or civilizations before the Greeks, or even having simultaneous histories after the Greeks, invented philosophy but, with not much contact between them, did not have philosophy—such as the Aztecs in the early sixteenth century, for example, or the Chinese, before the Greeks and during the Greek golden age of philosophical thinking. There is something odd in this historiographical picture, particularly because it is the result of an argument that positions philosophy as a good thing to have, a crucial achievement of which other cultures have been or are deprived.

You may be wondering at this point, what does all of this have to do with Latin American philosophy? A great deal, indeed, since I am talking around the colonial difference, and the colonial difference came into being during the so-called conquest of America, which is, in a different macro-narrative, the emergence of the Atlantic commercial circuit and of the modern/colonial world. But to explain this, I have to stay a little longer with the famous Greeks. Why, indeed, did León-Portilla title his book *La filosofía Nahuatl*, and why did people react to this title by asking whether Nahuatl-speaking people did or did not have philosophy? Why is Greek philosophy the reference point? And if Greek philosophy is not the reference point, then, what are we talking about? Perhaps we should change the perspective from which we think about this issue. Instead of assuming that there is something like philosophy, that the Greeks invented it, and that, thereafter, the rest of the planet had to deal with it, we should first ask, What was the "thing" that the Greeks called philosophy? Second, we should ask why, once the Greeks invented it, philosophy was appropriated by the West (since the Arabs were "first" to translate and pursue it) and then converted into a point of reference to establish borders between philosophy and its difference. Well, I am arguing that "philosophy and its difference" became an issue in the sixteenth century and that the issue was the making of the colonial difference.

Now, I do not know whether before the sixteenth century the problem encountered by León-Portilla was a common one. It may have been. Certainly, communities had their self-description and many ways of distinguishing themselves from other communities. But never before the sixteenth century had the differentiation acquired the dimension that it had in the modern/colonial world, a world that was made, shaped, and controlled by European powers, from the Spanish to the British empires and through Dutch, French and German colonialism. The European Renaissance (in southern Europe) and then the European Enlightenment (in northern Europe) did two things simultaneously. First, the self-image of the West began to be built by constructing the macro-narrative of Western civilization; second, the colonial difference began to be built with the philosophical debate around the humanity of the Amerindians. Certainly, Vitoria, Sepulveda, and las Casas did not ask themselves whether the Amerindians had philosophy. They assumed that they did not. And in this respect, León-Portilla made a brave and important move by assuming that there was a Nahuatl philosophy. But the problem lies elsewhere.

I am arguing that the problem León-Portilla had is the problem of the colonial difference. His contribution was bringing it to the foreground, even though, at that time (1959), the philosophical debate around decolonization was just at its inception. Frantz Fanon's *The Wretched of the Earth* was published in 1961. We will discuss why the debate around decolonization is important below. First, though, let's remember that León-Portilla's dilemma was not a problem for sixteenth-century Spanish philosophers or, even less, for eighteenth-century French philosophers, as we know because of the "debates on the New World" and Hegel's follow-up in his lessons on the philosophy of history. León-Portilla is Mexican, while Sepúlveda et al. were Spaniards, and the eighteenth-century philosophers, including Hegel, were either French, German, or British. This is not a problem of nationality, but of local histories—and of local histories from where you "feel" and "think," whether philosophically or not. León-Portilla may have felt the colonial difference when he decided to write *Nahuatl Philosophy*.

But what is this colonial difference? Robert Bernasconi is a specialist in Continental philosophy, and well versed in Heidegger, Levinas, and Derrida. Reflecting on the challenges that African philosophy currently poses to Continental philosophy, Bernasconi states, "Western philosophy traps African philosophy in a double bind: either African philosophy is so similar to Western philosophy that it makes no distinctive contribution and effectively disappears; or it is so different that its credentials to be genuine philosophy will always be in doubt."[3] Now, I am quoting Bernasconi not as an authority, to stamp with his quotation what I have been arguing so far, but as an ethnographic informant. Furthermore, I think that the elegance and force of his argument allow precisely for that. Otherwise, his argument would have been made at the pure level of the enunciated without putting at risk the very act of enunciation. That is, Bernasconi would have maintained the philosophical authority of someone who reports the difference without putting himself or herself at risk in the act of reporting. I am quoting Bernasconi because of the double bind in which Western philosophy has placed African philosophy. That double bind is the colonial difference, and the structure of power that maintains it is the coloniality of power. León-Portilla did not articulate the issue in that way. He argued for the existence of Nahuatl philosophy because Nahuatl philosophy has been negated since the very inception of conquest and colonization. What did his critics do? They questioned the pertinence of attributing philosophy to the Nahuatls. Which means that the quarrel was prompted by the colonial difference, the double bind between an excessive similarity and an excessive difference. Where do we go from here? Decolonization of philosophy and, more generally, of cultures of scholarship still seems to be a viable project. I quote Bernasconi again, this time on decolonization. What is new here is that as an expert in Continental philosophy he has heard the claim that philosophers, social scientists, and humanists in the Third World have been making for at least thirty years:

> The existential dimension of African philosophy's challenge to Western philosophy in general and Continental philosophy in particular is located in the need to decolonize the mind. This task is at least as important for the colonizer as it is for the colonized. For Africans, decolonizing the mind takes place not only in facing the experience of colonialism, but also in recognizing the precolonial, which establishes the destructive importance of so-called ethnophilosophy and sage philosophy, as well as nationalist-ideological philosophy.[4]

Decolonization, in the project of Moroccan philosopher Abdelkebir Khatibi, is the hidden side of the moon, the darker side of modernization. In its nineteenth-century version, modernization was linked to the civilizing mission; after World War II, it was linked to developmental ideology; and in the nineties it was linked to globalization and the market ideology, yet its hidden side was, and still is, colonization. While imperialism and globalization place the accent on the hegemonic forces of regulation and control, colonization (or, better, coloniality of power) places the accent on the receiving end of imperial and global designs. That is why decolonization as a project is most likely to come from the receiving end of global designs than from the local histories where global designs are drawn and implemented. For Khatibi, if decolonization is the darker side of modernization, it is also the irreducible complement of deconstruction. Khatibi conceived decolonization as a double critique, of Western and Islamic fundamentalism—a step that is beyond deconstruction, since deconstruction remains a critique of Western logocentrism by Western logocentrism itself.[5] In this sense, deconstruction runs parallel to postmodern critiques of modernity. Decolonization, as double critique, instead presupposes the colonial difference. It works precisely from the colonial difference, from the double bind between assimilation (say, Arabic philosophy is so similar to Western philosophy that it makes no contribution) and marginalization (it is so different that its credentials will be always in doubt). Decolonization, for Khatibi, is simultaneously an undoing and a redoing: an undoing (double critique) of the colonial difference and a redoing in terms of what I have elsewhere called "border thinking,"[6] as the ground of future epistemologies and political projects. Khatibi calls it "*une pensée autre*," "an other thinking," emerging from a double critique but, also, as a critique of Occidentalism from the perspective of the colonial history of North Africa, from the Spanish in the sixteenth century to the French in the nineteenth.

In Latin America, decolonization of scholarship arose in the middle to late sixties, with the impact of Frantz Fanon and of political decolonization in Asia and Africa. Philosophy of liberation was the philosophical version of what later became identified as decolonization. Decolonization invaded the social sciences as well. In the late sixties and early seventies, Colombian sociologist Orlando Fals-Borda was specifically arguing for decolonization of sociology.[7] In any event, in the seventies Dussel perceived the significant contribution of Emmanual Levinas's philosophy but pointed out its significant Eurocentric bent. Dussel observed in 1975,

> Speaking in person with Levinas in 1971 I could prove the degree to which our thinking was similar, but at the same time how a radical rapture had already taken place. He told me how his generation's great political experiences have been Stalin and Hitler (two dehumanizing totalizations, product of the European-Hegelian modernity). But when I pointed out to him that European modernity, with its conquistador ego, colonizers, and imperial culture, the oppressor of peripheral peoples, had been the experience of not just my generation but also of the last five hundred years, he could only grant that he never had thought that the "Other" could be the "indigenous peoples, Africans, or even Asians." The Other of the totality of the European world were all the cultures and humans which had been constituted as things ready at hand, instruments, known ideas, entities at the disposal of the "European (and later Russian-North American) will to power."[8]

At the time Dussel was saying this, philosophy of liberation was entangled in one of its most enduring periods of guilt, justly criticized by Horacio Cerutti-Guldberg.[9] Its complicity with political populism has left a bad taste in the memory of Argentina, in particular. The question is, however, that even the most enlightened New Left was not safe from such dangers. Be that as it may, there is another aspect of philosophy of liberation, particularly in Dussel's version, that has not been forgotten. Dussel's observations in 1975 are echoed, almost word for word, in Bernasconi's judgment of Levinas's philosophy in 1997:

> The Eurocentric view of philosophy is still largely intact, both in the institutional presentation of philosophy and in the declarations of some of Western philosophy's finest minds. Take Levinas, for example. In spite of the pluralism that his thought celebrates, Emmanuel Levinas was quite explicit that he was not willing to look beyond the Bible and the Greeks as models of excellence: "I always say but in private that the Greeks and the Bible are all that is serious in humanity. Everything else is dancing." Derrida does not exhibit the same prejudice, but insofar as Western metaphysics has from the outset been deconstruction's primary object, deconstruction has had little use for what falls outside Western metaphysics.[10]

If we think back to León-Portilla's book, we may see that it opened up a can of worms that, unfortunately, went unnoticed in Latin American philosophical circles, even in the late sixties, when the question of whether there was a Latin American philosophy occupied the minds of philosophers.[11] There was a parallel, at that time, between sub-Saharan African and Latin American philosophers who were becoming aware of the colonial difference. For to ask "Is there an African or a Latin American philosophy?" is to respond to the demands of the colonial difference. León-Portilla did it in this way, as an ethno-cultural historian and not as a philosopher. He did not ask whether the Nahuatl had philosophy. He assumed that they did, but in doing so, he had to make an enormous effort to put the Nahuatls next to the Greeks and then defend his move to his ferocious critics—that is, to the "malaise" produced by the colonial difference.

Now, the cards are on the table. Philosophy is a regional and historical practice, initiated in Greece and taken up by and in the making of Europe, from the Renaissance to the Enlightenment. Coupled with religious and economic expansion, philosophy became the yardstick by which other ways of thinking are measured. Perspectives have been changing, and now "philosophy" is located on the edge of the colonial difference. It is recognized because Western expansion has touched every corner of the planet, and displaced because what is good for one local history is not necessarily good for other local histories. To think from the colonial difference means, today, assuming philosophy as a regional practice and simultaneously thinking against and beyond its normative and disciplinary regulations.[12] After all, it was to a certain way of "thinking" that the Greeks called philosophy. In that sense, philosophy may have been invented by the Greeks, but thinking goes well beyond the Greeks—and beyond philosophy itself. The future demands thinking beyond the Greeks and Eurocentrism. Raúl Fornet-Betancourt, a Cuban philosopher residing in Germany, proposed "intercultural philosophy" to solve some of the puzzles presented by the colonial difference.[13] It is certainly a way of dealing with thinking beyond Eurocentrism. However, one of the issues that should be confronted is the translation of "cultural differences" into colonial differences and vice versa. The double translation will show that the very concept of "culture" is a colonial construction and that, indeed, "cultural difference" is the effect and the work of coloniality of power. Or, if you wish, "cultural difference" is basically a semantic question, while "colonial difference" underlines power relations, the coloniality of power, in the very making of cultural differences. The colonial difference is the underlying logic, and power relations holding together cultural differences have been articulated by the coloniality of power, from early Christian global designs to the current global coloniality driven by the metaphysics of the market. Intellectual decolonization, and in the case at hand the decolonization of philosophy, could help to undo the colonial difference and imagine possible futures beyond the alternative offered by global coloniality and the current reproduction (mass finances, mass mediation, mass migration) of the colonial difference.

NOTES

1. Miguel León-Portilla, *La filosofía Nahuatl* (Mexico City: Universidad Autonoma de Mexico, 1956).
2. Miguel León-Portilla, *Major Trends in Mexican Philosophy*, translated by A. Robert Caponigri (Notre Dame: University of Notre Dame Press, 1966). For philosophy in the Andes, see also Walter D. Mignolo, "Decir es fuera de lugar sujetos dicentes, roles sociales y formas de inscripción," *Revista de crítica literaria latinoamericana* 41 (1995): 9–32.
3. Robert Bernasconi, "African Philosophy's Challenge to Continental Philosophy," in Emmanuel Chukwudi Eze, ed., *Postcolonial African Philosophy. A Critical Reader* (Oxford: Blackwell, 1997), 188.
4. Ibid., 191.
5. Abdelkebir Khatibi, "Double Critique: I. Décolonisation de la sociologie." In Abdelkebir Khatibi, *Maghreb Pluriel* (Paris: Denoël, 1983), 43–63.
6. Walter D. Mignolo, *Local Histories/Global Designs. Coloniality, Subaltern Knowledge and Border Thinking* (Princeton, N.J.: Princeton University Press, 2000).
7. Orlando Fals-Borda, *Ciencia propia y colonialismo intelectual* (Bogota: Carlos Valencia, editores, 1987 [1970]).
8. Enrique Dussel, *Para una fundamentación filosofica de la liberación Latinoamericana* (Buenos Aires: Editorial Bonum, 1975), 8.
9. Horacio Cerutti Guldberg, *Filosofía de la liberación Latinoamericana* (Mexico City: Fondo de Cultura Economica, 1983.
10. Bernasconi, "African Philosophy's Challenge," 185.
11. Augusto Salazar Bondy, *Existe una filosofía en Nuestra America?* (Mexico City: Siglo XXI, 1996 [1968]).
12. See Chukwudi Eze, *Postcolonial African Philosophy*; Enrique Dussel, *The Underside of Modernity: Apel, Ricoeur, Rorty, Taylor and the Philosophy of Liberation*, trans. and ed. Eduardo Mendieta (Atlantic Highlands, N.J.: Humanities Press International, 1996); Enrique Dussel, *Postmodernidad y Transmodernidad. Dialogos con la filosofía de Gianni Vattimo* (México: Universidad Iberoamericana, 1999).
13. Raúl Fornet-Betancourt, *Filosofía Intercultural* (Mexico City: Universidad Pontifica de Mexico, 1994).

Part 3.
Neither Modern
nor Postmodern:
Postcolonial Globality

5. Borges and Postmodernity

ALFONSO DE TORO

The "Rhizomorphous" Producer and the Reader as "Literary Detective": The Adventure of Signs; or, The Postmodernity of Borgesian Discourse (Intertextuality-Palimpsest-Deconstruction-Rhizome)

> In all fiction, when a man is faced with alternatives he chooses one at the expense of the others. In the almost unfathomable Ts'ui Pên, he chooses—simultaneously—all of them. He thus *creates* various futures, various times which start others that will in their turn branch out and bifurcate in other times. [. . .] all the possible solutions occur, each one being the point of departure for other bifurcations.
> —Borges, *Ficciones*, 98[1]

> He believed in an infinite series of times, in a dizzily growing, ever spreading network of diverging, converging and parallel times. This web of time—the strands of which approach one another, bifurcate, intersect or ignore each other through the centuries—embraces *every* possibility.
> —Borges, *Ficciones*, 100

INTRODUCTION

Historically, the works of the Argentinean writer Jorge Luis Borges have usually been analyzed from philosophical, psychoanalytic, religious-mystic, or other standpoints. He has also been read in comparison with other authors, such as Valéry, Michaux, and, especially, Kafka.[2]

Beginning in the sixties, poststructuralist thinkers and the *Tel Quel* group devoted considerable attention to Borges. Today it is habitual to speak of his narrative texts as "postmodern."

Traditional literary science used to search (and still searches) for the "message" of Borges's work, which has constantly refused to be semantically decodified. Often extremely brief and sometimes trendy, many poststructuralist-oriented studies have concentrated on the description and functions of his narrative techniques, such as the literary description—understood by Ricardou and his school as a relatively traditional feature representing a transitional stage in the direction of the virtual, but essentially linguistic descriptions of the *nouveau roman* and the *nouveau nouveau roman*—textual productivity, reflections on writing, and so on. French authors apparently neglected the influence exerted by Borges's works on the development of literature starting in the fifties.[3] Whatever the case, the features that most attracted European authors—and most repelled the members of certain Latin American circles—were the sustained employment of several codes and the often misunderstood metatextual playfulness of Borgesian discourse. In my view, both features constitute the core of his work. In general terms, the analysis of Borges's "literariness" was neglected. For decades, it was considered blasphemous to describe the "literary playfulness" of a text or of its signifier without attributing to it a "deeper meaning."[4]

These tendencies seem to have been altered by the spread of semiotics in Ibero-American studies, and by the new approach to Borges's texts from the point of view of the debate on postmodernism. Similarly, it has been retrospectively observed, for example, that the philosophical enterprises of authors such as Lacan, Foucault, and Derrida are as postmodern as are those of Lyotard and Vattimo.

In my opinion, it is problematic that a considerable amount of the work which addresses so-called intertextuality in fact consists of traditional descriptions of the text's sources instead of semiotic analyses of its signifier. Observing that Borges cites, or implies the existence of, certain sources while refusing to explain their possible function within the text in which they appear does not take us very far. The description of intertexts is often limited to a mere list of external textual sequences, usually identified arbitrarily by means of the critic's specific literary knowledge.

Other theoreticians define Borges's works as postmodern either by emphasizing the forms of mimetic representation—as if postmodernism could be simply explained, in a *pars pro toto* fashion, by means of the "rediscovery of narrative mimesis"—or by focusing on the notion of discursive plurality. Unfortunately, it has not been noted that postmodernism was originally a North American cultural phenomenon dating from the sixties. It includes a vast range of cultural products, such as pop art, Westerns, and pornography.[5] Neither has a critique of the available categories used to define what belongs or does not belong to postmodernity been outlined. In any case, a difference should be established between the current categories and Ibero-American postmodernism as defined by Federico de Onís in the thirties.[6]

In a few of my previous studies, I considered several aspects of postmodernity in European and Latin American theatre, as well as in Latin American narrative. My purpose was to build a basic inter-subjective common ground on which the discussion about postmodernity could be established. I referred specifically to Borges in *Postmodernidad y Latinoamérica (con un modelo para la narrativa postmoderna)*, which was published in several journals beginning in 1990.[7] The following are the most important features of Borgesian discourse as analyzed in these studies:

1. The organization of signs and the ambiguous interaction between reality and fiction, and the relationship between object-language and metalanguage.

2. Presentation and development of the features that characterize Borges's work and that, in a certain sense, foreshadow basic tenets of the poetics of the *nouveau roman* and the *nouveau nouveau roman*. Examples of these features are textual productivity, the notion of writing as rereading, the dissolution of characters and of the narrator's identity, the metadiscursive and fictional levels, the revelation of fiction as fiction, and the double interaction between "object-discourse" and "metadiscourse," a feature that is shared with certain discourses of the *nouveau roman*—especially Robbe-Grillet's works—and with the *Tel Quel* group.

3. Borges and postmodernity.

My description of Borges's works is rooted in the following assumptions:

A. Borgesian discourse establishes a new form of aesthetics. His texts develop their own "defictionalization"—that is, the story is always revealed as an invention and no attempt is made to "make it concrete." Borgesian discourse evinces pluricodification, thus anticipating the notion of "double codification," identified by Fiedler in the sixties as a characteristic of the North American postmodern novel.[8]

Within this context, Borgesian discourse can be described in the following terms:

A.1. By means of the rhizome, a phenomenon extending far beyond that of intertext or palimpsest.

A.2. By means of deconstruction.

A.3. By means of *mise en abyme*, understood in the two senses specified by Gide: first, as a thematic treatment of the organization of the story (Borges, however, introduces a difference, since he emphasizes the diegetic organization of the signifier instead of that of the story); second, as the allusion to narrative procedures. Finally, the Borgesian *mise en abyme* also satisfies the meaning provided by authors of the *nouveau roman*, the *nouveau nouveau roman*, and the *roman Tel Quel*—that is, the destruction of the semantic level in a deconstructionist relationship with well-established genres.

A.4. By means of the habitual, virtual, or real dissolution of the narrator understood as a mediating category, a phenomenon that also affects the characters. It is thus possible to destroy the dual relationship between the "I-narrator" and the "I-actant," or to disperse the I-narrator into several I-narrators that may or may not be identified. The same applies to the "He-narrator" (i.e., the third-person narrator). We also observe a blurring of limits between the characters and the narrator, or between Borges the author and his narrators. Through these structure-dissolving techniques, the text becomes—at least virtually—anonymous and is reduced to itself. It is in this sense that Borges precedes the theories of the *nouveau roman* and the *Tel Quel* group regarding the self-generating nature of texts. The author becomes a "scriptor" intent on prompting the reader to act as a co-author, since the reader must continue to play the rhizomorphous game presented by the author and the narrator, thus establishing a parallel between the processes of writing and reading. Just as Borges concludes, from his reading of Kafka, that a writer is primarily a reader, it could be added that a reader is also a co-author.

B. Borgesian discourse deconstructs signifieds into signifiers. It is not a question of the search for sense—for a deep message—but of the search itself. The reader contemplates a true "adventurous journey" through several systems of signs. Repetition through time has eroded these systems' denotative capacity in such a manner that the only possibilities left are, first, that of looking for other containers of meaning and, second, that of radically turning the process into a search for pure signifiers. These signifiers are frequently employed in conjunction with "hook-acting" signifieds, which are afterwards revealed as semantically empty, since they are weakly codified.

It is obvious that in the pursuit and perception of these paradigms lies at least one of the most important methods for interpreting Borges's work: the discovery of its internal codification and its external decodification, which the author articulates at both the "object-discursive" and the "metadiscursive" levels.

C. Borges created a new paradigm in twentieth-century literature. Literature is no longer considered a "mimesis of reality," but a "mimesis of literature" and, specifically, a multiplication of codes organized according to the principles of the rhizome.[9] Borges thus forces readers to change their mode of reception. Traditional and coherent stories, mirrors of reality, and messages are not to be expected; rather, the text must be understood as its own reality, which is immanent in the period of reading. Its structure is a labyrinthine web containing an indeterminate number of well-known, little-known, unknown, or invented texts, which are valued by the culture's system—but not by Borges—as "universal," "trivial," or other categories. The addressee may accept this challenge by tracing back to specific references to people or works, quotations, and allusions; he or she may also let the flow of signifiers carry him or her away, and feel the attraction of a search which is inscribed within the text. Beyond his own personal taste, Borges does not seem to acknowledge distinctions between genres or objectifying evaluations of literature. For him, objectivity belongs only to signs—never to "works"—to phrases conceived of as motivating units. In this sense, he is a minimalist and a practitioner of fragmentariness. His readerly activity turns him into a producer of texts, rather than the opposite. His reading makes him a mediator between multiple signs, thus creating a rhizomorphous system.

Past literatures are activated through Borges the author by the text's implied reader. However, no attempt is made to provide the quoted text with a new and current sense in the realm of either production or reception of the text. Neither is the goal to reinterpret or to reconstruct these past texts, activities which were essential in the reception theory elaborated by the school of Constance. Texts are reproduced in a radically fragmentary manner. They function simply as a base on which to build a new text, which often bears no resemblance to the employed sequence. In my opinion, this is the core of Borges's poetics, the idea that led him to the notion that all texts have already been written and that his own work is a repetition of other written works, whether known or unknown to him, and a counterpart to these previous texts. This position is not merely a Borgesian flourish, but the basis of his literary system, in which a new theory of reception, distinct from the one that has so far been academically developed, is posited.[10]

Rather than mere content, Borges extracts structure from his sources, but the structure is placed at a different level and thus is transformed. When he generates an idea, each source seems to have only one sense; that is why he reveals his sources, which, whatever their type, always appear as fiction within the fiction.

D. Borges's postmodernity is based on his narrative techniques understood as a discursive plurality.

Besides the features mentioned above, postmodernity is characterized by the following terms: "deconstruction," "rhizome," the "metadiscursive game," "interculturality," "historicity," "cognitive reception," "ludic experience," "heterogeneity," "subjectivity," "re-creativity," "radical particularity," "diversity," and, in sum, "universality." One could add other features, such as minimalism, irony, humor, integrational fragmentation, collage, and dissolution of the separation between fiction and criticism, between art and non-art, between reality and fiction and, virtually, between the author and the reader.

1. TEXTUAL PRODUCTION AND THE NARRATOR'S METAMORPHOSIS: "EXTERNAL FICTION" AND "INTERNAL FICTION" AS LABYRINTHS

If the reader constantly stops reading in order to trace the quoted texts and the narrator's allusions, it can be said that Borges is placing the reader in a situation similar to that of the writer, who uses intertexts as literary digressions. This technique becomes manifest when the reader starts decodifying the quotations—in the case of texts and segments which actually exist—even if the identification does not help him or her. This method can be described as a collage or a literary montage; one must not understand both terms strictly in the pictorial sense, since the text lacks any element emphasizing simultaneity. Rather, the terms describe a collage and a syntagmatic montage that, although apparently coherent, never produce a causal sense. Pictorial simultaneity has been replaced by syntagmatic non-causality, in a process that ceaselessly tends toward the paradigmatization and rhizomatization of its terms and toward semantic-pragmatic destabilization.

In his short stories, Borges presents apparently traditional stories and structures, frequently built upon double *external* and *internal fictional levels*, reminiscent of the structure employed in the *Thousand and One Nights*. Within this articulation, an I-narrator (often called Borges) and/or a He-narrator act as mediators, assuring us that what is being told did actually happen (it might be added in passing that this type of technique is a quotation from the tradition of story-telling, especially in fantastic tales and first-person novels). In combination with this strategy, Borges deploys other techniques: footnotes, the "discovered manuscript," quotations from literary or scientific journals which include the exact dates, pages, and publication dates, and the mention of key situations given as real and transformed by the narrator of the "external fiction" into his true narrative goal to be presented to the reader. Through the use of all of these techniques, the narrator gives the impression that he is a chronicler who is presenting a report on something that has actually happened. This impression is enhanced by metadiscursive remarks. The overwhelming deluge of quotations, provided by a convincing narrator, create—especially when the reader is unable to control it—the dissolution of the separation between reality and fiction. In this manner, the names of people, countries, cities, and regions appear, whether they are real or not, as both real and purely fictional texts, and eventually as mere signs.

I will clarify the theories described thus far in the following examples.

Example 1: "*Tlön, Uqbar, Orbis Tertius*"

The "external fiction" of this story begins with the following explanations:

> I owe the discovery of Uqbar to the conjunction of a mirror and an encyclopedia. The unnerving mirror hung at the end of a corridor in a villa on Calle Gaona, in Ramos Mejía; the misleading encyclopedia goes by the name of *The Anglo American Cyclopaedia* (New York, 1917), and is a literal if inadequate reprint of the 1902 *Encyclopaedia Britannica*. The whole affair happened some five years ago. Bioy Casares had dined with me that night [. . .] (*Ficciones*, 17)

> The notes appeared to fix precisely the frontiers of Uqbar. [. . .] We read [. . .] that the literature of Uqbar was fantastic in character, and that its epics and legends never referred to reality, but to the two imaginary regions of Mlejnas and Tlön. (19)

The "external fiction" concludes with further explanations and additions:

> *Postscript of 1947.* I reprint the foregoing article just as it appeared
> in the *Anthology of Fantastic Literature, 1940*, omitting no more
> than some figures of speech, and a kind of summing up, which now
> strikes me as frivolous. So many things have happened since that
> date [. . .] I will confine myself to putting them down. (30)

> In March, 1941, a manuscript letter by Gunnar Erfjord came to
> light in a volume of Hinton, which had belonged to Herbert Ashe.
> The envelope bore the postmark of Ouro Preto. The letter cleared
> up entirely the mystery of Tlön. (30)

> About 1942, events began to speed up. [. . .] the Princess of Fau-
> cigny Lucinge had received her silver table service. Out of the re-
> cesses of a crate [. . .] fine immobile pieces were emerging [. . .]
> The metal case was concave. The letters on the dial corresponded
> to those of one of the alphabets of Tlön. Such was the first intru-
> sion of the fantastic world into the real one. [. . .] the second [. . .]
> [was] a shining metal cone [. . .] (32–33)

> Here I conclude the personal part of my narrative. [. . .] It is
> enough to recall or to mention subsequent events [. . .] About
> 1944, a reporter [. . .] uncovered, in a Memphis library, the forty
> volumes of the *First Encyclopaedia of Tlön*. (33)

The "external fiction" begins with an I-narrator who, by mentioning Bioy Casares,
reveals himself to be Borges. He informs us of the genesis of the story he is going
to tell. The I-narrator's position is retrospective, since he tells the story five years
after the dinner at the "quinta" in the calle Gaona. A mirror and an encyclopedia
are the starting points. Mirrors are defined as monstrous, which leads Bioy Casares
to remember a sentence by one of the heresiarchs from Uqbar, which he had read
in *The Anglo American Cyclopaedia* (New York, 1917). Immediately, Borges and
Bioy Casares begin to search for the article, which, after a series of difficulties, they
will find. It is crucial that the encyclopedia is fictitious and that Uqbar is a product of the imagination. In the article, Tlön is mentioned, and identified as a planet
invented by the inhabitants of Uqbar (this is a case of "double fictionality").

The search becomes prominent when Borges and Bioy unsuccessfully consult
volumes XLVI and XLVII of the set of *The Anglo American Cyclopaedia* in the
quinta. Later on, they find a trace in volume XXVI, in which they read:

> *Copulation and mirrors are abominable. [. . .] For one of those gnos-
> tics, the visible universe was an illusion or, more precisely, a sophism.
> Mirrors and fatherhood are abominable because they multiply and ex-
> tend it.* (18)

A few days later, Borges unsuccessfully consults an *Erkunde* by Ritter. The search comes to an end when Bioy discovers his volume XXVI, bound with false covers and with the letters "Tor–Ups" on its back; that is, the article "Uqbar," presumably, is missing. The reason is that the volume in the "quinta" set has 917 pages, whereas the one that Bioy brings has 921 pages, and thus includes the article in question. This article includes additional bibliographic indications, such as Silas Haslam's *History of the Land Called Uqbar* (1874) and Johannes Valentinus Andreä's *Lesbare uns lesenswerthe Bemerkungen über das Land Ukkbar in Klein-Asien* (1641).

At the end of the "external fiction," the editor–I-narrator informs us that he has reprinted his article on Tlön and Uqbar "just as it appeared in the *Anthology of Fantastic Literature*, 1940," in which an account is given about the origin of the encyclopedia and its fictional country. The dates of the *Antología* and the "Posdata," together with those noted in the "internal fiction," are important. After Herbert Ashe's death in 1937, the I-narrator discovers volume XI of the *First Encyclopaedia of Tlön* in Brazil, about which he had heard "two years since" (21). That means that the dinner with Bioy took place in 1935. Five years later, in 1940, the narrator publishes the article on Tlön, which is the actual year in which Borges and Adolfo Bioy Casares published their *Antología de la literatura fantástica*, and in which Borges's story first appeared, in *Sur* magazine. The short story was later reprinted in *The Garden of Forking Paths* (1941) and in the first edition of *Ficciones* (1944). It is also in 1944 that the complete set of the *First Encyclopaedia of Tlön* is "accidentally" found. Alien to all these dates is the "Posdata" of 1947, which, as a fiction within the fiction, does not refer to the article as printed in 1940, 1941, or 1944. It must have been added later, after the series of "discoveries" about the article ranging from 1941 to sometime after 1944. Borges is confronting us with the philological task of fixing the authorship, original dates, and printing dates of the discovered texts. The discoveries between 1941 and 1947 create a textual labyrinth that is finally explained in a letter by Gunnar Erfjord which was found in a book by Hinton that belonged to Herbert Ashe (this is a perfect example of the Borgesian labyrinth of people and authors). In the letter, Uqbar is described as the product of an invention directed by a secret society in the seventeenth century. Their original intention—that of creating a country and, later, a planet—was taken up again in 1824 in Memphis, and the complete final edition of the encyclopedia was not ready until 1914. Afterwards, the imaginary planet of Tlön emerges in the "reality of the fiction" in the form of several objects that were alluded to in the planet's encyclopedia and that now seem to have achieved real existence. In 1944, a journalist discovers the encyclopedia in Nashville, Tennessee. Tlön is thus revealed as a fiction within the fiction.

The "internal fiction" corresponds with the summary of the contents of volume XI, in which Tlön is described as a planet of idealists. There are accounts of, among other things, its philosophy, language, and literature and of the creation of objects by means of thought (the so-called *hrönir*). The entire summary is interspersed with quotations from real critics or philosophers, such as Leibniz, Hume, Berkeley, and Russell.

Example 2: *The Immortal One*

In *The Immortal One*, the "external fiction" is first constituted by the situation-ality of that which is narrated, then by a third-person narrator, an omniscient chronicler, and finally by an I-narrator.

Beginning of "external fiction"/constitutive metadiscourse:

He-narrator/I-narrator/editor-translator:

> In London, in the beginning of June 1929, the antiquarian Joseph Cartaphilus de Esmirna offered the Princess of Lucigne the six smaller volumes (1715–1720) of Pope's *Iliad*. The Princess acquired them; she exchanged a few words with him upon receiving them. He was, as she tells us, a consumed and earthy man who had gray eyes and a gray beard, with singularly undefined features. He man-aged to speak various languages with fluidity and ignorance; in only a few minutes he switched from French to English and from Eng-lish into an enigmatic combination of Spanish from Salónica and Portuguese from Macau. In October, the Princess overheard a pas-senger on the *Zeus* that Cartaphilus had died at sea while return-ing to Smyrna, and that he had been buried on the island of Ios. In the last volume of the *Iliad* she found this manuscript. The original is written in English and abounds in Latinisms. The version that we offer is literal. (*Labyrinths*, 105)[11]

End of "external fiction"/ deconstructionist "metadiscourse":

a) The "I-narrator"/character:

> {The troglodytes were the Immortal Ones { . . . }. Homer referred to those things [. . .]} I passed through new kingdoms, new em-pires [. . .]. I am mortal once again, I replicated myself, I am now like all men. That night, I slept until dawn.
> [. . .]
> [. . .] After two years' time, I have inspected these pages. I am cer-tain they reflect the truth, but in the first chapters, and even in certain paragraphs of the others, I seem to perceive something false.
> *The history I have narrated seems to be unreal because in it are mixed the events of two different men.*
> [. . .] Flaminio Rufus [. . .] Homer [. . .] there it is written that I fought at Stamford bridge [. . .] the narrator does not linger over warlike deeds [. . .]
> [. . .]

> When the end draws near, there no longer remain any remem-
> bered images; only words remain . . . I have been Homer. (*Laby-
> rinths*, 112–118)

b) The "First-person narrator"/character/narrator/author/Cartaphilus/Borges:

> *Postscript (1950)*. Among the commentaries elicited by the pre-
> ceding publication, the most curious, if not the most urbane, is
> biblically entitled *A Coat of Many Colors* (Manchester, 1948) and
> is the work of the most tenacious pen of Doctor Nahum Cordo-
> vero. It comprises some one hundred pages. The author speaks of
> the Greek centos, of the centos of Late Latinity, of Ben Jonson,
> who defined his contemporaries with bits of Seneca, of the *Virgilius
> evangelizans* of Alexander Ross, of the artifices of George Moore
> and of Eliot and, finally, of "the narrative attributed to the unique
> dealer Joseph Cartaphilus." He denounces, in the first chapter,
> brief interpolations from Pliny (*Historia naturalis*, V, 8); in the sec-
> ond, from Thomas de Quincey (*Writings*, III, 439); in the third,
> from an epistle of Descartes to the ambassador Pierre Chanut; in
> the fourth, from Bernard Shaw (*Back to Methuselah*, V). He infers
> from these intrusions or thefts that the whole document is apoc-
> ryphal.

In my opinion, such a conclusion is inadmissible. "When the end draws near," wrote
Cartaphilus, "there no longer remain any remembered images; only words remain." Words, displaced and mutilated words, words of others, were the poor pit-
tance left him by the hours and the centuries. (*Labyrinths*, 118)

We have, then, (1) a narrator who plays the role of reader-translator (first mediator); (2) the Princess as discoverer of the manuscript (second mediator); (3)
Joseph Cartaphilus, the antiquarian (third mediator) (Did you know that the
manuscript is there? Was this one written by him?); (4) as Part II informs us (p.
536), the author of the text is Marco Flaminio Rufo (fourth mediator), who has
in turn transformed himself into an Immortal (parts II and III); (5) one of the Immortals is Homer and is declared to be the equivalent of the "first-person narrator" (I = Marco Flaminio Rufo, Part V, p. 543), which is explicitly confirmed by
the "first-person narrator" (Part V, p. 544),who is the one in charge of the text
(and is thus the fifth mediator).

It is stated in *Posdata 1950* that the "first-person narrator" is Cartaphilus, since
the "third-person narrator," who transforms himself into an anonymous "first-person narrator (*"It is my understanding"*), attributes the words of the "first-person narrator" to Cartaphilus (= Marco Flaminio Rufo, Part V, pp. 543–544) (*Posdata
1950, p. 544*).

The new "first-person narrator" joins the "third-person narrator" from the beginning of the narration and ends with a sentence which is an interpretation of the epigraph attributed to Francis Bacon (*Essays LVIII*), which does not form part of the "external" or "internal" "fiction." Rather, it pertains to the authorial level, and so it pertains to Borges. As such, all the narrations return to their origin: Borges. It is he who uses craft, the ludic, metatextual game, to transmit his more diverse ideas/conceptions.

As we have seen, we have a Janus-headed narrator; in other words, he is atomized into various narrators:

BORGES
{M.F. Rufo = Immortal = Homer = Cartaphilus =
"First-person/Third-person Narrator"}

"Internal Fiction": the voyage of adventures:

1. After intensely asking about the river of immortality, the "first-person narrator" begins his search (534).
2. So as to realize his endeavors, he hires an army of mercenaries who experience the harshness of the desert in their trip through it. The soldiers see all kinds of monstrosities and discover the barbarians.
3. After his soldiers have been decimated and have deserted, the "first-person narrator," alias Flaminio Rufo, wanders until he finds the city of the pyramids and towers (535), where, beaten down by fatigue, he loses consciousness/lucidity and dreams of a labyrinth and a bucket of water that he cannot reach.
4. Upon waking, he finds himself tied up in a niche in the rocks, where he contemplates the city of the Immortals and dedicates a long description to it (535). The barbarians, gray characters in a state of ecstasy and absolute passivity, are truly Immortals who have not mastered language, but have mastered signs and live in a meditative state (538–539).
5. Upon drinking from the fountain, Flaminio Rufo becomes an Immortal and falls into a state of delirium after pronouncing a Greek phrase ("*The rich Trojans of Zelea that drink the black water of Esepo* [. . .]").
6. Upon waking for the second time, the first-person narrator begins a second voyage, a "micro-voyage" around the city, which is characterized by labyrinths, eternal galleries with no exit, inversely constructed, incomplete stairs (537), a highly heterogeneous architectonic structure.
7. The "first-person narrator" sets off on a third voyage to discover other kingdoms (541), and on the way he drinks from another river and is converted back into a mortal around 1792.
8. A year later, the first-person narrator writes and revises the manuscript describing his voyage. Even though he has discreetly lived through everything stated, something unbelievable still persists in the text.

The voyage in "internal fiction" is equivalent to that in "external fiction," as their common denominator is the "labyrinthine search" which does not lead to a final destination: the manuscript is declared to be unreal (questionable) and written by a collective conscience. That which is described has originated from the dreams and delirium of the "first-person narrator." The texts cited in *Posdata,* to which we will return later, clarify only certain technical aspects of the narration. What has been for the "first-person narrator" of "internal fiction" adventures and dreams, the immortal and mortal being, has been the text for the "First-person/Third-person narrator of external fiction." The voyage through the desert, especially the trip around the immortal city, is found in metonymic relation to the words that Borges works with in the books.

Example 3a: *The Garden of Forking Paths*

The "external fiction" in this text is set up by an anonymous I-narrator who reveals himself retrospectively only at the beginning of the story. He does not need to add his own commentaries at the end, since the "external fiction" is explained by the development of the "internal fiction." The starting point is page 242 of Liddell Hart's *History of the European War,* in which there is mention of a British military attack during World War I that was postponed from July 24 to July 29, 1916, because of heavy rainfall. This version of the events is put into question by a report—from which two pages are missing—written by Dr. Yu Tsun, former professor of English at the Hochschule in Tsingao.

The I-narrator, Dr. Yu Tsun, a relative of Ts'ui Pên (the author of the novel *The Garden of Forking Paths*), controls the "internal fiction." He is a spy working for the Germans who kills Stephen Albert in a town called Ashgrove. When the papers publish the news about the murder, the name of the victim reveals to the German secret service the name of the town that is scheduled to be attacked. After ensuring delivery of this communication, Dr. Yu Tsun is caught and later executed by the English secret service.

A large portion of this story constitutes a poetics of Borgesian writing—an aspect that I will discuss below. This circumstance is established not only by a metadiscourse, but by the fact that Ts'ui Pên, the author of the novel *The Garden of Forking Paths,* is, in a certain sense, Borges himself.

Example 3b: *Ibn Hakkan al-Bokhari, Dead in his Labyrinth*

The "external fiction" begins with a conversation between Dunraven and his friend Unwin in 1914. The former tells the latter of an episode that happened during his childhood: an Arab leader was killed by his cousin Zaid in a labyrinth-house in Pentreath. The "external fiction" ends with the analysis of the narration, which, in the opinion of Unwin, is not convincing and lacks verisimilitude. Unwin then proposes a different version, which both he and Dunraven accept.

Once again, this is a case of the birth and deconstruction of a fiction, which is confirmed by Allaby, the director of the school, who considers Ibn Hakkan's version within the "internal fiction" "fantastic." Unwin notes that the basic structure comes from the myth of the Minotaur and from the genre of mystery novels.

The editor explains in the postscript to the *El Aleph* collection—dated May 13, 1949—that the story is a variation on *"The Two Kings and their Two Labyrinths,"* which had been added by the copiers of *One Thousand and One Nights."* One should not neglect the epigraph from the Koran XXIX, 40, which relates the terms "house" and "spider" through the act of "building"—that is, erecting and composing in a labyrinthine fashion. This is how Borges reveals his metadiscursive game, his method of writing and his poetics, rendered absolutely transparent by his own explication of the text. He thus avoids the propensity to search for the profound or hidden elements, for the allegory in the textual game.[12]

The "internal fiction"—the first version, as told by Dunraven, which is also the one that the assumed Ibn Hakkan tells Allaby, and the one that Allaby tells the narrator—can be summarized as follows:

After a popular uprising, a tyrannical and daring king escapes together with his cousin Zaid, who is a coward. They bring a treasure with them. In the night, while Zaid peacefully sleeps, Ibn Hakkan dreams of a net of snakes suffocating him, which, in reality, is a cobweb lightly touching his body. He wakes up, kills Zaid and Zaid's servant, and destroys the former's face with a stone.

While he flees, he dreams that Zaid has condemned him to be chased and killed. Ibn Hakkan builds a labyrinth-house on a rock overlooking the bay and paints it crimson.

One day, Zaid appears and kills the lion, the slave, and al-Bokhari, destroying all of their faces.

The second version—Unwin's—is a rewriting of the first one that corrects several gaps in "narrative logic," thus revealing the narrative traps, which may have been overlooked by the reader but not by Unwin—the primary addressee of the story—and which generate some suspicion. For him, it is not the story but the way in which Dunraven has narrated the story that is an invention.

The first thing that he finds is that Ibn Hakkan does not kill Zaid; rather, Zaid runs away with a part of the treasure while Ibn Hakkan sleeps. Subsequently, Zaid pretends that he is Ibn Hakkan. The reason for this change of identity is that Zaid was reputed to be a coward, which troubled him and did not let him either fall asleep or kill Ibn Hakkan. Zaid builds the house in a prominent area, and he paints it crimson in order to attract al-Bokhari and kill him. Al-Bokhari reaches Pentreath, Zaid lures him into his trap and kills him, as well as the lion and the slave. He destroys all of their faces so that the change of identity may not be noticed; if he had disfigured only one of the murdered, it would have raised suspicions. After that, Zaid runs away.

The treatment of the question of identity and difference causes the two stories to be built upon "rhizomorphic correspondences." The labyrinth is mythologically present in the story of the Minotaur; the net corresponds with the network of runners in the Minotaur's cave and with Ariadne's thread, both of which coincide with the net of runners in Zaid's labyrinth-house and with the net of spiders in al-Bokhari's dream (which is directly caused by the light grazing of a spiderweb). These "nets" are also equivalent to the net of different solutions to a crime available to a detective in a murder mystery. On the other hand, they are also the nets of agents transmitting the message: Zaid, Allaby, Dunraven, Unwin, and the text's editor. They are equally the potential for variation inherent in Unwin's version and, finally, the author's itinerary through the narrative adventure and the reader's path through the reading adventure. On the basis of this set of correspondences, Zaid may turn into Ibn Hakkan and vice versa. Only Zaid knows that he dreamt he was a king. In his own right, the narrator turns into a reader and vice versa.

One of the senses of the term "net" is "rhizome," which expresses not imitation or similarity between two nets united by a common signifier, but the rhizome-specific principle of "non-parallel" lines.[13] This meaning of "net" generates the narration and dissolves several identities, including the narrator's.

In Borges's short stories, "external" and "internal" fictions do not play a traditional role. They neither make the narrative framework stable nor try to explain what has just been narrated. Rather, they create at the level of the signifier a labyrinth that misleads the reader by forcing him or her to adopt a strong and radically active readerly attitude while at the same time deconstructing his or her own narration and erasing its narrative character. The transformation of the narrator is a means to effectively abolish the separation between fiction and reality, between producer and addressee of the text, inasmuch as the narrator is always a reader who edits, or informs of, a given text—this factor is neatly exemplified by "Tlön, Uqbar, Orbis Tertius." Borges never ceases to write about the roles of both communicational instances: that of the author and that of the reader.

2. INTERTEXT, PALIMPSEST, RHIZOME

Before reviewing Borges, it is necessary to review the terms in the above heading, as they have acquired different meanings since Kristeva coined them.

Kristeva[14] first takes the writings of Bakhtin as her motivation, and from them the term or concept of "dialogism,"[15] which has little or nothing to do with the earlier concept of intertextuality, defined as "mosaique de citations, tout texte est absorption et transformation d'un autre texte. À la place de la notion d'intersubjectivité s'installe celle d'*intertextualité*, et le langage poétique se lit, au moins, comme *double*."[16]

This discussion appears to arrive at a primary culmination in the work by G. Genette, *Palimpsestes*,[17] in which he starts with five categories based on the term transformation that drives at the constitution of "hypertexts," which in turn discard their relation to "hypotexts." The five categories which appear are:[18]

1. *Intertexuality* = "relation de coprésence entre deux ou plusieurs textes [. . .] par la présence effective d'un texte dans un autre; ex.: citation, plagiarism, allusion."

   The criterion is of the external text type: the relation between Text A and Text B, between hypotext (= Reference text: A) and hypertext (= new text which takes a previous text as reference: B).

2. *Paratexuality* = "relation généralement moins explicite et plus distante, que [. . .] le texte proprement dit entretient avec [. . .] son *paratexte:* titre, sous-titre, intertitres, préface, postfaces, avertissement, avant-propos [. . .] notes marginales, commentaires," and so on. It deals with an "avant-texte," a "pre-text" (schema, project, etc.).

   The criterion is the "internal text:" Parts of a text, such as preface, title, postface, epigraph, special types of texts within the text—for example, in "Tlön, Uqbar, Orbis Tertius," the verses taken from *Hamlet*.

3. *Metatextuality* = "type de transcendence textuelle . . . relation . . . de commentaire, que unit un texte à un autre texte dont il parle, sans nécessairement le citer [. . .] sans le nommer"—for example, Hegel in his *Phenomenology* includes Diderot's *Le Neveu de Rameau.*

4. *Architextuality* = "relation tout à fait muette, que n'articule [. . .] qu'une mention paratextuelle [. . .] ou [. . .] infratitulaire"—for example, poetry, essay, novel, and so on.

   The criterion is the "external text," which deals with relations among genres and literary types. For example, one finds this phenomenon in Borges when he suggestively plays with elements from political novels or historical, fantastic, or regionalist short stories/novels.

And finally,

5. *Hypertexuality* = "toute relation unissant un texte B (= *hypertexte*) à un texte antérieur A (= *hypotexte*)," where a previous text is not inserted as a commentary, but in "second degree" form. Hypotexts and hypertexts also may be scientific. Text B does not discuss Text A, but includes it, thus making A part of B; it results in a transformation.

   The criterion is the "external text." The hypertext is usually fictional, which is to say that it is derived from another fictional text. Not all intertextuality is hypertextuality, and each hypertext may be read in its totality, as a text with autonomous significance. Each hypertext signifies an elaboration, a project: "faire du neuf avec du vieux." A new function superimposes itself onto an older one and the dissonance between the two is what constitutes the new work. Hypertextuality is a perpetual circulation of texts.

   This project reveals a palimpsest attitude, an imposition of the ludic: "accomplissement intellectuel et divertissement." The palimpsest is a "littérature livrèsque, de second degré."

According to Genette, the serious transformation is the most important of all hypertextual practices, due to its vast historical field and its varied possibilities. Genette posits that the intertextual work is always a work which deals with texts as unities unto themselves, not as mere allusions or ideological "echoes." This thereby discards the terms "transformation" and "imitation."

Departing from this base and considering the international discussion concerning the present subject, I propose the following definitions and redefinitions as the first objective for an adequate model of Borges's works. I indicate that Genette's category 5 is practically the same as category 1: it is the form by which intertextuality is constituted (operatively):

I define *hypotextuality* etymologically, in the sense of minor intensity. Here it is minor functional intensity, which we separate from a mere relation, such as the mention of a name, a title, a word, and so on.

I define *hypertextuality* as an intertextual work, a transformation which presupposes a major or minor codification by the author of the text and the major or minor possibility of its decodification by the reader. This definition discards the terms "transformation" and "imitation."

Instead of Genette's hypotext, I employ the term "*pre-text*," and I replace hypertext with "*posttext*."

I would like to refer to the *result* which emerges from the relation between a pretext and a posttext—in other words, the intertextual work—as *intertext*. I reserve the term "*intratext*" for the relations within a determined text and define it as such: when, for example, Borges explains the beginning of a story or explains its (pseudo) origins at the end. Intratext may be metatextual or objetotextual, which is to say, it may discuss the text or refer to anecdotes.

I summarize the material in the following schema. I also indicate that a paratext may be given in relation to internal or external texts. The verses from *Hamlet* at the beginning of *El Aleph* refer to a work outside of the posttext; its possible function in the posttext forms an intratext (see fig. 5.1).

Outside of the rhizome, what we find to be the most definitive in describing the narrative method of Borges within the categories developed by Genette "are additive oulipism or additive contamination" and "autopastiche." Genette defines the first one as:[19]

> Oulipisme/contamination . . . techniques de mixage, contamination additives   et substitutives. La forme la plus traditionnelle (préoulipienne) de la   contamination additive est le *centon*, qui consiste à prélever un vers ça et là pour constituer un ensemble aussi cohérent que possible.

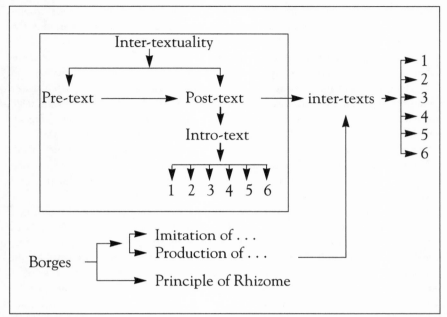

Figure 5.1

or:

> . . . transformation ludique. Le garant de lucidité est ici caractère
> purement "machinel" du principe transformateur, et donc fortuit
> de résultat. C'est le hasard qui opère, aucune intention sémantique
> n'y   préside, rien de "tendancieux" ni de prémédité. Dans la par-
> odie classique (et moderne), le "jeu" consiste à détourner un texte
> de sa signification initial vers   une autre application connue d'a-
> vance, et à laquelle il faut l'adapter   *soigneusement*. . . . La paro-
> die est un jeu d'adresse; l'oulipisme est un jeu de hasard, comme la
> roulette. Mais . . . cette récréation hasardeuse ne peut manquer
> longtemps de devenir *récréation*, car la transformation d'un texte
> produit toujours un autre texte, et donc un autre sens.

He defines the second category in the following way:

> L'autopastiche: Lorsqu'un auteur accentue son idiolecte en multi-
> pliant ou en   exagérant les traits caractéristiques, il est tentant
> (et courant) de le taxer, ou plus   exactement de feindre de le
> soupçonner d'autopastiche ironique, ou comme on   dit plus
> couramment, d'"autoparodie."

I find the "pseudo-conclusion," or "fictive conclusion," simulated from an imaginary text, to be of central importance in Borges's work. This may be defined as the synthesis of indirect repetition and textual commentary.[20]

I would like to define the term *deconstruction* in the following way. I use Genette's definition of palimpsest as a basic concept related to intertextuality, as well as to deconstruction: *the intellectual endeavor of reading a text from its deep-seated structure, which is to say, reading a text in a linear fashion, also taking into account what the author was thinking. This sheds light on the motivation for its composition and its relation to the epistemologies of different time frames.* To read the "palimpsest way" is to be involved in deconstruction: to discover the metatextuality of a text, its epistemological transgressions. Deconstruction is to read the text in light of its time frame; it is to read *with* the text and *against* the text. We may define this reading/activity as an epistemological semiotics.

On a certain level, postmodern deconstruction is a superimposed reading, a *para-reading*, whose objective is to use other texts as the basis for motivation until one reaches the point of forgetting or eliminating the point of reference.[21] Deconstruction is to read the text with mistrust, to put everything into question; it is to explore the most remote recourse or possibility so as not to judge, but to offer up a hypothesis. It is a reading which privileges difference—which is related to the discovery of ruptures, evasions, zero semiotic positions. Postmodern deconstruction tries to subjugate metaphysical binarism, oppositions such as "interior (soul-breath-word-thought-logos) vs. exterior (body-writing-material)," which began with Platonism and continued with Rousseau and even Saussure. It does not seek out the "pure idea," but, rather, its *"différence"*—that is, its original impurity (Heidegger/Levinas). This focuses on the decentralization of the subject in favor of transformations against a totalitarian structure. In this theory, thought, like speech, is treated as a *game* of infinite substitutions within a limited totality. Derrida develops his thought in a radical manner in *Glas* (1974), *La vérité en peinture* (1978), *La carte postale de Socrates à Freud et au-delà* (1980), and *Parages* (1986), for which he was accused of "charlatanry."[22]

Returning to Borges, he resorts to the method of palimpsest in the sense mentioned above. He treats it as a ludic game of extratextual, motivating structures which apparently employ certain pre-texts and use diverse types of textual insertions, which employ other texts and authors of varied works and different time frames. The attitude is palimpsest/deconstructionist, but it appears that only pre-text is used. Palimpsest does not lead us to a version, transformation, or reversal of the given themes; rather, it creates a text that cannot be reduced to an already codified structure, for if it is separated from the traditional course of palimpsest (which always presupposes a transformation of codified structures), we will find ourselves in a cul-de-sac. Nor is the original text used as an actualized, newly concretized rereading. This is also what follows in regard to the posttext. It does not produce a new signified (an intertext) in the inserted syntagmatic space, nor does it connect the signified of the pre-text within the new context; rather, the signifying structure is what is used. This is clearly illustrated in Borges's stories, which resist an interpretation on the basis of the signified, thereby leaving the impression of emptiness and radical segmentation.

According to my assessment, Borges takes the forms of palimpsest and intertext to the limit—that is, to their irreconcilability—by means of a radical heterogeneity, fragmentation, and aparallelism. Palimpsest and intertext presuppose a literary mimesis—that is, a copy—a principle of unity that appears heterogeneous but is not, just as the different branches and bifurcations of a tree are not. What we do see as a clear procedure is a strong tendency toward the rhizome[23]—that is, toward a type of organization in which an element finds itself connected with another of a very different structure, producing an ahierarchical, disunited, open, and ever-developing proliferation. Speaking metaphorically, we have a network of knots from which emerge roots that connect themselves to other knots. It is not the relationship of signifier/signified that matters, but the type of relationship at the level of the signifier. In other words, the significance of the syntagm does not matter; what matters is how it is connected. Borges's literature likes to lead us to believe that it is mimetic (Cervantes accomplished this in *Don Quijote*), or that it imitates literature (*Don Quijote* also achieves this). In reality it only *cites the world and literature, producing virtually rhizomorphic texts which are a subtle deconstruction of the cited models, not a parody of them, which was the system of deconstruction in* Don Quijote.

In my view, Borges carries the techniques of the palimpsest and the intertext to their limits by making both unrecognizable through the use of radical heterogeneity, fragmentation, and a lack of parallelism. Both palimpsest and intertext presuppose a mimetic notion of literature—that is, the notion of the copy, a principle of unity which, despite appearances, is not heterogeneous in the same way that the different branches and bifurcations of a tree are unique. What one finds indeed is a strong tendency to the "rhizome," a kind of organization in which one element is connected with another belonging to a very different structure, thus producing a non-hierarchical, disjointed, open, and ever-developing proliferation. In graphic terms, there is a network of knots out of which spring roots that are connected to other knots. In these connections, it is not the signifier–signified relation that is important, but the relations at the level of the signifier: the question is not what the signified of the segment is, but how the segment is connected. Borges's literature pretends that it imitates the world, but, like Cervantes's *Don Quijote*, it does something else. It also pretends that, again like *Don Quijote*, it imitates literature. However, Borges's literature merely *quotes from the world and from literature, thus producing virtually rhizomorphic texts that subtly deconstruct the quoted models instead of parodying them, as Cervantes did according to Don Quijote's deconstructive principle.*

Deleuze and Guattari define the rhizome through six principles: "connection," "heterogeneity," "multiplicity," "nonsignifying rupture," "cartography," and "decalcomania." The first two principles refer to the proliferation of the rhizome in all dimensions of n-1, to its changes in shape, its accidental quality, and to its refusal to form genealogical trees, dualities, or deep structures. Rhizomes are chains of different codifications and of different biological, economic, political, or cultural systems. The third feature ("multiplicity") is understood to be the absence of an object and a subject—one can only apprehend a rhizome through determination, quantity, and dimension. In symbolic terms, the rhizome is a network, a fabric in which only lines with no supracodification exist. Rhizomatic lines of discourse are unique and simple, since they totally cover the dimension of the rhizome and need no further additions. Deleuze and Guattari describe the ideal book as one endowed with a page-long plan in which the totality of a vast variety of elements (experiences, historical determinations, concepts, individuals, groups, and social formations) could be put together.

This notion is perfectly exemplified by Borges's "The Analytic Language of John Wilkins," mentioned by Foucault as the starting point for his famous *The Order of Things* (xv–xxiv). Borges's text includes a reference to a Chinese encyclopedia in which a set of heterogeneous items has been assembled:

> In its remote pages it is written that animals are divided into: (a) belonging to the Emperor, (b) embalmed, (c) tame, (d) suckling pigs, (e) sirens, (f) fabulous, (g) stray dogs, (h) included in the present classification, (i) frenzied, (j) innumerable, (k) drawn with a very fine camelhair brush, (l) et cetera, (m) having just broken the water pitcher, (n) that from a long way off look like flies. (*Obras completas* II, 86)

We cannot consider here the previous or the following paragraphs, which further intensify the radical nature of multiplicity. Borges's work is shaped as a mere sketch, as the representation of certain "writing materials" which, in fact, are the writing or narration themselves.

The fourth principle introduces the possibility of interrupting or destroying a rhizome and the impossibility of having dualities. Rhizomes "deterritorialize" prominent cultural items and "reterritorialize" them within the rhizomorphous system. There is no imitation or similarity, but an explosion of at least two heterogeneous series consisting of a single rhizome and not subjected to a higher system; for example, the crocodile does not adopt the shape of a tree trunk and the chameleon does not take the color of its skin from its environment. These animals do not imitate or reproduce; rather, they paint the world in their colors. They "produce" rhizomes; they produce worlds.

Criteria five and six highlight the absence of a genetic axis, a deep structure, and objective units. The rhizome is a card of many entries, not a "copy of." It is open to any dimension, it is productive rather than reproductive; it springs from performance rather than from competence.

The theory of rhizomes is an utopia of postmodern philosophy, led by the desire to go beyond "metadiscourses," duality, and hierarchical systems. This utopia may be attempted, but not achieved—or at least in the case in science. As presented by authors such as Lyotard and Vattimo, it is a virtual possibility in philosophy, as it is in art and literature.

Returning to Borges's texts, a few examples will show how he replaces traditional forms of palimpsest and intertextuality. In "The Garden of Forking Paths," we can identify several roots branching from a single rhizome:

a':   the British attack in 1916 (a military event);

b':   in connection with this, the events in a case of espionage;

c':   Dr. Yu Tsun's version of these events;

d':   Dr. Yu Tsun's visit to Stephen Albert;

e':   Ts'ui Pên's text, which is also a theory of textual production and of the possibilities inherent in reading at the metadiscursive level. At the same time, it is a theory of labyrinths or of rhizomatic or temporal structures. In sum: a theory of what literature may be.

In the beginning, Dr. Yu Tsun believes that the labyrinthine structure of his ancestor's book could be described as a circular structure similar to that in *The Thousand and One Nights*. According to this notion, one must reject certain possibilities when making specific choices ("In all fiction, when a man is faced with alternatives he chooses one at the expense of the others" [*Ficciones*, 98]). The methods of textual production and reception proper to Dr. Yu Tsun are traditional and derive from the principle of the genealogical tree. That is why he speaks of the evolution or inheritance of a text, which can be preserved, restored, updated, and, finally, understood by means of the palimpsest: "I also imagined a Platonic hereditary work, passed on from father to son, to which each individual would add a new chapter or correct, with pious care, the work of his elders" (97).

After his failure to interpret his ancestor's work, Dr. Yu Tsun realizes that Ts'ui Pên's principle of composition is "simultaneous," or, in our terms, nonparallel and rhizomorphous: "He thus *creates* various futures, various times which start others that will in their turn branch out and bifurcate in other times. This is the cause of the contradictions in the novel" (98).

Hence the infinite possibilities of combination of events and endings. Terms that usually stand opposed can now coexist: "In Ts'ui Pên's work, all the possible solutions occur, each one being the point of departure for other bifurcations. Sometimes the pathways of this labyrinth converge. For example, you come to this house; but in other possible pasts you are my enemy; in others my friend" (98). The expression "each [solution] being the point of departure for other bifurcations" shows that, in a non-causal way, each knot produces other knots and bifurcations.

Albert's observations about Dr. Yu Tsun's ancestor show that, for him, this text is a masterpiece, even though the novel has traditionally been undervalued as a literary genre. If Ts'ui Pên chose to write a novel, it was because he was a brilliant

man of letters, and not merely a novelist, thus reaching beyond given genres and
structures of classification. The chosen themes (metaphysics, mysticism, philosophy) were pretexts for him to engage in another topic—time, which, being "simultaneous" or "non-parallel," obeys rhizomorphic principles.

The rhizome can be detected at two different levels: encoded in a series of military and espionage events, on the one hand, and in a theory of writing and non-
metaphysical thought, on the other (the mention of Plato is revealing in the
latter case). These two levels are connected in a non-parallel manner after being
deterritorialized. In the "external fiction" the situation is similar: the military attack initially has no connection with the visit to Stephen Albert. It is suggested
that the agent working for Germany wants to escape the imminent danger after
having been discovered. Equally, his ancestor's work has no connection with the
texts mentioned at the beginning. For the agent, the labyrinth/rhizome consists
of both escaping and sending the information; for Ts'ui Pên, it is his book; for Albert, it is his interpretation of the book; and for the reader, it is detecting and understanding the system of the signifier devoid of its signified. A parallel is
established: Dr. Yu Tsun and Ts'ui Pên are the producers of the internal fiction regarding the events and the text, while Borges's and Ts'ui Pên's texts play that role
at the metadiscursive level. On the opposite pole of communication, Dr. Yu Tsun
and the reader are the addressees of the "internal fiction" and/or the "external fiction." In the process, the deconstruction affects not only the literary genres of espionage and war novels, but also the text's structure, as is the case in *The One
Thousand and One Nights*. All of these structures are mentioned as hypothetical
starting points in order to be discarded. The cited texts offer no help either in interpreting the signified or in fixing a signifier—they are merely quotations that
demonstrate the opposite of what they say. These structures do not reverse or alter
the signifieds/signifiers, which were present in the books as insinuations; rather,
they form a rhizome, something new, a unique and unrepeatable self-negating
system.

In "Death and the Compass," Borges reveals the loose and unconnected materials that he employs: "I have woven it, and it holds: the materials are a dead
writer on heresies, a compass, an eighteenth-century sect, a Greek word, a dagger,
the rhombs of a paint shop" (139).

In "Theme of the Traitor and Hero," Borges connects "Chesterton's mysteries"
with "Leibniz's pre-established harmony" to compose his text. "Story of the Warrior and the Captive" begins with a Latin epitaph, attributed to B. Croce, about a
military event, which means that this starting text is also of a critical nature. According to the narrator, in *History of the Decline and Fall of the Roman Empire*, XLV,
177–688, Gibbon also describes this event about a Lombard warrior who defects
during the siege of Ravenna and dies while defending the Roman city, which he
had previously attacked on the barbarian side. The second pillar of the text—the
story of an English woman turned indigenous—is told to Borges by his grand-
mother. The relation—or, rather, the non-parallel connection between both sto-

ries—consists of an inversion of places of origin. Borges explains the mechanism thus:

> The figure of the barbarian who embraced the cause of Ravenna, the figure of the European woman who chose the wasteland, may seem antagonistic. And yet, both were swept away by a secret impulse, an impulse more profound than reason, and both heeded this impulse, which they would not have known how to justify. Perhaps, the stories I have related are one single story. The obverse and the reverse of this coin are, for God, the same. (*Labyrinths*, 130–131)

In "The Babylon Lottery," the lottery-like character of Borges's textual organization is stressed: "Such is the symbolic scheme. In reality, *the number of drawings is infinite*. No decision is final, all diverge into others" (*Ficciones*, 70).

The fact that the quoted texts are useless at the level of the signified and become merely a skeleton at the level of the signifier is exemplified by the mention of Johannes Valentinus Andreae (1586–1654) in "Tlön, Uqbar, Orbis Tertius." Borges attributes to him *Lesbare und lesenswerthe Bemerkungen über das Land Ukkbar in Klein-Asien* (19).

Texts are never quoted in order to be inserted at the level of the signified or to be recalled, which means that the possibility of a reception understood as a new concretization is rejected. This is evident in "Pierre Menard, Author of Don Quijote" and in "Averroes' Search." In the former text, Menard undertakes a remake of *Don Quijote*. Two methods are open to him: the first is to try to bring the text up to date, but the distance in time and the loss of the text's determining factors do not allow it. The second is to copy the work word by word, which, although apparently producing a tautology or a copy, creates a new text once it has been inserted in the present tense of writing: in contemporary time, textual signifiers produce completely different signifieds. The text is totally new, and eventually destroys the original work belonging to Cervantes:

> The initial method he conceived was relatively simple: to know Spanish well, to re-embrace the Catholic faith, to fight against Moors and Turks, to forget European history between 1602 and 1918, and to *be* Miguel de Cervantes. Pierre Menard studied this procedure (I know that he arrived at a rather faithful handling of seventeenth-century Spanish) but rejected it as too easy. Rather because it was impossible, the reader will say! I agree, but the undertaking was impossible from the start, and of all the possible means of carrying it out, this one was the least interesting. To be, in the twentieth century, a popular novelist of the seventeenth seemed to him a diminution. To be, in some way, Cervantes [. . .]

seemed to him less arduous [. . .] than to continue being Pierre
Menard and to arrive at *Don Quixote* through the experiences of
Pierre Menard. (49)

The I-narrator uses a letter by Menard to reconstruct his method, but also fails.
What remains is the introduction of a new literary method based on the palimpsest, ambiguity, error, anachronism, and, ultimately, the generating principles of
the rhizome: "Menard (perhaps without wishing it) has enriched, by means of a
new technique, the hesitant and rudimentary art of reading: the technique is one
of deliberate anachronism and erroneous attributions" (54). The I-narrator speaks
here both of the act of the reading and of textual production, since the terms
"anachronism" and "attributions" were previously mentioned by the author.

In "Averroes' Search," the Arab philosopher tries to translate the terms "co-
moedia" and "tragoedia" in Aristotle's *Poetics*, but fails, as his cultural system does
not include these terms. Neither can the I-narrator figure out who Averroes really
is: "I felt that Averroes, wanting to imagine what a drama is without ever having
suspected what a theater is, was no more absurd than I, wanting to imagine Averroes" (*Labyrinths*, 155).

These mechanisms turn Borges into a postmodern *avant la lettre* who creates a
new form of deconstruction in which the literary referent, and even its motivating origin, disappear. Thus emerges a new text, but, unlike *Don Quijote*, its literary referent is never clearly defined. Borges is not properly an intertextual author;
rather, he *imitates* and quotes intertextuality, in the same way that he quotes the
"reality vs. fiction" polarity or the mechanisms of fantastic literature.

3. "OBJECT-DISCOURSE" AND "METADISCOURSE," OR, THE CANCELLATION OF THE "REALITY VS. FICTION" OPPOSITION

Moreover, I would like to use some examples to demonstrate that many of
Borges's texts, not only the works compiled in *Ficciones* and *El Aleph*, possess a
double codification within the total structure of the text: at the level of "object-
discourse" of the narrated account, and at the level of "metadiscourse." These discourses consist of particular observations regarding the text in question, along
with general questions concerning the type of literature. I will categorize the different examples of "metadiscourse" into three groups: the "text within the text"
which arises from the proceedings of textual organization, the "text within the
text" as textual producer, and the "text within the text" as thematization of textual reception.

The "I-narrator" of *The Immortal* comments on the "internal fiction" in the text
written about his experiences. His commentary forms part of the "object-discourse" as well as the "metadiscourse," since he tells us about the "*contamination*"

of his history with unreal facts derived from poets. He qualifies his history as "fantastic," and states that its structural beginning lies in the "Centón."[24]

When the "I-narrator" tells us about his dream, which focuses on an interminable, horrific labyrinth, filled with pseudo-symmetries so as to deliberately confuse people, corridors with no exit, windows that are out of reach, doors that lead to a cell or a well, inverse stairs that lead to the sky, and so on, he is also discussing the rhizomorphic processes of his work (diverse manuscripts, authors, themes) and of the reader's experience.[25] On a more general level, he qualifies the text as a production of signs, in which there is no difference between real and unreal: "I can no longer distinguish whether this or that detail is a transcription of reality or of the forms which designed my nights."[26]

The city of the immortals (= "object-discourse") is equivalent to the book, and is qualified as such:

> . . . a chaos of heterogeneous words, the body of a tiger or a bull, in which teeth, organs, and heads monstrously germinated, conjugating and loathing each other, they may very well be like images.[27]

The troglodyte ("object-discourse") is the equivalent of the writer ("metadiscourse") and his writing is "barbaric," which reflects the strangeness with which the reader receives the narrative discourse. This is why the "first-person narrator" wants to teach the impatient barbarian (= the relationship between Borges and the reader):

> The man designed them, looked at them, and corrected them. He suddenly   erased them with the palm of his hand and his forearm, as if the game were   frustrating him.   [. . .] that night I realized the purpose of teaching him to   recognize, and perhaps repeat some words.[28]

"To trace," "to look," and "to correct" are terms which do more than reveal part of the production. They also reveal the reader's intentions in regards to comprehending the text, as illustrated in the following passage:

> I thought that Argos and I participated in different universes; I thought that our perceptions were the same, but that Argos combined them in a different way and constructed different objects with them; I thought that objects did not exist for him, rather, a vertiginous and continuous game of very brief impressions. I thought of a world without memory, without time.[29]

The situation represented the difficulty encountered in the relationship of producer and recipient with respect to the novelty of that which is narrated ("same perceptions vs. combination/different construction").

The "object-discourse" remains hermetic; it appears to resist an allegorical interpretation of semantic weight.[30] It takes on the characteristics of pre-text for the
rhizomorphic semiotic game, in which the structure is like that of a wheel, not circular, but without beginning and without end, where one element engenders another, without determining the other, without ever reaching unity.[31]

In *The Theologians*, the narrator characterizes the writings of Juan de Panonia as
"vast and almost inextricable periods, disturbed by punctuation marks, where neg-
ligence and syntax errors appeared to be forms of disdain. From the cacophony he
made a polished, universal instrument"[32] reflected in reading the beginning of a
text or the text at face value, which is later discovered to be the rhizome. The only
pleasure left for the recipient seems to be the mere discovery of citation, how it is
reflected in the character of Panonia, and what it establishes: that his writings
come from other writings. The conclusion is that the text "did not seem to be
written by a concrete person, rather by any man, or maybe by all men,"[33] which
accentuates collective textual productivity in the face of an individualized one
which calls attention to originality and newness.

We find a final example in the passage in "Tlön, Uqbar, Orbis Tertius" in which
Borges and Bioy Casares describe the characteristics of the article from the encyclopedia about Uqbar ("object-discourse") which are those of the story itself
("metadiscourse"):

> We carefully read the article. The passage that Bioy remembered
> was possibly the only surprising one. The rest seemed the same, ad-
> justed to fit the general tone of the work and (naturally), a little
> boring. Rereading it, under its rigorous writing we discovered a
> fundamental vagueness. We only recognized three of the fourteen
> names ambiguously interspersed in the geographic part of the text.
> [. . .] We only recognized one name from the historical names: the
> impostor Esmerdis the Magician,[34] probably used as a metaphor.
> The note appeared to delineate the border of Uqbar, but its nebu-
> lous points of reference were rivers and craters and chains of the
> same region.[35]

In reality, the text is coherent and convincing. Why can't a recipient believe
that *The Anglo-American Cyclopedia* exists? Furthermore, why should he doubt
that Uqbar exists? It could be the ancient name of a city that exists today. Outside
of this, there is a massive citation of texts, places, and authors which functions to
give credence to that mentioned above. It is clear that the narrator reveals the fictive nature of the account in another place; in the beginning he sustains that *The
Anglo-American Cyclopedia* is "fallacious," stemming from a republication of the
Encyclopaedia Britannica. Later on, the geographical places and current persons, or
post quam that are easily described as mere fiction.

The *language and literature* section was brief. Only one memorable detail: it noted that the literature from Uqbar was fantastic in character and that its epics and legends never referred to reality, but to the imaginary regions of Mlejnas and Tlön.[36]

In this passage, Borges refers to his own text as a pure invention, as fantastic, thereby giving us the instrument by which to understand his interpretation.

I now had in my hands a great methodical fragment of the entire history of an unknown planet, with its architectures and cards, with the awe of its mythologies and the rumor of its languages, with its emperors and oceans, with its minerals and birds and fish, with its algebra and fire, with its theological and metaphysical controversies. Everything articulated, coherent, lacking, visible doctrinal purpose or parodic tone.

. . .

The fact that all philosophy is fist and foremost a dialectical game, a *Philosophie   des Als Ob,* has contributed in its multiplication. Incredible systems abound,   but of pleasant architecture or the sensational type. The metaphysicists of Tlön do not search for the truth, nor even verisimilitude: they search for, wonder. They judge metaphysics to be a branch from fantastic literature. They know that a system is nothing more than the subordination of every aspect of the universe by any other object.

. . .

Books are also different. Fictional books only work with one argument, with all its imaginable permutations.[37]

In this case we have a "text within a text" in the story "Tlön, Uqbar, Orbis Tertius," given that the content of the fantastic encyclopedia is equivalent to the content of the "internal fiction," thereby discovering it as fantastic. Not only in this story, but in "The Lottery in Babylonia," "An Examination of the Work of Herbert Quain," "The Library of Babel," "The Garden of Forking Paths," and "The Form of the Sword" do we find a great number of "metadiscourses" which constantly comment on the "object-discourse."[38]

4. ANTICIPATING THE *NOUVEAU ROMAN,* THE *NOUVEAU NOUVEAU ROMAN,* AND *TEL QUEL*

This analysis is primarily intended to be an interpretation of the system of Borges's short stories on the basis of their signifiers. It also reveals that Borges anticipated some central ideas of the *nouveau roman*, the *nouveau nouveau roman*, and *Tel Quel*, together with some features of postmodernity.

The eclectic activity of perceiving several systems is the core of Borges's aesthetics, as it relates to both the producer and the recipient of the text. The producer is an addressee who turns his or her experience as a perceiver into writing, thus reproducing reading by means of a rhizomorphous organization. The reader may also reproduce this game, but he or she can also remain at the level of immanent readings or trace the text back playfully as a "literary detective" would. When searching for clues at the level of the signified, one will encounter disappointment. When engaged in a labyrinthine signifier-oriented search, one will experience a pleasurable adventure through several systems that cannot be reduced to a coded suprasystem. The narrator dissolves between the hinges as a result of the rhizomorphous quality of his writing; he also reveals the "secret" of his text by means of a "metadiscourse" which interprets the "discourse-object" in a continuous "text-within-the-text" act of description. Borges goes beyond intertextual practices and the aleatory techniques of the *nouveau roman*, both of which presuppose a unified system of signs. He shifts from the straightforward palimpsest of "Pierre Menard" to the rhizome in "The Garden of Forking Paths." Literature thus achieves the epitome of its own referential powers and autonomy, and is confronted with reality, understood now as merely a quotation, and with other texts, which are deconstructed.

5. BORGES'S POSTMODERNITY

Rather than writing on the "reality vs. fiction" opposition, Borges disposes of the former part of the dichotomy and divides the latter into a "mimesis of fiction vs. fiction" confrontation. This is why his short stories are always the result of a (pseudo)intertextual activity. The reality that is taken for granted is frequently one that was created by other texts; hence the fact that Borges's texts cannot be properly described as fantastic according to Todorov's categories. The stories in *Ficciones* and *The Aleph* must be viewed as a "quotation" of the opposition between reality and fiction and as a "mimesis of fiction." Literature, and not reality, is now the referent, which is constituted by signs. In this sense, Borges's stories are not usually ambiguous regarding the traditional "reality vs. fiction" opposition. At best, they may be taken to belong to what Todorov terms the "marvelous fantastic" or the "strange fantastic."

The term "fantastic," as proposed by Todorov in a general fashion, is not valid. If applied to Borges, its sense must be changed: "The fantastic would thus be equivalent to "literature" (i.e., built, invented, a structure of words, texts, names, referents, quotes). In this sense, the fantastic involves the dissolution of the referent called "reality" as a basic element of literature, which now becomes a quote of other texts."[39]

As I observed above, postmodernity is a phenomenon that began in the sixties in the United States and was later exported to Europe and Latin America, primarily in the seventies. Chronologically, Borges does not belong to postmodernity; systematically, it is different, for his stories really anticipate the phenomenon. This is why, after examining several forms of knowledge and art that existed prior to postmodernity, one can identify authors who already "thought" in that particular direction. Borges is not only a predecessor of postmodernity, but also—as I hope to have shown in my analysis—a postmodern author in the most genuine sense of the term.

After examining several theories of intertextuality and a few Borgesian stories ("Tlön, Uqbar, Orbis Tertius," "The Garden of Forking Paths," "Story of the Warrior and the Captive," "Pierre Menard, Author of Don Quijote") we reach the conclusion that Borges is not, strictly speaking, an intertextual author. Rather, he quotes and deconstructs the principles of intertextuality, which are replaced by the notion of the rhizome. If intertextuality is understood to be based on the principle of transformation, the intertextual operation will be possible only if one can detect in the new text a lexeme (the author's name and/or the title of a work, even a poetologic term), a sequence or a series of sequences (full or partial quotations taken from a work), or a structure (a sequence of agents, characters, or narrative modes). These intertextual insertions may be effected through direct or indirect imitation, through parodies or transvestitism, or through complementation, distortion, or negation of the previous text. In any case, the inserted unity must play a role in the new text. Borges does not usually follow the method in this sense. In most cases, his abundant quotations are simply eclectic mentions with a single purpose: to become *motivating* structures of writing that retrieve an idea often unconnected to the quoted passage. The texts alluded to by Borges frequently share the features of his own discourse: they are eclectic, fragmentary, miniature, and esoteric. They mix erudition and dilettantism, elevated and colloquial language, metaphysics, physics, theological allusions, and more. As his quotations are the result of his readings, so the act of writing is treated as a mere appendage to his readerly activities.

I will end by summarizing the main features of Borges's postmodern textual techniques classified according to either the type of discourse or the narrative mode. The list of types of discourse includes:

a) Literary discourse: deconstructive intertextual games, quotations from other authors of fiction or from anonymous fictional texts: Homer, Shakespeare, Cervantes, Flaubert, Joyce, Valéry, Chesterton, Kafka, *The Arabian Nights*, D'Annunzio (these quotations are not restricted to Western culture and systems).

b) Fantastic literary fictional discourse ("The Aleph," "Tlön, Uqbar, Orbis Tertius," "The Zahir," "The Babylon Lottery," "The Immortal").

c) The discourse of philosophy, metaphysics, scientific theory, or logic: quotations of, and references to, philosophers such as Lull, Leibniz, Descartes, Berkeley, Hegel, Spengler, and Kant.

d) Theological discourse: Saint Augustine and the debates on the existence of God and the structure of the universe.

e) Mystic/religious discourse ("The Theologians," "The God's Script").

f) Philological discourse: "Averroes' Search," quotes from the *Revista de Filología Española* or from the *NRF*, encyclopedias, maps, and so on.

g) Genre-bound discourses, such as the essay or literary discourse ("An Examination of the Work of Herbert Quain").

h) The discourse of detective novels ("Ibn Hakkan al-Bokhari, Dead in His Labyrinth," "The Waiting," "The Man on the Threshold," "The Garden of Forking Paths," "Death and the Compass").

i) The discourse of adventure stories ("The South," "The End," "Ibn Hakkan al-Bokhari, Dead in His Labyrinth").

j) (Pseudo)realist discourse ("The South," "The End").

k) The discourse of (pseudo)ordinary life: quotes from newspapers and magazines.

l) Metadiscourse ("Pierre Menard, Author of Don Quijote," "The Aleph," "The Immortal," "The House of Asterion," "The Other Death").

m) Narrative discourse full of parody and humor.

n) The discourse of history.

At the level of the narrative modes one can detect:

a) A scientific tone—or, rather, a mimesis of science conceived of as a game superseding nineteenth-century realism, which was in fact a scientific mimesis taken seriously: quotations from philological journals, and from authors and texts both existent and nonexistent.

b) An omniscient author.

c) A coherent *fabula*, with well-defined locations, times, and characters which eventually are displaced by deconstruction, masks, dissolution, and diffuseness.

d) Ambiguity and resistance to interpretation.

e) Unresolved allusions.

f) Self-deconstruction and the deconstruction of created signifieds.

g) Autobiographical allusions.

h) A full mixture of reality and fiction lacking ontologic implications.

i) Reflections on writing and narrative.

j) Pseudo-local color: pseudo-neocostumbrism and pseudo-realism.

k) Myth, located between history and language: semiotization, dissolution, dissemination of the myth.

l)   The dissolution of the third-person narrator, who gets lost among the contradictions of a first-person voice: use of several identities and of no identity, narrator/character double status, in relation to himself or unrelated.

m) Collective quality and repetition: the disappearance of the creator and of the myth of the genius, the text viewed as the origin of productivity.

n)   The reader as an active co-author: decoding, second-degree deconstruction.

Deconstruction, eclectic rhizomorphous games, paralogic or aparallel structures, the non-hierarchization of used systems, the dissolution of the narrator, and thus of the virtual identification between narrator and addressee, the mention of the author Borges as a fictional character, quotations of a vast array of texts with varying degrees of intrinsic quality: these features help to cancel and to refute ontological categories such as "reality vs. fiction" and art vs. non-art, and blur the limits between literature and criticism, thereby turning Fiedler's notion of the "double codification" into a *multicodification*. The form of Borges's discourse is radically open, heterogeneous, intercultural, ironic, humorous, and full of parody. His minimalist, fragmentary, and idiosyncratic thought promotes the universal dimension of discourse, which, in his case, abolishes the frontiers between languages and nationalities.

The often-debated question of Borges's "Latin American features" must then be included in a larger, universal system of signs, which, in the long term, is the most durable aspect of cultures. This semiotic universality is what has prompted the erroneous labeling of Borges as a "European" author or his exclusion from Latin American culture. This situation is absurd, especially if one considers that Borges is probably the only internationally renowned Latin American author to have lived in his native country, with the exception of the period between 1914 and 1919, almost until his death (which, as is well known, was in Geneva). Borges was always faithful in his consideration of Latin America as part of Western culture and to his view of universal culture as open to all. This, in itself, is a highly postmodern attitude.

TRANSLATED BY JOSÉ GARCÍA AND CHRISTINA LLOYD

NOTES

This is a translation of an edited version of a longer work originally published in two parts: "El productor 'rizomórfico' y el lector como 'detective literario': la aventura de los signos o la postmodernidad del discurso borgesiano (intertextualidad-palimpsesto-rizoma-deconstruction," in Karl Alfred Blüher and Alfonso de Toro, eds., *Jorge Luis Borges: Procedimientos literarios y bases epistemologicas* (Frankfurt: Verlag Klaus Dieter Vervuert, 1992),

145–183, and "Borges y la 'simulación rizomática dirigida': percepción y objetivación de los signos," *Iberoamericana* 18. Jahrgang 53, no. 1 (1994): 5–32.

1. Jorge Luis Borges, *Ficciones* (New York: Grove Press, 1962).

2. See M. B. Boegeman, *Paradox Gained: Kafka's Reception in English from 1930 to 1949 and His Influence on the Early Fiction of Borges, Beckett, and Nabokov* (Los Angeles: University of California Press, 1977); B, Belitt, "The Enigmatic Predicament: Some Parable of Kafka and Borges." *Tri-Quarterly* 25 (1972): 268–291; Karl Alfred Blüher, "La crítica literaria en Valéry y Borges," *Revista Iberoamericana* 135/136 (1982): 121–135; E. Geisler, "Paradox und Metaphor: Zu Borges's Kafka Rezeption," *Romanistische Zeitschrift für Literaturgeschichte* 1 (1986): 219–244; J. Nuño, *La filosofía de Borges* (Mexico City: Fondo de Cultura Económica, 1986); and Jaime Alazraki, *La prosa noarrativa de Jorge Luis Borges*, 2nd ed. (Madrid: Gredos, 1974), especially the bibliography.

3. It is important to note that *Ficciones* was translated into French by P. Verdevoye in 1951. In addition, between 1923 and 1955 (that is, before the *nouveau roman* achieved popularity) several important authors wrote works on Borges, most of them in French and/or in France, which were published in well-known literary journals and magazines. These authors were later to study the *nouveau roman*, thus making the amnesia of French authors and criticism all the more striking. Some of these early French studies were R. M. Albérès, "J. L. Borges ou les deux bouts du monde," *Affinités* 2 (1953): 84, 85, 92; P. Bénichou, "Kublai Khan, Coleridge y Borges," *Sur* 236 (1955): 57–61; M. Brion, "D'un autre hémisphère," *Le Monde* (26 Mar. 1952), and "J. L. Borges et ses Labyrinthes," *Le Monde* (18 Aug. 1954); Roger Caillois, "Soldat de la liberté," *Opéra* (30 Jan. 1952); M. Carrouges, "Le gai savoir de Jorge Luis Borges," *Preuves* 13 (1952): 47–49; Max Daireaux, *Panoramas des Littératures Contemporaines* (Paris: Kra, 1930); A. Hoog, "Au delà de l'énigme. Jorge Luis Borges: *Ficciones*," *Carrefour* (26 Mar. 1952); R. Kemp, "La vie des livres. Vérités et Fictions," *Les Nouvelles Littéraires* (20 Mar. 1952); and M. Nadeau, "Un écrivain déroutant et savoureux: J. L. Borges," *L'Observateur* 94 (28 Feb. 1952).

4. A few exceptions to this general trend are Gérard Genette, "L'utopie littéraire," in Gérard Genette, *Figures* (Paris: Seuil, 1966), 123–124; P. Macherey, "Borges et le récit fictif," in P. Macherey, *Pour une théorie de la production littéraire* (Paris: François Maspero, 1971), 277–285; W. D. Foster, "Borges and Structuralism: Toward an Implied Poetics," *Modern Fiction Studies* 9 (1973): 341–352; A. Echavarría, *Lengua y literatura de Borges* (Barcelona: Ariel, 1983); Ulrich Schulz-Buschhaus, "Borges und die Décadence: Über einige literarische und ideologische Motive der Erzählung 'Tlön, Uqbar, Orbis Tertius,'" *Romanische Forschungen* 96 (1984): 90–100, and "Das System und der Zufall. Zur Parodie des Detektivromans bei Jorge Luis Borges," in Erna Pfeiffer and Hugo Kubarth, eds., *Canticum Ibericum* (Frankfurt am Main: Klaus Dieter Vervuert Verlag, 1991), 382–396; I. Nolting-Hauff, "Die Irrfahrt Homers. Abentuer der Intertextualität in 'El inmortal' von Jorge Luis Borges," in I. Nolting-Hauff and J. Schulze, eds., *Das fremde Wort. Studien zur Interdependenz von Texten* (Amsterdam: Gruner, 1988), 411–431; and M. Lafon, *Borges ou la réécriture* (Paris: Seuil, 1990).

5. See Leslie Fiedler, "Cross the Border—Close the Gap," in Marcus Cunliffe, ed., *American Literature since 1900* (London: Barrie & Jenkins, 1975), 344–366; idem, "The New Mutants," *Partisan Review* 32, no. 4 (1965): 505–525.

6. Regarding postmodernism in the context of Hispanic culture, see Federico de Onís, *Antología de la poesía española e hispanoamericana* (Madrid: [Hernando], 1934); Octavio Corvalán, *El postmodernismo, la literatura hispanoamericana entre dos guerras mundiales* (New York: Las Américas Publishing Co., 1961); Pedro Salinas, "El cisne y el buho: apuntes para

la historia de la poesía modernista," in idem, *Literatura española, siglo XX. 2. ed. aumentada* (Mexico City: Antiqua Libreria Robredo, 1949), 45–65; and Beatriz Sarlo, "La poesía postmodernista." *Historia de la literatura argentina* 3 (1980): 98–113.

7. See Alfonso de Toro, "Semiosis teatral postmoderna: Intento de un modelo," *Gestos* 9 (1990): 23–57; idem, "¿Cambio de paradigma? El "nuevo" teatro latinoamericano o la construcción de la postmodernidad espectacular," *Iberoamericana* 15, no. 2–3 (1991): 70–92. Regarding the term "postmodernity" and Borges, see also U. Schulz-Buschhaus, "Das System und der Zufall," in Erna Pfeiffer and Hugo Fubarth, eds., *Canticum Ibericum. Neuere spanische, portugiesische und lateinamerikianische Literatur in Spiegel von Interpreation und Übersetzung. Georg Rudolf Lind zum Gedenken.* (Frankfurt am Main: Klaus Dieter Vervuert Verlag, 1991), 382–396.

8. See note 4.

9. This is why Borges's short stories can hardly be viewed as "fantastic" according to Todorov's epistemologic definition in *Introduction à la littérature fantastique* (Paris: Seuil/ Points, 1970). Such a definition is grounded precisely on the vagueness or ambiguity derived from the opposition between "fiction" and "reality." In this respect, see Alfonso de Toro, "Überlegungen zur Textsorte 'Fantastik' oder Borges und die Negation des Fantastischen. Rhizomatische Simulation, 'dirigierter Zufall' und semiotisches Skandalon," in Alfonso de Toro et al., eds., *Fantastik* (Leipzig: Stauffenburg Verlag, 1996), 11–74.

10. Borges states clearly in the prologue to *Ficciones* (ed. Anthony Kerrigan [New York: Grove Press, 1962]) that "a better course of procedure is to pretend that these books already exist, and then to offer a résumé, a commentary. Thus proceeded Carlyle in *Sartor Resartus*. Thus Butler in *The Fair Haven*. These are works which suffer the imperfection of being themselves books, and of being no less tautological than the others. More reasonable, more inept, more indolent, I have preferred to write notes upon imaginary books" (15–16). This is why I think that Borges does not foreshadow the reception theory as systematized by the Constance school, as Jauss notes; rather, he proposes a form of reception which, beginning with a word contained in past works, can produce an absolutely new text. Consequently, literature from the past is irrecoverable, as Pierre Menard shows. It would be more precise to observe, as Jauss himself notes in the same work, that Borges inaugurates the theory of intertextuality, palimpsest, and deconstruction, although he turns these methods into rhizomatic techniques.

11. Jorge Luis Borges, *Labyrinths: Selected Stories and Other Writings*, ed. Donald A. Yates and James E. Irby (New York: New Directions, 1964).

12. Allegory is a classic and well-known mode of interpretation in Borgesian research, as in virtually every study by Alazraki. The present analysis intends to show that Borges either opposes semantic allegory continuously or destroys it after evoking it, thus making an arbitrary exercise of any kind of semantic reading that is superimposed onto the literal one.

13. The expression "non-parallel lines" is used by Deleuze and Guattari from Chauvin's studies; see Gilles Deleuze and Félix Guattari, *Rhizom* (Berlin: Merve Verlag, 1977). It describes the relation between two beings which, although they may have common parts, evolve in a completely different way. Examples are the presence of certain animal genes in the human body, and the AIDS virus, which was spread among a certain type of monkey before it expanded to human beings, thus affecting the human, but not the monkey's, organism.

14. J. Kristeva, "Bakhtin, le mot, le dialogue et le roman," *Critique* 23 (1967): 438–465; idem, "Problèmes de la structuration du texte," in *Théorie d'ensemble* (Paris: Seuil, 1968), 297–326; idem, *Semeiotike; recherches pour un sémanalyse* (Paris: Seuil, 1969); idem, *Le texte*

du roman. Approche sémiologique d'une structure discursive transformationnelle (Paris: Mouton, 1976).

15. M. Bakhtin, *Literatur und Karneval: Zur Romantheorie und Lachkultur* (München: Ullstein, 1969); idem, *Ashthetik des Wortes* (Frankfurt am Main: Suhrkamp, 1979). The Bakhtinian term is based on the "plurality of voices" (heteroglossia) or the polyphony of the novel, and has two points: (1) dialogism, understood as the open and free debate between divergent opinions within the text, and (2) monologism, understood as the security and establishment of authority or tradition. These voices may be directed toward objects or actions, or exercised between narrator and characters or among characters themselves, thus synthesizing the ideology of a certain time frame. Forms of polyphonic prose are irony, parody, the processes of distancing (*ostranenie*), subtle polemics, and replicas. These processes relativize the word, the message, which, in turn, loses its position as absolute truth; canonized truths disappear. The term "dialogism" corresponds with this, along with the "perspective" of modern narratology, and has nothing to do with "intertextuality" created by Kristeva, which refers to the relation between two or more texts.

16. Kristeva, *Semeiotike*, 146.

17. G. Genette, *Palimpsestes. La littérature au second degré* (Paris: Seuil, 1982). It is fitting to mention the following miscellanies in German: R. Lachmann, ed., *Dialogizität. Theorie und Geschichte der Literatur und der schonen Künste* (München: Wilhelm Fink Verlag, 1982); W. Schmidt and W. D. Stempel, eds., *Dialog der Texte: Hamburger Kolloquium zur Intertextualität* (Wien: Gesellschrift zur Förderung Slawistischer Studien, 1983); K.H. Stierle and R. Warning, eds., *Das Gespräch. Poetik und Hermeneutik* (München: Wilhelm Fink, 1984); M. Pfister and U. Broich, eds., *Inter-textualität. Formen und Funktionen, anglistische Fall-studien* (Konzepte der Sprache und Literaturwissenschaft. 35) (Tübingen: Max Niemeyer, 1985). Particularly cf. M. Frank, "Einverständnis und Vielsinnigkcit oder: Das Aufbrechen der Bedeutungs-Einheit im *eigentlichen Gesprach*," in Stierle and Warning, *Das Gesprach*. 86–132; R. Lachmann, "Ebenen des Intertextualitätsbegriffs," in Stierle and Warning, *Das Gespräch*, 133–138; R. Lachmann, "Bachtins Dialogizität und die aksmeistische Mythopoetik als Paradigma dialogisierter Lyrik," in Stierle and Warning, *Das Gespräch*, 489–515; R. Lachmann, "Zur Semantik metonymischer Intertextualität," in Stierle and Warning, *Das Gespräch*, 517–523; U. Schick, "Erzählte Semiotik oder intertextuelles Verwirrspiel? Umberto Eco's *Il nome della rosa*," *Poetica* 16 (1984): 138–161; K. H. Stierle, "Werk und Intertextualität," in Stierle and Warning, *Das Gespräch*, 139–150; M. Pfister, "Konzepte der Intertextualitat," in Pfister and Broich, *Inter-textualität*, 1–30. Recently published is M. Worton and J. Still, eds., *Intertexuality. Theories and Practices* (Manchester and New York: Manchester University Press, 1990).

18. Cf. Genette, *Palimpsestes*. 7–14.

19. Ibid., 49–64, 135–136.

20. Ibid., 294–297.

21. J. Derrida, *De la grammatologie* (Paris: Minuit, 1967); idem, *L'écriture et la différence* (Paris: Seuil, 1967); idem, *La dissémination* (Paris: Seuil, 1972).

22. In regard to Anglo-Saxon deconstructionism, cf. J. Culler. *The Pursuit of Signs: Semiotics, Literature, Deconstruction* (Ithaca, N.Y.: Routledge & Kegan Paul, 1981); idem, *On Deconstruction: Theory and Criticism after Structuralism* (London: Routledge & Kegan Paul, 1983); C. Norris, *Deconstruction: Theory and Practice* (London: Hutchinson, 1982); and V. B. Leitch, *Deconstructive Criticism: An Advanced Introduction* (London: Methuen, 1983).

23. According to botany, the rhizome is a subterranean bulb, similar in appearance to a root, but it has membranous leaves and embryonic seedlings which generally lie in the horizontal position, like the common lily.

24. Jorge Luis Borges, *Obras completas* (Barcelona: Emecé Editores, 1989), vol. 1, 543–544.

25. Ibid., 535–538.

26. Ibid., 538.

27. Ibid.

28. Ibid., 538–539.

29. Ibid., 539.

30. Ibid., 538: "Moreover, none of the forms were the same, which excluded or distanced the possibility of their being symbolic."

31. Ibid., 540.

32. Ibid., 551.

33. Ibid., 552. Cf. also "Tlön, Uqbar, Orbis Tertius" in Borges, *Obras Completas*, vol. 1, 439: "The idea of plagiarism does not exist: it has been established that all work belongs to only one author, who is not temporal and is anonymous. Criticism insists on inventing authors: it elects two dissimilar works—the *Tao Te King* and *1001 Nights*, let's say, and attributes them to the same writer and later determines the psychology of that interesting *homme de lettres* . . ."

34. Greek name of the Persian prince Bardiya, second child of Cyrus, whose throat was cut by his brother Cambises II.

35. Borges, *Obras Completas*, vol. 1, 432.

36. Ibid.

37. Ibid., 434, 436, 439.

38. Ibid., 459–480, 496.

39. Tzvetan Todorov, *The Fantastic: A Structural Approach to a Literary Genre*, trans. Richard Howard (Ithaca, N.Y.: Cornell University Press, 1975), 26.

6. Colonialism, Modernism, and Postmodernism in Brazil

AMÓS NASCIMENTO

> Os males do Brasil são muita saúva e pouca saúde.
> (The problems of Brazil are too many sauba ants and
> not enough health.)
> —Mário de Andrade, *Macunaíma*

Dwelling on recent discussions on postmodernity, I want to propose a historical reconstruction of the project of modernity in Brazil. Although I will use the adjectives "modern" and "postmodern" loosely, I differentiate between "modernization" as a certain social-economic or political process, "modernism" as a cultural and aesthetic movement, and "modernity" and "postmodernity" as more general terms. My purpose is to show that there is a deficit of contemporary discussions on postmodernity in Brazil, since they abstract from differences and particularities, ignoring especially the African American situation.

One important task in my reconstruction is a critique of three aspects of modernization: the *ideology of colonialism*, the *ideology of syncretism*, and the *ideology of nationalism*. Along these lines, another task is to pay special attention to the parallel struggles and efforts made for the inclusion and recognition of differences within modernity. In order to have a specific point of reference, emphasis is given here to African and African American experiences of displacement as we follow the corresponding historical movement from *slavery*, through *civil rights*, to the struggles in creating a *multicultural community* within the Brazilian context. I think that this double line of reconstruction and critique has consequences not only for the Brazilian case, but also for the debate on postmodernity in Latin America and for the transcultural debate in general.

I. MODERNITY AND THE POSTMODERN DEBATE IN BRAZIL

I want to start by noting four problems with abstraction on different levels. The first problem arises because of the fact that Latin America is left out of the general international discussion, even though "postmodernism" is a Latin American term that mirrors the Latin American culture and situation. The second problem is that, even in the Latin American debate, the Brazilian discussion on postmodernity seems to be considered irrelevant. The third problem is a reduction that takes place within the Brazilian context itself. The main actors in the public debate of postmodernity and cultural identity do not recognize the many presuppositions in their own discourse and leave out the import and implication of many groups that are marginalized in the official definition of modernity. The final problem—which could be subdivided into others—arises because these marginalized groups are in fact the central subject of the debate, but are left out of the discussion. Without claiming to represent them, I want to bring attention to the African American case.

1. Postmodernity and the Quest for a Modern Identity

The first reductive abstraction is that Latin America is left out of the international or transcultural postmodern debate, even though the very word "postmodernism" has its origins in this Latin American context. The term was known in Hispanic American literature by the early twentieth century; in 1934 Federico de Onís used it in his *Antología de la Poesía Española e Hispanoamericana* to qualify a tendency that came after "modernism" and had no specific stylistic characteristics.[1] Perhaps because of this ambiguous definition, some authors who comment on the postmodern debate and mention Onís avoid referring to Latin America, arguing that this reference does not contribute to the understanding of the contemporary discussion.[2] However, if one looks at the movements mentioned by Onís, there is a clue for understanding postmodernism: the majority of the authors he cited were members of minorities at the margins of society: emancipated women, Natives, ex-slaves, homosexuals, and foreigners who dared to bring their art to the public. In this sense, *post*modern is not what comes after, but what is outside of the official definition of modern.

Even in the internal debate on postmodernism and postmodernity in Latin America, there is another reductive abstraction, because little has been said about the Brazilian contribution to this debate. However, after the notion of "postmodernity" gradually gained relevance in Anglo America between the forties and the sixties, it was in Brazil that the first discussions of the theme in a Latin American context took place.[3] One early debate was initiated by José Guilherme Merquior, who used the term "postmodern" in relation to the cultural and philosophical situation of Brazil in an article for the newspaper *O Estado de São Paulo* on November 7, 1976. He turned to literature of the Brazilian *Modernismo* and rediscovered the important contributions of writers such as Mário de Andrade, Manuel Bandeira, and Jorge de Lima, contrasting them with what was being produced at the same time in Europe. Merquior not only developed an internal discussion concerning literary production in Brazil, but he also tried to come to terms with the European aesthetics of the sixties, which were represented by structuralism, an emerging post-structuralism, and the Frankfurt School. This is docu-

mented in his paper "Modernisme et après-modernisme dans la littérature brésili-
enne," which he presented at the Colloque de Cérisy. Here we find a certain vague
focus placed upon the modernist Brazilian author Mário de Andrade. Merquior's
postmodern argument in this case was simple: we are also modern![4]

Following a Brazilian tradition of literary and cultural criticism that goes back
to Sílvio Romero and the members of the Recife School in the nineteenth century, Merquior was above all a polemist and opened a controversial discussion on
the status of Brazilian art, especially literature, which led to equally polemic debates on the meaning of national identity. This debate could be followed in the
most important newspapers, especially *Folha de São Paulo,* and involved intellectuals such as Roberto Schwarz, Augusto de Campos, Haroldo de Campos, and
Mario Chamie. The discussion focused on certain technicalities of high modernism and concretism in poetry. Mário de Andrade was a point of reference, for
he was taken by the "concretists" to be a symbol of modernity. Augusto de Campos sealed the debate with a satirical poem, "Póstudo," an epigram that plays with
the polysemy of the words *mudo* (change, mute, dumb) and *tudo* (all, everything)
to point to the aporias of postmodernity.[5]

In another newspaper, *O Estado de São Paulo,* the philosopher Sérgio Paulo Rouanet debated with Merquior on the meaning of modernity and modernism, turning to Max Weber, Michel Foucault, and Jürgen Habermas to propose modernity
as a project of rational criticism. In two essays for the journals *Tempo Brasileiro* and
Revista do Brasil, titled "Do Pós-Moderno ao Neo-Moderno" and "A Verdade e
a Ilusao do Pós-Moderno," as well as in his books, especially *A Razão Cativa: As
Ilusões da Consciência de Platão a Freud* and in *As Razões do Iluminismo,* Rouanet
summarized the basic lines of the debate on postmodernity in the United States
and Europe, connecting them with the Brazilian discussion. All this may seem unrelated to the previous internal discussion in Brazil. However, in a less well-known
text published in *Folhetim* on November 17, 1985, "Verde-amarelo é a cor do nosso
irracionalismo," the discussion on national identity erupts from the basic topic expressed in the phrase "The problem of Brazil is . . ." in which the blank is to be
filled by a qualifier. In 1927 Mário de Andrade said, cryptically, "The problems of
Brazil are too many sauba ants and not enough health" (*Os males do Brasil são
muita saúva e pouca saúde*). Rouanet fills the blank with the word "irrationalism."[6]
The point is: modernity is the condition to ascribe the predicate "rational" to
Brazilians.

There were some other discussions, which were more independent from the debate initiated by Merquior but also responded to the above claims. In 1986 two
authors summarized the basic discussions in terms of cultural criticism: Jair Ferreira dos Santos, in *O que é pós-moderno,* and José Teixeira Coelho Neto, in *Moderno Pós-Moderno.* Reflecting upon the philosophical debate on epistemology in
Europe and in Brazil, Manfredo de Oliveira had a different reading of Habermas
and Karl-Otto Apel and discussed the impact of the crisis of rationality and its
ethical consequences in general in *Ética e Racionalidade Moderna.* With attention
to these discussions, Otília Arantes slowly built her point and brought it to the

public with O *Lugar da Arquitetura depois dos Modernos*, which centered more on the role and place of architecture. In a country that is home to Brasília—the modern city par excellence—she posited that there is architecture in the periphery! These are just some examples of the plurality and simultaneity of the basic issues concerning the discussions of modernity and postmodernity in Brazil and their theoretical import.[7]

There is yet another distorting abstraction in the Brazilian debate, for Merquior had turned above all to elite intellectuals and had no regard for the importance of popular cultural expressions in Brazil. Others followed in Merquior's footsteps, but also, independent of his controversial claims, there was an ongoing debate on postmodernity in Brazil that tried to correct this point. For instance, after the impact of dependence theory and the discussions on culture and art at the Institute for Higher Learning in Brazilian Studies (ISEB—*Instituto Superior de Estudos Brasileiros*) during the fifties and sixties, the theme arose in the context of the theology and philosophy of liberation. Enrique Dussel used the term in 1974 to denote the new thinking emerging in Latin America, and in 1977 Gustavo Gutiérrez expressed his position on the theme.[8] A similar yet very different point was made by Leonardo Boff. He presented the claims of liberation theology in an audacious form and had to face the censorship of Rome in the same way that Galileo had. Boff's point was simple: there is a Latin American and, more specifically, a Brazilian way of being religious, which involves the need to cope with different cultures and syncretism.[9]

Another contributor to the postmodern debate in Brazil was Renato Ortiz, who followed the anthropological approach of Roger Bastide and researched the interaction between Africans and Europeans in Brazil to show that something genuinely Brazilian came out of this process which cannot be found anywhere else and is expressed above all in popular culture and religion. In this case the argument was obvious: we have a cultural identity![10] And out of the discussion on cultural identity in Brazil arose the internal opposition between popular culture and elite culture (*cultura popular e cultura de elite*). Here I can point out the contribution of Marilena Chauí, who had a political reading of the debate and criticized the model of national cultural identity as being both fabricated by an elite that wanted to integrate the nation and abstracted from daily life. Opposing the elitism and conservatism that reflected a whole tradition that Merquior shared was the argument that the national was the popular! Chauí had another line of criticism of modernity: she pointed to the conservative political ideology of conciliation and integration in Brazilian history, made a claim for democratization, and insisted upon the role of women in this process.[11] Chauí's argument echoed in the streets after decades of military dictatorship: we need democracy now!

These examples give us a panoramic view of the debate. In discussing "postmodernity in Brazil" we could follow the lines sketched above and bring in other unknown stories which would complement the Latin American discussion and integrate it into the wider framework of transcultural dialogue involving other contexts. Nonetheless, we need to recognize that while the above initiatives were critical of specific aspects of modernity and modernization, they were also limited by certain contingencies, which I have called reductive abstractions. The discussion on postmodernity in the so-called international arena abstracted reductively from Latin America. The Latin American discussion was equated mostly with Hispanic America, leaving out the part that was colonized by the Portuguese—that is, Brazil; the Brazilian discussion was dictated by members of a certain aristocratic group and centered in cities such as São Paulo and Rio de Janeiro. An internal contingency in relation to the part that popular culture plays in this totality was not recognized.

Even if we take all these aspects into account, there is yet another challenge. Over all, I am more concerned about the distinct lines of discussion in Brazil that show different projects of modernity and postmodernity as attempts to define what Brazil is or, more specifically, as attempts to define the modern Brazilian identity. However, these attempts do not account for the consequent plurality of "Brazils" expressed in the debate itself. To deal with "postmodernity in Brazil" with an eye on aspects of plurality and identity, I want to take a different avenue that is intrinsic to the above discussion but has not yet surfaced: the question of Brazilian identity as a sum of Native, European, and African aspects. To indicate where I am headed, I will stress the issue of plurality and center my attention on the African American element implicit in the discussion.

2. Projects of Modernization and the Plurality of Identities

The adjective "modern" and the generative "modernity" are old enough and have such multifarious meanings that anything is possible when talking about these issues in relation to Brazil. Therefore, I want to speak, from the beginning, of a necessary differentiation. There are a plurality of "Brazils" that become sedimented and occluded by so many distinct layers of meaning. In pointing to the process of modernization, I want to explore and reflect on this polysemy and sedimentation in light of a threefold task: to present the economic project of modernization in relation to the *ideology of colonialism*; to show the ethnic and political aspect of the modern project as represented in the constitution of nation-state and the *ideology of syncretism*; and turn to the cultural project of modernization as it is found more recently in the *ideology of nationalist populism*. My thesis is that these elements underlie the whole theoretical discussion above and that they surface in the unanswered question of Brazilian identity, beyond other aspects that are important and have consequences for the postmodern discussion at large.

My discussion of these three projects will show that, despite the seemingly positive evolution that can be noted in going from one historical stage to another, there is a line of continuity that needs to be examined in order to reveal identities behind this veil, which allows us to point to regressions. And here I present a double criticism: on the one hand, with regard to continuity I reject the historicist conception of modernity as a linear development that follows a necessary determined positive progression; on the other, for the same reason, I present my doubts about the prefix *post* as a sufficient correction to problems that we may find in aspects of modernity. What I am looking for is, rather, what is "outside of" or "beneath" the official definition of modernity and is rarely identified. I ask, In which sense can we talk about "postmodernity in Brazil" and deal with the unanswered question of identity? I will try to answer this question in a constructive process below.

II. IDEOLOGIES OF MODERNIZATION
AND THE QUEST FOR IDENTITY IN BRAZIL

As point of departure I shall take a multicultural perspective, arguing that it is necessary to make room for differentiation and simultaneity in order to see the distinctive character of cultural and political movements in Brazilian history. There have been ideologies of domination and representation, but there have also been movements which have criticized colonialism, syncretism, and nationalism. Thus, the notion of *post* may be misleading. That is, we need to recognize that what we call "postmodernity" may be simultaneous with modernity. Following this proposed revision of the notion of postmodernity, and centering my attention above all on a neglected African American perspective and contribution to this debate, I maintain that as we question the assumptions of the traditional view of Brazilian history and their echoes in the discussion of modernity and modernization, the way is cleared for perspectives in an exchange that can be properly called postmodern, not because these perspectives come after modernity, but because they recognize and bring with them the histories and situations that are simultaneously at play all through history, but have been denied or forgotten. In what follows I shall proceed more or less in chronological order, so that I may present the historical information upon which I base my arguments.

1. The Ideology of Colonialism and Its Discontents

My understanding of modernization in relation to colonialism aims essentially at proving that there are many questions still to be answered regarding the opposition to ideologies, which cannot be reduced to a single period, economic system, or form of discourse. A serious analysis also has to look at institutions and contexts from distinct perspectives. There are at least two justifications for this: colonialism is still present in Brazil as a continuous challenge; similarly, critical sources that confront colonialism have emerged, and still emerge, primarily in times of cholera. This justifies the need for a continuous form of criticism.

In his book *A Ideologia do Colonialismo*, Nelson Werneck Sodré has developed detailed studies on the ideology of colonialism in Brazil.[12] Brazil was a Portuguese colony starting in 1500, declared its independence from Portugal in 1822 to become the first and only monarchy in the Americas, and adopted the status of a republic through a coup d'état in 1889.[13] Over this period, American Natives were slaughtered (1500–50), Africans were brought as slaves (circa 1550–1850), and the poor and undesirables were expelled from Europe to become colonists in an immigration wave that lasted until the beginning of the twentieth century (broadly, 1800–1900).[14] Therefore, four out of the last five centuries of history have been marked by violent forms or aspects of colonialism such as genocide, slavery, and expatriation. This confirms that it is necessary to amplify our understanding of colonialism, instead of limiting it to a given crystallized period.

a) Three Institutions of the Ideology of Colonialism

There is no doubt that colonialism was one of the pillars of a European hegemonic economic system[15]—a system that included the structures of feudalism, mercantilism, and slavery. Beyond this, I am also concerned with some institutionalized discourses that justified this system within Brazil. In the sixteenth century, for instance, three institutions were at work and functioned as complementary pieces in the ideology of colonialism in Brazil: the monarchy, the church, and the juridical structure.[16]

The Portuguese monarchy. From the sixteenth century on, Portugal imposed upon its American colony the characteristics of the political forms of feudalism and traditional monarchism. One aspect particular to the Brazilian context in relation to other Latin American colonies is that the Brazilian intelligentsia was educated at the University of Coimbra in Portugal, which was founded in 1286 and provided unity to all Portuguese colonies, insofar as all bureaucrats, whether they were in Goa, India, or Bahia, Brazil, had the same educational background and administrative skills.[17] This fact had a definite effect on cultural issues. For instance, while books were printed in Mexico City as early as 1535 and in Lima in 1584, the Portuguese Crown did not allow printing in the colony at all. Only after 1808— when the Portuguese king transferred the Court to Brazil in order to escape from Napoleon—were military academies and schools of medicine and law created, but culture was not privileged.[18]

The ecclesiastic system. In Latin America, missionary activity is normally understood to have been the right hand of colonization, as well as of the Inquisition. Although the Inquisition was not established in Brazil, representatives were sent to the colony. Independent of this process, there was, after 1511, a systematic installation of ecclesiastic orders—especially Jesuits, Franciscans, and Dominicans— which were also responsible for colonial expansion in the Americas.[19] The Jesuits founded schools, imported the scholastic method in philosophy, and focused on the interpretation of Aristotle's *organon*. In contrast to the Spanish colonies, in Brazil there was no academic system during the colonial period or interest by Portugal in establishing seminaries or universities there. For example, dioceses were established in Mexico City around 1527 and in Lima around 1540,[20] the first seminary was founded in Santo Domingo in 1538, and universities were founded in Mexico City and Lima in 1551, and in Bogotá in 1573. Moreover, Jesuit schools were established on the Pacific coast, reaching California in the nineteenth century. In Brazil, however, the first seminary was not founded until 1748, and the first large universities were established only in the twentieth century; Universidade de São Paulo, for instance, was founded in 1932.[21]

With the establishment of Jesuit *reduções* or *pueblos*, Natives, colonists, and religious leaders were brought together in centers of commercial, political, and religious life, where missionary attention was focused on the children; this explains, in part, the lack of institutions of higher education.[22] We should not necessarily equate this initiative with political power. The orders had some independence, but they were still hierarchically below the representatives of the Portuguese monarchy and therefore were subsumed under the manorial system. Because the Portuguese Crown could install bishops and dispense mediation on theoretical discourse, the authority of the king was affirmed as being above the ecclesiastic institutions. In the end, the Jesuits were expelled from Brazil by Pombal in 1759— shortly before their expulsion from Hispanic America, in 1767.

The juridical bureaucracy. The other arm of colonialism was the juridical institution implemented by Portugal.[23] Beyond the medieval model, Portugal had the mediation of lawyers to establish its bureaucracy, thus separating it from the military, political, and ecclesiastic functions, and it relied upon the aristocracy to perform administrative duties. This characterizes another aspect of the ideology of colonialism and colonization, insofar as it was through negotiation and conciliation of interests that the Portuguese Crown established the guidelines for colonial expansionism. As Thomas Flory affirms, the Portuguese sent lawyers and not military troops to reinforce royal decisions in the colonies.[24] In the colony of Brazil it was no different, at least until the establishment of the *Relação da Bahia* as the superior court in El Salvador in 1609. The fact that jurists were not necessarily aristocrats but were taken from lower classes, together with the fact that they had administrative experience but no complete formal education, gave even more power to the king.[25]

It is necessary to differentiate the autonomous activity of lawyers and judges from that of ecclesiastic leaders and the representatives of political institutions established by the Royal Court. In fact, Portuguese law decreed that the governor and the courts were autonomous and had the power to impose taxes. Judges had more independence and would show their power by contradicting decisions made by bishops and governors. Nevertheless, their action was distant from the controlling power of the monarchy and, in the end, this led to a form of mutual agreement in many cases, in a strategy of compromise that remained as a cultural inheritance of colonialism.

b) Opposition to the Ideology of Colonialism

I have described these institutions in some detail in order to show their power and impact, as well as to indicate that they remained in place in later periods. Nonetheless, despite the power of the ideology of colonialism in connecting these institutions, there were also movements that opposed this ideology, though not always successfully. There is a need to consider them analytically and in more detail, but here I shall mention three distinct opposition movements of utopian inspiration : the Guarani in their search for a land without evils,[26] the Jesuit missions—which must be distinguished from other ecclesiastic projects[27]—and the African slaves who escaped from captivity and formed communities called *quilombos*. All of these movements confronted colonialism from the sixteenth to the eighteenth century and projected libertarian hopes that would be reflected in the ideals that were defended later in the Enlightenment. I will now focus my attention on the case of the *quilombos*.[28]

The African quilombos. These rural centers were established by runaway slaves deep in the northeastern Brazilian jungle. The most famous was Palmares, in the state of Pernambuco. It was formed in 1604 by forty runaway slaves and resisted decades of constant attacks by the Dutch and Portuguese, until November 20, 1695, when it was destroyed and its leader, Zumbi, was killed.[29] Three hundred years after the death of Zumbi, this day became a national holiday, and public attention has turned to some groups of African ancestry that still live in small villages of difficult access throughout the Brazilian territory, from the southern states of São Paulo and Mato Grosso, through Minas Gerais, Goiás, and Bahia, north to many regions in Sergipe, Maranhão, and the Amazon. One of the first *quilombos* to receive attention was Cafundó, close to the city of São Paulo. In 1989, the existence of a *quilombo* near the Trombetas River in the Amazon became known internationally, as mining companies and farmers invaded the surrounding land.[30]

In all of these cases, the striking fact is that the slaves and their descendants were for centuries able to remain hidden and maintain their language and culture, while even in Africa many of the original tribal groups lost their historical references. Through these new findings, researchers of African American history in Brazil have concluded that there was a much greater resistance to slavery than once thought, and that the formation of *quilombos* seems to have been a continental phenomenon.[31] In light of this, there is also a suspicion that what was recorded in Brazilian history as an army campaign against Canudos, a whole city of rebels, in the late nineteenth century may have been the persecution and destruction of another *quilombo* where ex-slaves congregated after the abolition of slavery. This was also the case with other movements that wanted to establish a political structure independent of the nation, which were considered an "African Republic" with socialist characteristics within Brazil.

More research is needed on this issue. However, I would like to draw some preliminary conclusions based upon the above information. As I stated above, four out of the last five centuries of history in Brazil and Latin America were marked by violent forms or aspects of colonialism, such as genocide, slavery, and expatriation, which took place simultaneously with a period defined as modernity in Europe that included humanism and the Enlightenment as its philosophical expressions. I want to stress the word "simultaneously." The opposition to colonialism does not need to be thought of historically as a moment yet to come, defined as modernity. Modernity in Europe was parallel to colonialism. In the Americas, including Brazil, emancipatory ideals related to modernity were being expressed in opposition to colonialism in the utopia of the Guaranis, the Jesuit missions, and the African *quilombos*.

In the *quilombos* there was strong opposition to colonialism, despite the power of the colonial institutions and the ideology that maintained the network of these institutions. A critique of colonialism in Brazil must include these distinct experiences, show the confrontation and communication of simultaneous unities, and reflect upon them. Using the example of communities of ex-slaves that were able to maintain their identity over centuries, I have attempted to show that they provided resources for a critique of the ideology of colonialism that can be revived. Unfortunately, this has not been done to any large extent. In his book *A Ideologia do Colonialismo*, Sodré concentrated on the main representatives of the colonial ideology. I propose that now is time to concentrate on those who criticized it. Like colonialism itself, the stereophonic echoes of those who were and are discontent with it still reverberate.

2. The Ideology of Syncretism and Forms of Resistance

The word "syncretism" is derived from a Greek word meaning "the unification of all Cretans against a common adversary." In the context of the Americas, this term has been used to imply the encounter of and interaction among Native, African, and European cultures and the forging of a new identity in the New World. Syncretism is therefore a key issue in the discussion on the Brazilian identity and constitution as a modern nation, and it is expressed in the slogan "racial democracy." This slogan has parallels in other Latin American countries—for instance, in the idea of "Mestizo society" in Colombia and "Café con Leche" in Venezuela.[32] However, if we look at this process in Brazil from a critical perspective, "syncretism" appears as a powerful ideological tool that displaces Natives and assimilates Africans in the "diaspora," as it imposes one biological, historical, linguistic, or cultural ideal of "nation" that remains European and suspends the pluralistic perspectives and claims of different groups and subjects.

The political independence that Brazil achieved from Portugal in 1822 ran parallel to the efforts for liberation by other South American countries. However, although a series of popular movements—including groups of free Africans and proletarians—were engaged in the revolutionary struggle for democratic ideals and citizenship, the results of independence in Brazil were not similar to those in the revolutions led by Simón Bolívar in other countries. In Brazil, there was the astonishing establishment of the first and only independent monarchy of South America under D. Pedro I, who was, and remained, Portuguese. This is one among many puzzling contradictions in Brazilian history.[33] In light of these facts, it is not surprising that the new regime clung to a policy of expansionism, bringing European colonizers, slaughtering Natives, and maintaining slavery in order to demarcate the territory. I would like to point to some problems in the assimilatory process which I call the *ideology of syncretism*. From the above, different forms of

syncretism—political, scientific, cultural, and religious—and their ideological
unity can be discerned.

a) The Assimilatory Character of Syncretism

Following independence from Portugal, the question in Brazil was how the territory and identity of the new nation were going to be defined. My point of departure lies in the contradiction between the movements for liberation and
independence, on the one hand, and slavery, on the other. As this contradiction
became evident to important intellectuals of the nineteenth century, they proposed *political syncretism* as a solution. It is in relation to this issue and to the integration of ex-slaves into society that debates about miscegenation, hybridity, and
syncretism in Brazil arose. In the synthesis of Native, African, and European elements, African culture was not taken as a constitutive part of the nation-building
process; in fact, it was argued that it represented a pernicious element that should
be avoided.[34] This demonstrates the negation of African identity and its assimilation into a larger definition of culture through the process of constructing a national identity in Brazil.

The appropriation of Native culture. At the time of independence in Brazil there
were a series of rebellions that indicated the level of instability—"nervous states,"
in Bhabha's felicitous expression. The idea of "fusion," taken from chemistry, was
simply an allusion to the need for a common political denominator. The melting
of different ethnic groups into the same pot would bring about a "new race," and
such a program for cultural and ethnic identity would guarantee unity and national security. But the question was, Which model should be used? Neither the
Europeans (in this case, the Portuguese as colonizers) nor the Africans (as slaves)
offered an acceptable model, for the former would be a regression to colonialism
and the latter to a primitive stage. Since neither of them represented civilization
or modernity, the only option left was the already destroyed indigenous Guarani
culture, and national identity was thus to be found in the distant *Indio*, the *bon
sauvage*.[35]

This romanticization à la Rousseau, referred to as Indianism (*indigenismo*), is
considered a high point in modern Brazilian literature and was the theme for Carlos Gomes's operas. This process is typical of other Latin American countries as
well, such as Mexico and Ecuador.[36] But in fact, most of the Natives within the
eastern part of the Brazilian territory with whom contact might have been possible had been exterminated in an invasion of the interior that pushed many other
tribes toward the west. The idea was purely a literary fiction, and soon there was
a change of tone, conveyed by the slogan "We are not Indians, we are Brazilians."
In the end, the caboclo or mestizo was taken as the genuinely Brazilian synthesis
between the Native and the European.

The problem of the African inheritance. The African contribution was left aside
during these discussions. It was only with *Abolicionismo*, a movement that opposed
monarchy and used the English charge against the slave trade as a pretext, that
African participation in forming the Brazilian culture was recognized, but this was

not without problems. For instance, José do Patrocínio wrote in the daily *Gazeta da Tarde* on May 5, 1887 that Africans were part of "the fusion of all races" in the Brazilian culture and warned about the risk of a civil war if there was no abolition of slavery. Although he defined himself as mulatto, his arguments show how he was prey to the ideology of political syncretism. The political instrumentalization of the theme is seen clearly in the most important abolitionist, Joaquim Nabuco, a liberal in the Brazilian parliament who opposed the conservatives who supported the monarchy. There was a disguised Eurocentric motivation behind his initiatives, which contradicted his supposed humanitarian aims. He defended a process of "whitening" for Brazil, complained that the country was colonized by the Portuguese and not by the Dutch, deplored the fact that Africans had to be brought as slaves, and saw the immigration of Europeans to Brazil as the only alternative for the beginning of an emancipating and civilizing process that would lead to a genuine Brazilian.[37]

The abolition of slavery in 1888 was the condition for the establishment of the Brazilian Republic in 1889 without a civil war, but with a coup d'état. Because this process was led by the positivism of the military academy (which represented the bourgeoisie, as opposed to the aristocracy), there was practically no change in the situation of Brazilians of African ancestry after abolition (ex-slaves became the poor and went to the cities). Under the positivistic influence of *scientific syncretism*, the debate on national identity this time was not about people and nations—the locus of egalitarian republicanism—but was reduced to "race." With the tools of the new sciences, syncretism was understood in the more objective terms of "racial miscegenation" between Natives, Africans, and Europeans. In this process there was an actualization in the forms of the ideology of syncretism! Between 1870 and 1930, the scientific syncretism of military positivism was behind the installation of scientific academies, museums, research institutes, and hospitals which concentrated their interest on the "racial question." Disciplines at the turn of the century, such as phrenology, eugenics, anthropometry, craniology, criminalism, and ethnology, followed a Darwinistic determinism to establish a hierarchy of the races and arrive at the synthesis of "racial perfectibility."[38]

Philosophy and literature were instruments of such a synthesis. As Alvares de Azevedo noted, without a corresponding national philosophy and poetry, nobody could purify the blood of the nation. Philosophers, writers, and anthropologists were now in search of an ideal Brazilian.[39] Along these lines, the problematic idea of political identity in terms of race was conveyed in terms of a *cultural-anthropological syncretism*, as defended by the Brazilian philosopher Sílvio Romero. He was representative of the most important philosophical tendency in the nineteenth century, the School of Recife, whose constant attacks on metaphysics led to positivism. Translating this discussion into the terms of literary criticism, Sílvio Romero affirmed, polemically, "All Brazilians are mestizos, if not in their blood, then surely in their ideas."[40] Following this train of thought, the physician Nina Rodrigues was the first to develop an ethnological study about the presence of Africans and of the Yoruba religion in Brazil. His book *Os Africanos no Brasil* (pub-

lished posthumously) is a rich source of data, despite its limitations, because it reveals the ideological presuppositions in the politics, science, and culture of syncretism. This triple heritage is obvious at the beginning of his book, where he
approvingly quotes Sílvio Romero: "It is a shame for Brazilian science that we have
not consecrated our efforts to the study of African languages and religions. . . .
[We] have this material in our own house, [we] have Africa in our *kitchens*, the
Americas in our *forests*, and Europe in our *salons*."[41]

Here we find a conjunction of previously mentioned aspects. Rodrigues was interested in the interaction between African and Christian religions and understood this phenomenon in neuropathological terms, which he used to define the
"criminality of Negroes" in El Salvador. Observing how the "most underdeveloped
Negroes" took the saints of Popular Catholicism to disguise their "fetish cults" and
polytheistic beliefs, he warned against the inefficiency of evangelization and
alerted the church to the dangers of syncretism.[42] Note that there had been now a
turn in the application of the term, as syncretism is seen as something negative
and ascribed to a defective African American appropriation of European elements
that somewhat contaminates what could be defined as the Brazilian identity. In
order to understand the process that was taking place at the beginning of the
twentieth century, other authors followed this same path as they did historio-
graphic and ethnographic research in the communities of ex-slaves that still existed at that time.

Finally, despite the Greek origins and long history of the term "syncretism" and
despite its application in Brazil through different types of discourses, the most po-
lemical discussion in which the concept appears concerns *religious syncretism*. This
theme is important not only because of the development of missionary techniques
of evangelization, but also because in the early twentieth century anthropological
approaches to African culture served as a transition from ethnology to subsequent
sociological debate on religious syncretism. Among the most interesting themes
was the question of how the Yoruba were able to maintain their Orishas religion unified in a Brazilian movement, Candomblé.[43] This question prompted interest in Afro-Brazilian studies after the abolition of slavery in 1888 and gained
more relevance in the twentieth century, reaching an even wider public in the
sixties.

b) Resistance to the Ideology of Syncretism

African slaves lived not only in rural areas, but also in the cities, where a slave
could buy liberty (*Alforria*). For this reason, there was a concentration of slaves
and ex-slaves in many large cities, where the African population outnumbered
those of European origin. One of the forms of association allowed for slaves was
the religious network of brotherhoods and sisterhoods, provided that they were
converted to Catholicism—in other words, provided that they were assimilated
into one of the institutions of colonialism. In Vila Rica, persons of African origin
belonged to the Order of St. Ifigenia.[44] There were also groups of intellectuals and
artists in these cities, and the most famous artist was the composer José Maurício

Nunes Garcia.[45] These groups were connected to the struggles of applying Enlightenment ideals in Brazil at that time, so it is not surprising that they took part in movements for political independence.[46]

Nevertheless, many others were still outside this realm. Although they were in cities, they were excluded because they were not members of such societies, or because they professed a different religion. Moreover, many rebellions occurred in Brazilian colonial cities between 1780 and 1840—that is, during, and after, the struggle for political emancipation from Portugal—and many of them were ascribed to low-level workers or to specific groups of Africans, such as the Revolution of Tailors (1798), the Inconfidence in Minas Gerais (1789), the Revolution in Pernambuco (1817), and the Rebellion of the Malês (1835). But even though these rebellions involved different groups—the bourgeoisie, manual workers, and slaves—in the fight for independence, in the end Africans and African Americans were left out of the libertarian process and could not become citizens.[47]

The above shows that resistance to colonialism existed as early as the time of the struggle for national independence, but it became more of an issue when it was related to the establishment of a liberal republic and the abolition of slavery. As emancipated slaves at the beginning and end of the nineteenth century searched for their roots and considered their situation within an exclusivist Brazilian society, they had two options: either separatism and turning to an "African nation" (as happened in Nigeria—after Nigerians lost all connection to Europe—and in the *quilombos* hidden in Brazil), or assimilation into Brazilian society. But since African culture was not taken as a constitutive part of the nation-building process, based on the argument that this would represent a pernicious element that should be avoided, alternative communities were created.[48]

There is a connection between these events and the arrival in the cities of slaves from Yorubaland. Their involvement in the resistance movement is suggested by the fact that they were highly politicized through their experience with the Oyo Empire and their contact and confrontation with Christians and Muslims in Africa.[49] With this, there was not only the maintenance of *quilombos* and the creation of African brotherhoods in the church and groups related to musical and intellectual academies, but also the constitution of new groups, related above all to the cultural and religious tradition of the Yoruba. This found its expression in the Terreiros de Candomblé, which escaped the assimilatory character of Christian missionaries, and shows how the negation of African identity and culture in the process of constructing a national identity in Brazil created ghettos that tried to escape different aspects of the ideology of syncretism.

In these ghettos, we find a connection to the discussion on cultural tradition, modernity, and postmodernity. From some of these very ghettos came key artists and intellectuals who have remained in the background of Brazilian history and of the discussion on postmodernity in Brazil. Most people turn to the Baroque art of Minas Gerais, to the salons of Rio de Janeiro, or to the philosophy of the School of Recife, as Sílvio Romero did, but they do not reflect upon the influences underlying these movements. Aleijadinho and José Maurício Nunes Garcia are con-

sidered the most important artists of the cultural environment of Minas Gerais between the seventeenth and nineteenth centuries; both are of African origin, and
Nunes Garcia always emphasized that his mother was an ex-slave.[50] Machado de
Assis, one of the greatest Brazilian writers, was also of African American origin,
but was accused of being a foreigner in Brazil. For this reason, the Indianist romance of José de Alencar, politician and member of the conservative fraction of
the Brazilian northeast, was chosen as representative of the Brazilian culture.
Moreover, many forget that Tobias Barreto, the founder of the School of Recife
and the first Brazilian philosopher to discuss Kant and Marx—as well as being the
first Brazilian to publish his essays in Germany—always insisted that he came from
a family of slaves from a *quilombo* in the state of Sergipe.[51] But for many, Barreto
was not a national intellectual because he turned to Kant and Marx instead of following the Brazilian tradition. Surprisingly, Nina Rodrigues was also of African
inheritance, and his ideas of syncretism were heard, read, and quoted by W. E. B.
Du Bois in the United States.[52]

   The problem concerning slavery was at the center of the question regarding national identity that divided Brazil during the nineteenth century. For liberals, it
was incompatible with the idea of a democratic country and an embarrassment in
matters of foreign relations, while for slaveholders, the idea of abolishing slavery
was something imported and foreign, disconnected from Brazilian reality. In view
of Brazilian history, one of the greatest mistakes anyone could make was not to be
a genuine Brazilian. This charge was made against those who, ironically, represented some of the best achievements in Brazilian intellectual history. In this context, between the metaphysical obscurantism of one side and the positivistic
blindness of the other, the question concerning African slavery and the African
American contribution was considered to be less relevant. In short, independent
of the ideological choices of a series of authors and politicians who insisted on the
tradition of, or a turn toward, modernity to define the Brazilian identity, most of
them abstract from the African and African American inheritance and resistance
as part of Brazilian culture, society and politics.

3. The Ideology of Nationalism, Culture, and Populism

   After the independence of Brazil in 1822 and the republican declaration in
1889, the question concerning identity within a national framework remained, as
did tension with identities which were not considered part of the whole. This
problem manifested itself in many ways, one of them presented in the question, Is
there a Brazilian culture? Another, more specific question asked was, Is there a
Brazilian literature (or philosophy, or art)? The important thing in all these questions was the adjective: it had to be genuinely Brazilian.

a) Culturalism and Integralism

   It is not surprising, therefore, that an anthropological turn—represented by the
studies of Gilberto Freyre and other foreign researchers, such as the Americans

Melville Herskovits and Donald Pierson and the Frenchmen Pierre Verger and Roger Bastide—taken by authors such as Darcy Ribeiro and Roberto Da Matta was centered around this idea. Freyre came to be the most famous of the "culturalists." He reconstructed different aspects of Brazilian culture (food, health, climate etc.) to see how they reached synthesis and "conciliation." With this perspective, Freyre brought many previous issues of Brazilian history together in his views on culture.[53] In *Casa Grande & Senzala* he analyzed the influences of colonialism and the manorial system in the manners and morals of the Brazilian elite, especially in the northeast, and saw a religious element as constitutive of Brazilian culture, expressed in the syncretism of African and Arabian aspects in the Jesuitic method of catechizing: the use of liturgy, feasts, and dances.[54]

The same categories were applied to religious issues. Based on his reconstruction of Brazilian history, Freyre inferred that "Catholicism was really the cement of our unity."[55] He used the same scheme to explain the Brazilian particularity in political matters: in comparison to the United States, Brazil was a "racial democracy." Despite his emphasis on the "sexual ethics" that allowed this mestizage and led to the "racial democratization of the country," and despite his sympathetic interpretation of the African influence in Brazil, his cultural analysis was elitist and did not address the problems of Brazilian society, but justified and generalized the regional context of the northeast as representative of the whole. Thus he was criticized by a generation of Marxist sociologists who questioned the idea of "racial democracy" and studied the situation of African Americans at the bottom of a class society.[56] In the field of art, as defended by Freyre, we find the same conciliatory elements that got him labeled as a traditionalist. The ideologies of colonialism and syncretism, in their various forms, remain in his work and in other important artistic expressions in Brazilian history—for instance the literary style that comes precisely from the northeastern context that Freyre was trying to describe, regionalism (*Regionalismo*). This style not only defended traditional particularities of Brazilian culture—defined in terms of an anthropological description of geographic differences—but was also a reaction against *Modernismo* and the Week of Modern Art (*Semana de Arte Moderna*) in 1922, which prompted the realization of the first congress of regionalists of the northeast in 1926 under Freyre's influence. It is interesting to note that in each region there was a given central character for art and literature: *cangaceiros* in the northeast, *gaúchos* in the south, *indios* and *caipiras* in the west.

At this time, the political situation in Brazil seemed to be reflected in these ideas. In the first decades of the twentieth century, a period defined as the Old Republic (*República Velha*), national politics was led by oligarchic groups, opposed by a series of movements, including attempts at separatist revolutions, for example, in São Paulo. All these movements and groups show that the old dreams of national unification and the establishment of a univocal identity were illusory. As it had at the time of independence from Portugal and at the time of the abolition of slavery and the declaration of the republic, the question concerning unity, homogeneity, and identity came to the surface once more in a country of continental proportions. Even though the transition was made, it led to the New State (*Estado Novo*), which was simply the dictatorship of the *gaúcho* Getulio Vargas from 1930 to 1945 and inaugurated a populism parallel to that in Argentina in the *Integrismo* of the thirties and in Peron's dictatorship after 1946.[57]

In the Brazilian context, we find intellectuals attempting to justify the dictatorship by proposing an integration of the parts into a whole, without recognizing differences. The most relevant movement was integralism (*Integralismo*), which played an important part in articulating the program of centralization proposed by Getúlio Vargas and reflected the integralism of Carl Schmitt in Germany. Part of its task was precisely to maintain ideological unity. The integralist movement was definitely authoritarian, strongly emphasized categories such as patriotism and nationalism, and revived nineteenth-century romanticism and syncretism. As part of a program defined as "objective politics" by Oliveira Viana, one of the leaders of the movement, it defended European ideals, but not with Iberian references, for Iberian, Native, African, and syncretic groups were intrinsically corrupt, in Viana's opinion.[58] Ironically, in the search for an intellectual hero in the national philosophy of the nineteenth century, these authors turned to the African American Tobias Barreto.

It is useless to search for any trace of egalitarianism or acceptance of Africans and African Americans in these models, or for any trace of a positive acceptance of Natives. Unfortunately, the ideologies of colonialism and forms of syncretism were still present in ethnic culturalism and cultural nationalism. The inclusion of differences within the Brazilian national and cultural identity was instrumental and conditioned to assimilation through a progressive process of degeneration and disappearance, so that identities were not revealed. For these reasons, I speak of a continuity and "selective affinities" between colonial, syncretic, nationalist, and culturally conservative tendencies: they all proposed either a systematic abstraction or an assimilation of differences, but *not* recognition of the historical particularities of Natives (whose culture was annihilated) and Africans (who were victims of slavery) or Europeans who were expatriated and by no means represented the "high culture" of an aristocratic elite. As I noted, these positions opposed *Modernismo*. Let us then take a look at this tendency.

b) Modernismo *as an Aesthetic Pièce de Résistance*

One of the central moments in the attempt to respond to the question of Brazilian identity without falling into traditionalism or the traps of modern ideologies was the Week for Modern Art in the Teatro Municipal in São Paulo, in 1922. This event was contemporary and expressed somewhat the rebellions that were occurring at the time, as well as actualizing the echoes of the earlier emancipatory currents that were part of the movement for independence in 1822. In this event, a group of young authors and artists related to the avant-garde movement radicalized the search for a Brazilian intellectual movement, especially through experimentation and the rejection of authoritarian models, including foreign ones. Distinct from the concept of "modern" and the definition of "modernism" in the culture and literature of Hispanic America, *Modernismo* does not necessarily indicate a certain bourgeois fin-de-siècle style, but is a reaction to this tendency without appealing to a conservative tradition.[59]

Despite its name, which may mislead many interpreters, Brazilian *Modernismo* represented an early reaction to the ideologies of modernity. One should not oversimplify the movement, for it included writers such as Oswald de Andrade, the leader of the anthropophagic movement (*Antropofagismo*), who came from an aristocratic family, had a conservative political orientation, and developed a form of cultural anarchism that did not contribute to the recognition of the occluded aspects I am trying to reveal. It was precisely in the turn to a forgotten and repressed African and African American tradition that this movement gained its critical impetus. African rhythms and musical structures of daily life can be heard in the pieces by Heitor Villa-Lobos. African and African American images are seen in the paintings of Tarsila do Amaral.[60] Surprisingly, the cities where *Modernismo* found expression were primarily São Paulo, Rio de Janeiro, and Recife.

In search of African American expressions of modernism, I now turn my attention to Mário de Andrade, the leader and most important member of the modernist movement. De Andrade was a musician, a professor of aesthetics and history of art in São Paulo, and a writer. In ethnological and anthropological research, he developed many empirical studies in different regions of Brazil, collecting and recording motifs of daily life that he later used in his work. He also experimented with painting, drawing, and photography. There are a number of issues to be discussed in de Andrade's work, but I want to call attention to the fact that in all of his work he was rediscovering and recording African and African American culture that had been, until then, neglected. It is not surprising that as important an author as Guimarães Rosa found de Andrade's art too plebeian and others defined it as too primitive.[61] The same can be seen in his linguistic work, as he observed the phonetics of simple people and constructed a system of phonetics and semantics upon this base, thus rejecting the established linguistic canon, and he used this system consistently in his own literary work. Similarly, for years, de Andrade collected musical motifs, especially of ex-slaves in the Brazilian northeast, and used them when he wrote a series of musicological texts. He left unpublished the first dictionary of the Brazilian language.[62]

Although I cannot indulge in an analysis of this material here, it is easy to see that the work of the most important Brazilian modernist intellectuals reflects precisely what has been negated throughout Brazilian history, and even in the debates on postmodernity, of which de Andrade himself has been the central theme. Despite the fact that de Andrade tried to avoid a simple politicization of art, he clearly rejected the three ideological moments of modernization described above. In his first work, the anti-war anthology of poems entitled *Há uma gota de sangue em cada poema* (1917), he vehemently opposed conservatism and clung to pacifism. Another example of his turn to African American motifs in his early literary texts was *A Escrava que não era Isaura*, an ironic paraphrase of a previous book by Bernardo Guimarães, published in 1875, which pictured Brazilian society at the time of slavery.[63] Merquior deals with these texts, but, surprisingly, he is not interested in de Andrade's most important book, *Macunaíma*, published in 1927.

In *Macunaíma*, which de Andrade defined as "rhapsody" and saw as a "symptom of the national culture," he presented a critique of colonialism in the very proposal to "discover" Brazil and the consistent avoidance of references to Europe, except to depict exploitation. But above all he opposed the national ideology of syncretism, coining the term "fable of the three races." In the background, overlain by a series of motifs and parodies, we can find the cosmogony of Genesis as de Andrade relates the origin of ethnic groups in Brazil, bringing them together and at the same time differentiating them in such a way that he prompted the reaction of conservative nationalists. They described the book as a mix of "*caboclo*, nigger, and white . . . that lacks truth" and as a fiasco. In the book's cryptic message, ethnic differences arise as various people bathe in the same water, and those who come later are darker because the water is dirty. Thus, Macunaíma, the anti-hero, also forms a provocative critique of nationalism, precisely because he cannot be attached to a certain time, group, geography, or type.

In an unpublished introduction to the book, de Andrade explains that he needed to "invent" a Brazilian who would mirror reality: "I am interested in Macunaíma because he expresses the essence of the Brazilians."[64] But in the end, as Haroldo de Campos notes, the definition and characterization of Macunaíma are so open that he becomes a Latin American hero—originally a member of a Native tribe in the Amazon, born in a place that could be identified as Brazil or Venezuela, related to Peru, confronted with an Italian immigrant.[65] The anti-hero does not fit the ready-made identity established in colonialism, syncretism, and nationalism, and for this reason the book, as well as de Andrade himself, is still open to new interpretations. In the end, we still hear the echo of the sentence that Macunaíma repeats all through the book: "The problems of Brazil are too many sauba ants and not enough health" (*Os males do Brasil são muita saúva e pouca saúde*).

III. BACK TO MODERNISM AND POSTMODERNITY IN THE BRAZILIAN CONTEXT

Mário de Andrade somewhat summarizes the themes we have discussed. His work was the pièce de résistance for authors such as J. G. Merquior, Haroldo de Campos, Renato Ortíz, and Marilena Chauí, and it brings to the surface a series of issues in relation to African Americans in Brazil. In this perspective, we can return to the debate on postmodernity in Brazil as presented at the onset and draw some conclusions. In historical terms, colonialism, syncretism, and nationalism could be used to denote periods and processes that reflect one specific heteronomous power of assimilation without any recognition of differences. These processes occur differently, but they all lead to a similar result: the annihilation of Natives, the rejection of Africans, and the partial integration of expatriated Europeans, taking from them the right to participate in or contribute to a debate. The problem of the Brazilian debate is that, like sauba ants, many people are living underground and are not visible. My aim was not to represent these groups, but to acknowledge that they exist, even though I concentrated on the African American experience and tried to call attention to the systematic exclusion performed in an ideological process of discursive formation. What de Andrade conducts is an anti-discourse that recovers what was left out.

Now the question is, What is the relationship between these themes and the discussion of postmodernity? Or, more precisely, as I asked at the outset, in what sense can we talk about postmodernity in Brazil? There is indeed an ongoing debate on postmodernity in the Brazilian context, but if we analyze just what is being discussed, I still think that much more needs to be brought to light. The theme of the authentic Brazilian identity remains the central question, but this question is misleading, insofar as it has abstracted from identities at play in an ongoing debate in Brazilian history.

I first expanded the scope and put a series of fragments together in order to show the need to differentiate how the ideologies of colonialism, syncretism, and nationalism form a veil that covers a series of issues and is still at work today. These ideologies express reductionistic models, contradict plurality, and exclude simultaneous perspectives that have always existed. Moreover, I tried to show that in the specific case of Brazil, the "African American" search for identity in the process of slavery, the struggle for civil rights, and the search for a multicultural identity indicate a continuous force of resistance to these ideologies. If on the one side there is a veil covering the whole, on the other—the underside—we find a form of resistance that has been expressed above all through art and culture and has accumulated in sedimented layers. These forms of rebellion and initiatives of resistance such as the *quilombos* that are found here and there, the religious expression of Candomblé, the music of José Maurício Nunes Garcia, the subversive polemics of Tobias Barreto—despite the appropriation of his work by conservative tendencies—the "rhapsody" of Mário de Andrade, and others erupt from time to time in modern discourse.

Now let me give a more direct answer to the question concerning the sense of talking about postmodernity in Brazil and the unanswered question concerning identity. Although many analysts and key figures in the debate on postmodernity in Brazil have criticized aspects of what I call the ideologies of modernization, a number of issues are still overlooked. In fact, a central issue has been blatantly left out of the postmodern discussion, because in every discussion about Brazilian identity and culture, there is no recognition of other factors at play or of an approach to the issue from a pluralist perspective. I think that the postmodern debate still has to include the variety of perspectives—the African American perspective, among others—which are actually the basis of the whole discussion. As the debate on postmodernity has Mário de Andrade's *Modernismo* as its point of departure, the progressive and cumulative history of resistance to ideologies of modernization also leads to Mário de Andrade. To talk about postmodernity in Brazil presupposes a coming to terms with *Modernismo*. At least in relation to the misleading search for identity, *Modernismo* is far ahead of postmodernity or postmodernism.

This final answer would point to a possible correction of one of the reductive abstractions I mentioned at the beginning of this text, which is unique to the Brazilian debate. But since I have given enough evidence that colonialism is similar and distinct in the countries of Latin America, and that missionarism and syncretism, as well as Indianism and populism, are also distinctly Latin American, perhaps this answer could help to solve other reductive fallacies as well.

NOTES

1. I have presented some arguments on this theme in "Una genealogía de la Postmodernidad en el Contexto Latinoamericano," *Disenso* 1 (1995): 63–69.

2. For example, see M. Koehler, "Postmodernismus: Ein Begriffsgeschichtlicher Ueberblick," *Amerikastudien* 22 (1977): 8–18. Jean-François Lyotard starts his *La condition postmoderne* (Paris: Minuit, 1979) by mentioning the historical reconstruction made by Koehler, but then concentrates on questions around science and cybernetics. See also W. Welsch, *Unsere postmoderne Moderne* (Weinheim: Acta Humaniora, 1987), 13, who quotes the same source but adds that the reference to Latin America is irrelevant.

3. See C. Rincón, *La no simultaneidad de lo simultáneo. Postmodernidad, globalización y culturas en América Latina* (Bogotá: EUN, 1995), the chapter "Los comienzos del debate sobre lo postmoderno en el Brasil," 103ff.

4. See the texts by J. G. Merquior in the *Suplemento Cultural* to *O Estado de São Paulo*, no. 4, and in Jacques Leenhardt, ed., *Littérature latino-américaine d'aujourd'hui [colloque de Cerisy : du 29 juin au 9 juillet 1978, tenu au]. Centre culturel international de Cerisy-La-Salle* (Paris: Union générale d'éditions, 1980). The argument about Brazilian postmodernity is developed by J. G. Merquior in *Formalismo e Tradição Moderna* (Rio de Janeiro: Nova Fronteira, 1977), *O Fantasma Romântico e outros ensaios* (Rio de Janeiro: Nova fronteira, 1980), and *As Idéias e as Formas* (Rio de Janeiro: Nova Fronteira, 1981). There is a need to recognize that Merquior was a pioneer not only in the debate on postmodernity, but in many other regards. He was one of the first to write about structuralist aesthetics and about the aesthetics of the Frankfurt School in the sixties. See J. G. Merquior, *A Estética de Lévi-Strauss* (Rio de Janeiro: Civilização Brasileira, 1967), *Arte e Sociedade em Marcuse, Adorno e Benjamin* (Rio de Janeiro: Paz e Terra, 1969); idem, *From Prague to Paris: Poststructuralist Itineraries* (London: Verso, 1983). The same is true of his discussions of liberalism in Europe.

5. For a more detailed view of this theoretical debate, see C. Rincón, *La no simultaneidad de lo Simultáneo. Postmodernidad, Globalización y Culturas en América Latina* (Bogotá: EUN, 1995).

6. See S. P. Rouanet, *A Razão Cativa: As Ilusões da Consciencia de Platão a Freud* (São Paulo: Brasiliense, 1985); idem, *As Razões do Iluminismo* (São Paulo: Cia. das Letras, 1987).

7. Cf. J. F. Santos, *O que é pós-moderno* (São Paulo: Brasiliense, 1986); J. T. Coelho Neto, *Moderno Pós-Moderno;* M. Oliveira, *Filosofia na Crise da Modernidade* (São Paulo: Loyola, 1989); idem, *Ética e Racionalidade Moderna* (São Paulo: Loyola, 1993); O. Arantes, *O Lugar da Arquitetura depois dos Modernos* (São Paulo: EDUSP, 1993).

8. See E. Dussel, *Historia de la Iglesia en América Latina* (Barcelona: Nova Terra, 1974) and the introduction to his *Filosofía de la Liberación* (Mexico City [Distrito Federal]: Contraste, 1989 [1st ed. 1977]), as well as G. Gutiérrez, *La Fuerza Histórica de los Pobres* (Salamanca: Sígueme, 1979).

9. Leonardo Boff, *Igreja, Carisma e Poder* (Petrópolis: Vozes, 1981).

10. Renato Ortiz points to the example of the Umbanda religion. Cf. R. Ortiz, *A Morte Branca do Feiticeiro Negro* (São Paulo: Brasiliense, 1990); idem, "Du Sincretisme à la Synthèse: Umbanda, une religion brasilienne" *Archives de Sciences Sociales des Religions* 20, no. 4 (1975): 89–97. For his discussion on culture, see idem, *A Consciencia Fragmentada. Ensaios de Cultura e Religião* (Rio de Janeiro: Paz e Terra, 1980); idem, *Cultura Brasileira e Identidade Nacional* (São Paulo: Brasiliense, 1985); idem, *A Moderna Tradição Brasileira* (São Paulo: Brasiliense, 1988).

11. See M. Chauí, *O que é Ideologia?* (São Paulo, Brasiliense, 1984); idem, *Repressão Sexual: essa nossa (des)conhecida* (São Paulo: Brasiliense, 1985).

12. Cf. N. W. Sodré, *A Ideologia do Colonialismo. Seus Reflexos no Pensamento Brasileiro* (Petrópolis: Vozes, 1984).

13. For a general critical view, cf. R. Faoro, *Os Donos do Poder. Formação do Patronato Político Brasileiro* (São Paulo: EDUSP, 1975), 2 vols. See also N. W. Sodré, *Formação Histórica do Brasil* (Rio de Janeiro: Civilização Brasileira, 1976), 175–181.

14. The immigration of Germans and Italians to the Americas was guided by the doctrines expressed in R. Malthus, *An Essay on the Principle of Population as It Affects the Future Improvement of Society with Remarks on the Speculations of Mr. Godwin, Mr. Condorcet and Other Writers* (London: Penguin, 1976).

15. For the case of Brazil, see C. Furtado, *Formação Econômica do Brasil* (Rio de Janeiro: Fundo de Cultura Econômica, 1959).

16. Here I follow N. W. Sodré, *A Ideologia do Colonialismo. Seus Reflexos no Pensamento Brasileiro* (Petrópolis: Vozes, 1984).

17. On this, see S. Schwartz, *Sovereignty and Society in Colonial Brazil: The High Court of Bahia and Its Judges (1609–1751)* (Berkeley: University of California Press, 1973). For this reference and for juridical information I am indebted to discussions with Martônio Mont'Alverne Lima.

18. On this topic, see S. Buarque de Holanda, *Raízes do Brasil* (Rio de Janeiro: J. Olympio, 1936). The move of the Portuguese Crown to Brazil needs to be recognized as profoundly significant for understanding the difference between Brazil and other South American nations, because this made it the only monarchy in the Americas. Dom Joao VI was the only monarch to escape from Napoleon, bringing to Brazil all the structure and information about the Empire and its colonies in which the French were interested. With the establishment of the Court in the colony and, shortly thereafter, with the declaration of independence, there was political autonomy. Also for this reason, the structures of colonialism in Brazil are to be seen as internal.

19. Cf. P. Dressendörfer, "Hacia una reconsideración del papel del clero en la 'conquista espiritual' de América," *Jahrbuch für Geschichte von Staat, Wirtschaft und Gesellschaft Lateinamerikas*, vol. 22 (1985): 23–28.

20. Cf. J. Carrato, *Igreja, Iluminismo e Escolas Mineiras Coloniais* (São Paulo: Editora Nacional, 1968). See also A. Paim, *História das Idéias Filosóficas no Brasil* (São Paulo: Grijalbo, 1974); W. Martins, *História da Inteligencia Brasileira: 1550–1794* (São Paulo: Cultrix, 1977–1978), vol. 1.; and G. Freyre, *Casa Grande e Senzala* (Rio de Janeiro: J. Olympio, 1933), 69–70 . See also R. Faoro, *Os Donos do Poder* (São Paulo: EDUSP, 1975), vol. 1, 176–203.

21. Cf. CEHILA, *Historia General de la Iglesia en América Latina* (Salamanca: Sígueme, 1982), vol. 2, 472–516. See also J.-H. Prien, *Historia del Cristianismo en América Latina* (Salamanca: Sígueme, 1985), 101–110. For more details on the Brazilian case, see E. Hoornaert, *Formação do Catolicismo Brasileiro: 1500–1800* (Petrópolis: Vozes, 1974). It was around this seminary in Mariana and the main colonial cities in Minas Gerais that educational activity oriented toward humanist and liberal values could be found. In fact, many intellectual movements for independence started in this region in the late eighteenth century.

22. Cf. CEHILA, *Das reduções latino-americanas às lutas indígenas atuais (XI Simpósio, Agosto de 1981, Manaus, AM)* (São Paulo: Paulinas, 1981). See also H.-J. Prien, *Historia del Cristianismo en América Latina* (Salamanca: Sígueme, 1985), 197–213, and CEHILA, *Historia General*, vol. 2, 490ff.

23. Stuart Schwartz studied the background of 103 of the 168 judges sent to Brazil between 1609 and 1758 and discovered that only 23 came from families with an educational background. Cf. Schwartz, *Sovereignty and Society*, 382ff.

24. Cf. T. Flory, *Judges and Jury in Imperial Brazil (1808–1871): Social Control and Political Stability in the New State* (Austin: University of Texas Press, 1981), 31.

25. On this, cf. Schwartz, *Sovereignty and Society*, 270ff.

26. The Guaranis had their own set of beliefs and, in view of the European invasion, retreated farther west, in search of a land beyond the Andes where there would be no evil. In many cases, when they were dominated by the Portuguese the Guaranis would commit collective suicide. This was seen by many philosophers in Europe as positive, since they saw in this act an anti-slavery principle that allowed the Guaranis to maintain their dignity at any cost. The practice of collective suicide as the final response to oppression and repression still exists today. For details, see E. Schaden, *Aspectos Fundamentais da Cultura Guarani* (São Paulo: Difusão Européia do Livro, 1962); L. Cadogan, *Ayvu rapyta: textos míticos dos Mbyia-Guarani del Guara* (São Paulo: Faculdade de Filosofia/USP, 1959). See also A. Metraux, "The Native Tribes of Eastern Bolivia and Western Mato-Grosso," *Bulletin 134* (Washington, D.C.: Bureau of American Ethnology, Smithsonian Institute, 1942), pp. 1–182; idem, "Les messies de l'Amérique du Sud," *Archives de sociologie des religion 2*, no. 4 (1957): 108–112; M. I. Queiroz, *O Messianismo no Brasil e no Mundo* (São Paulo: Alfa-Omega, 1977). Further, cf. H. Clastres, *Terra sem Mal* (São Paulo: Brasiliense, 1978), and C. Lugon, *A República 'comunista' cristã dos Guaranis* (Rio de Janeiro: Paz e Terra, n.d.).

27. The Jesuit scholastic system of higher education was not transferred to the colony; instead, the Jesuits concentrated on the education of children. At the beginning of colonization alternative institutions were also established that led to the famous utopian "Jesuit missions." These were the attempts at bringing people who were dispersed in different parts of the colony to live together in a village, where the priests could develop a different approach to mission—bringing the Natives to perform what was conceived as "integral salvation" by providing an education in the liberal arts and an introduction to human studies and politics. In fact, music and art comprised a way to attract the Natives, and this practice was maintained in the missions. In Paraguay, the result of this work was documented by the architecture in Tobati and Yaguaron. The political and economic experiment was more akin to socialism and was rejected by the very European colonists and governors, and this sealed the end of the utopian initiative. Cf. CEHILA, *Das reduções latino-americanas*; Prien, *Historia del Cristianismo en America Latina*, 197–213, 255–282; idem, *Historia General*, vol. 1, 490ff.

28. The displacement of Africans through colonial slavery has been explored by Pierre Verger in *Flux et Reflux de la traité des Nègres entre le Golfe de Benin et Bahia, du XVII au XIX*

siècle (Paris: Mouton, 1968), and by Paul Gilroy in *The Black Atlantic: Modernity and Double Consciousness* (Cambridge, Mass.: Harvard University Press, 1993), although the case of Brazil is not touched on directly in Gilroy's book.

29. See D. Freitas, *Palmares: A Guerra dos Escravos* (Rio de Janeiro: Ed. Movimento, 1982). For a general view, see J. Chiavenato, *O Negro Brasileiro. Da Senzala à Guerra do Paraguay* (São Paulo: Brasiliense, 1987), especially 57; A. Russel-Wood, *The Black Man in Slavery and Freedom in Colonial Brazil* (New York: St. Martin Press, 1982).

30. Article 68 of the Transitory Clauses of the 1988 Constitution grants possession of these areas to the original settlers of the *quilombos*.

31. Much has been written and much research is yet to be done on this theme, especially on an analytic differentiation between *cangaço, quilombo*, and other messianic movements. Cf. M. V. Queiroz, *Messianismo e Conflito Social* (São Paulo: Atica, 1981), D. T. Monteiro, *Os Errantes do Novo Século* (São Paulo: Duas Cidades, 1974), and J. S. Martins, *Os Camponeses e a Política no Brasil* (Petrópolis: Vozes, 1983).

32. For Brazil, see Freyre, *Casa Grande e Senzala*. For Colombia, see P. Wade, *Blackness and Race Mixture: The Dynamic of Racial Identity in Colombia* (Baltimore: Johns Hopkins University Press, 1993). For Venezuela, see W. R. Wright, *Café con Leche: Race, Class and National Images in Venezuela* (Austin: University of Texas Press, 1991). For a critique, see A. Nascimento and J. Sathler "Black Masks on White Faces: Liberation Theology and the Quest for Syncretism in the Brazilian Context" in D. Batstone et al., eds., *Liberation Theologies, Postmodernity and the Americas* (London: Routledge, 1997), 95–122.

33. Cf., for example, R. Faoro, *Os Donos do Poder. Formação do Patronato Político Brasileiro* (São Paulo: EDUSP, 1975), vol. 1, 298; and M. S. Carvalho Franco, *Homens Livres na Ordem Escravocrata* (São Paulo: IEB, 1969).

34. Cf. N. Rodrigues, *Os Africanos no Brasil* (Brasília: Ed. Universidade de Brasília, 1988). For a general description, see T. Skidmore, *Black into White: Race and Nationality in Brazilian Thought* (New York: Oxford University Press, 1974). For a recent critique, see L. Schwarcz, *O Espetáculo das Raças* (São Paulo: Cia. das Letras, 1992).

35. Cf. V. Lanternari, *As Religiões dos Oprimidos* (São Paulo: Perspectiva, 1974); M. I. Queiroz, *O Messianismo no Brasil e no Mundo* (São Paulo: Alfa-Omega, 1977). See also E. Schaden, *Aspectos Fundamentais da Cultura Guarani* (São Paulo: Difusão Européia do Livro, 1962).

36. In Alencar's *O Guarani*, the strong and beautiful Peri is the ideal partner for the blond daughter of a Brazilian landowner of European origins. In *Iracema*, his portrait of the Indian in the central role has had so much influence that even today the name Iracema is a synonym for "pretty woman." It should be noted as well that the Tupi name "Iracema" is an anagram for the word "America." For Mexico, cf. T. G. Powell, "Mexican Intellectuals and the Indian Question: 1876–1911," *Hispanic American Historical Review* 48, no. 1 (Feb. 1968): 19–36; and W. Raat, "Los intelectuales, el positivismo, y la lucha indigena," *Historia Mexicana* 20 (1971): 412–427. For Ecuador, see R. Ball, Jr., "Ecuadorean Indigenismo and Its Literary Manifestations," *Discurso* 12, no. 2 (n.d.): 19–28.

37. Cf. J. Nabuco, *O Abolicionismo* (London, 1883), in which he states, "What we visualize is not emancipation of the slave, but emancipation of the nation." For details, see P. Beiguelman, *Teoria e Ação do Pensamento Abolicionista* (São Paulo: Pioneira, 1967).

38. See R. Ortiz, *Cultura Brasileira e Identidade Nacional* (São Paulo: Brasiliense, 1985), 13, and Schwarcz, *O Espetáculo das Raças*, 43–66.

39. See J. A. Haddad, "A Filosofia de Alvares de Azevedo," in *Anais do III Congresso de Nacional de Filosofia* (São Paulo: Instituto Brasileiro de Filosofia, 1960), 63–68. For a gen-

eral view of the context and of the influence and importance of the School of Recife, see A. Crippa, ed., *As Idéias Filosóficas no Brasil* (São Paulo: Convívio, 1978); and A. Paim, *A Filosofia da Escola de Recife* (Rio de Janeiro: Saga, 1966). Cf. also W. Martins, *História da Inteligencia Brasileira: 1877–1896* (São Paulo: Cultrix, 1979), vol. 6.

40. S. Romero, *O Naturalismo em Literatura* (São Paulo: Lucta, 1882), 85, 149. These ideas have parallels beyond Brazil's borders—for example, in Argentina, where José Ingenieros defended ethnic cleansing, and in Mexico, where the hybrid inheritance of the Malinches was defined in terms of a proud "cosmic race" by the philosopher José Vasconcelos.

41. N. Rodrigues, *Os Africanos no Brasil* (Brasília: Ed. Universidade de Brasília, 1988 [1904]), xv.

42. Ibid., 255ff.

43. R. Bastide, *As Religiões Africanas no Brasil* (São Paulo: Pioneira, 1973); and P. Verger, *Orixás. Deuses Iorubás na Africa e no Novo Mundo* (Salvador: Corrupio, 1981).

44. For details, see Bastide, *As Religiões Africanas no Brasil.*

45. See A. d'Escragnole Taunay, *Uma Grande Glória Brasileira: José Maurício Nunes Garcia (1767–1830)* (São Paulo: Melhoramentos, 1930); and C. Mattos and E. Barbosa, *O Ciclo do Ouro, o Tempo e a Música do Barroco Católico* (Rio de Janeiro: PUC/MEC/FUNARTE/XEROX, 1979).

46. J. Carrato, *Igreja, Iluminismo e Escolas Mineiras Coloniais* (São Paulo: Editora Nacional, 1968).

47. See J. J. Reis, *Rebelião Escrava no Brasil. A História do Levante dos Malês: 1835* (São Paulo: Brasiliense, 1987).

48. For a description and critique of some aspects of this issue, see T. Skidmore, *Black into White*, and Schwarcz, *O Espetáculo das Raças.*

49. Cf. D. Apter, *Black Critics and Kings: The Hermeneutics of Power in Yoruba Society* (Chicago: University of Chicago Press, 1992).

50. For a general account, see L. Machado, *O Barroco Mineiro* (São Paulo: Perspectiva, 1969); A. Avila, *O Lúdico e as Projeções do Barroco Mineiro* (Sao Paulo: Perspectiva, 1971); C. R. Boxer, *A Idade de Ouro no Brasil* (São Paulo: Companhia Editora Nacional, 1963); and G. Bazin, *L'Architecture religieuse baroque au Brésil* (Paris: Éditions d'Histoire de l'art/Librairie Le Blon, 1956). Cf. d'Escragnole Taunay, *Uma Grande Glória Brasileira*, and Mattos and Barbosa, *O Ciclo do Ouro.*

51. Most studies on Tobias Barreto and on the School of Recife are by conservative authors who have an interest in rescuing what is genuinely Brazilian, and research into and interpretation of the aspects I am trying to emphasize is still needed. In any case, besides Barreto's own writings see P. Mercadante, *Tobias Barreto na Cultura Brasileira* (São Paulo: Grijalbo/EDUSP, 1972).

52. Cf. W. E. B. DuBois, *Against Racism: Unpublished Essays, Papers, Addresses, 1887–1961*, edited by H. Aptheker (Amherst: University of Massachusetts Press, 1985), 69ff.

53. See Freyre, *Casa Grande & Senzala.* For a critique, cf. F. Fernandes, *A Integração dos Negros na Sociedade de Classes* (São Paulo: Ed. Atica, 1978).

54. See Freyre, *Casa Grande & Senzala*, 54, 87.

55. Ibid., 30.

56. For a critique of Freyre's position, cf. F. Fernandes, *A Integração dos Negros na Sociedade de Classes* (São Paulo: Ed. Atica, 1978); F.H. Cardoso, *Capitalismo e Escravidão* (São Paulo: Difusão Européia do Livro, 1962); Thales de Azevedo, *Cultura e Situação Racial no Brasil* (Rio de Janeiro: Civilização Brasileira, 1966); O. Ianni, *Escravidao e Racismo* (São

Paulo: Atica, 1978); and A. Nascimento, *O Genocídio do Negro Brasileiro* (Rio de Janeiro: Paz e Terra, 1978).

57. Cf. E. Carone, *A República Velha* (São Paulo: Difel 1970), vol. 1; idem, *A Primeira República (1889–1930)* (São Paulo: Difel, 1973). See also S. Miceli, *Intelectuais e Classe Dirigente no Brasil (1920–1945)* (São Paulo: Difel, 1979).

58. Cf. work by proponents of integralism: P. Salgado, *O Integralismo Perante a Nação* (Rio de Janeiro: Ed. Liv. Clássica Brasileira, 1950); P. Salgado and M. Reale, *Cartilha do Integralismo* (Porto Alegre: AIB, 1933); and Oliveira Viana, *Problemas de Política Objetiva* (Rio de Janeiro: Record, 1974).

59. See W. Martins, *O Modernismo* (São Paulo: Cultrix, 1964).

60. Cf. J. G. Merquior, "Drei Schriftsteller des 'Modernismo': Mario de Andrade, Manuel Bandeira und Jorge de Lima," in M. Strausfeld, ed., *Brasilianische Literatur* (Frankfurt: Suhrkamp, 1984), 121–158.

61. M. Andrade, *Macunaíma. O Herói sem Nenhum Caráter* (São Paulo: EDUSP, 1989 [critical ed. of 1927 original]).

62. T. Lopez, *Mário de Andrade: Ramais e Caminho* (São Paulo: Duas Cidades, 1972); J. Dassin, *Poesia e Política em Mário de Andrade* (São Paulo: Duas Cidades, 1978).

63. See these works in M. de Andrade, *Obras Completas* (São Paulo: Ed. Martins/INL, 1967.

64. M. Andrade, *Macunaíma.*

65. See H. Campos, *Morfologia de Macunaíma* (São Paulo: Perspectiva, 1973).

7. Continental Philosophy and Postcolonial Subjects

OFELIA SCHUTTE

As a field of specialization in the United States, Continental philosophy generally refers to French and German philosophy in the post-Kantian era. A few great thinkers other than French and German philosophers are included in its canon—for example, Denmark's Kierkegaard and Italy's Croce and Gramsci. Rarely does Continental philosophy extend its borders to Spain; Spanish philosophers in the Continental tradition remain unacknowledged in most anthologies. In recent years, advocates for diversity have raised the question of the importance of including philosophers from various parts of the world in teaching and research practices. While I believe that it is important to engage with philosophers from underrepresented parts of the world, including Africa, Asia, and Latin America (as well as Spain, which occupies a privileged place vis-à-vis the others yet is still unrecognized), this is not the principal topic of this paper. Instead, I propose to deal with a related and perhaps more subtle issue. The issue that I will attempt to develop addresses the "resonance factor" of postcolonial subjectivity in Continental philosophy. This, too, may be considered an issue of inclusion, but the type of inclusion to be considered is of a wholly different kind. The question here concerns the effects, if any, on the Western subject of the consequences of Western colonization of other continents and peoples. This kind of question requires that we take a critical view of Western history in its colonialist expansionist phases. The purpose is not to reject the past or to attempt to annihilate its consequences but to shed a critical light on practices in which we are engaged today. These practices are both, to some extent, a product of the past and ways of acting that define the way we look at the future.

As we enter the twenty-first century, there is much discussion about ongoing processes of "globalization." The world is interlinked via technology, mass-media, and communications networks, economic agreements, and political conventions in ways that call for an analysis of Western ideological and philosophical constructs as these interact with subjects in both Western and non-Western societies. Closer to the field of Continental philosophy, the question deals with the construction of postcolonial subjects and their interpellation with the philosophical tradition that calls itself "Continental." It asks that the specialist in Continental philosophy begin to think, or to imagine, what it is like to read French and German philosophy in a world in which readers are located at many different physical points. In this view, if "identity" is considered a cultural construct, then the "subject" of philosophy cannot be presumed to sustain a homogeneous set of metaphysical characteristics (whether these characteristics are represented in the form of a Kantian self or a Heideggerian *Dasein*). Postcolonial critical theory, challenging the cultural location of the Continental thinker, raises the basic questions, Is there a difference between European philosophy and Eurocentrism? Can one be a Continental philosopher and a critic of Eurocentrism simultaneously? Is one to think that unless a philosopher specifically states something to the contrary, to teach Continental philosophy is to support and defend Eurocentric thought?

I will briefly define Eurocentrism as the cultural presumption that European thought and values—however these are defined—contain the essence of civilized or rational thought.[1] I should clarify that my critique of Eurocentrism in the context of doing philosophy is contextual rather than absolute. What I am after is not strictly Eurocentrism as such, but any pattern of thinking and acting that takes for granted the cultural and scientific hegemony of procedures and values established in the most powerful nations on Earth. That European nations—or at least some of them, such as France and Germany—have occupied this position of power over others is a fact of history, just as Britain and the United States have dominated Anglocentric thought and cultural projects throughout the world. The greater the power of a nation or nations pursuing global political agendas, the more questionable the corresponding form of "centrism" becomes. The reason is that such concentrations of power have proven historically either to violate the rights of others outright or, at a minimum, to disregard the experiences and contributions of the less powerful, including women and those who are socially and economically marginalized. The result has been, on one hand, to propose as comprehensive a less-than-universal form of knowledge and, on the other, to fail in the ethical responsibility to listen to those others whose voices may clash with the sources of epistemic legitimation established in the central parts of the world.

What has Continental philosophy to do with this? There is probably an unstated sociocultural (possibly also professional) assumption associating the teaching of Continental philosophy with some form, at least a mild one, of Eurocentrism. For example, it is not easy (and perhaps it is not considered appropriate) to engage in a discussion of developing countries in a Continental philosophy class. Students taking these courses generally want to know more about France and Germany or about European thought. They do not come to a class on Heidegger, for example, expecting an answer to questions regarding readings of Heidegger in the Third World, or regarding Germany's heritage as a colonial power. There is a distinction between questions regarding colonialism and the rest of European politics. Questions regarding colonialism and its sequels are presumed to remain outside the epistemic/cultural horizon of the Continental philosophy class.

It does not require much reflection, however, once the omission has been identified, to realize that European colonialism must have some effect on Europe's intellectual history. This effect may be both subtle and indirect. While there may be no explicit mention of colonialism in a philosopher's work, the absence of a critique of colonialism could in itself point to a silent acceptance of the colonialist project. It is therefore important to pay special attention to the way in which our interest in the field of Continental philosophy is defined. For example, is there an excessive concern with keeping the field of Continental philosophy methodologically pure and delimited to certain nonnegotiable questions? Or is there a willingness to be open to new and hybrid constructions of Continental thought that can accommodate philosophers and thinkers from the West's internally diverse populations and its cultural peripheries?

Unless learning encompasses an analysis of the relations of power between central and peripheral cultures, the argument claiming that Continental philosophy is Eurocentric in nature cannot be easily dismissed. In defending one's philosophical practice against the charge of Eurocentrism, one could say that there is a distinction between reading texts from dominant cultures and promoting the dominance of such cultures over others. In my view, this is a valid distinction, but by itself it is insufficient to guarantee that a practice is free from Eurocentric effects. One could say, for example, that just because one is a specialist in Heidegger or Nietzsche this does not make one an accomplice of Western hegemony or Eurocentrism. One could even make an argument on behalf of knowledge for its own sake and the importance of engaging with important texts, regardless of political or cultural issues, for these are the kinds of arguments and forms of reasoning that we embrace when, pursuing our scholarly interests, we detach a piece of knowledge from the intellectual history of the world's peoples. Indeed, I myself have often engaged in justifications of this nature. I begin my pedagogic practice from the conviction that teaching Nietzsche does not make me an accomplice of Eurocentrism. But how do I know that it does not? Or how can I be sure that precisely because I do not teach Nietzsche in such a way as to promote Eurocentrism, someone might not judge that my teaching is lacking in some basic sense?

One line of defense against equating Continental philosophy with Eurocentrism is to argue that some Continental philosophers have attempted to be critical of a Eurocentrist philosophy. It is not clear, however, that a very strong case can be made on this ground given that even if Eurocentrism is challenged on some fronts, it may well remain unchallenged on others. Still, as an example of this type of challenge, I will mention Sartre insofar as he is known for his political opinions against colonialism, including France's colonization of Algeria. Another strategy might be to claim that the *effects* of reading some Continental philosophers could be to deconstruct or undermine (at least to some extent) the ideology of Eurocentrism. This is a much more promising approach. With it, one could take some threads out of an otherwise Eurocentric text to disentangle the fabric of Eurocentrism and point toward otherness. In this regard, I will address a reading of Nietzsche's views on history before I move on to examine properly postcolonial readings of Continental thought.

Using the second strategy, aside from Nietzsche one could equally address many others in the field. For example, Heidegger, despite his Nazi leanings, offered a strong critique of technology and European modernity, thereby distancing himself from certain core elements of the Eurocentrist historical project. Derrida, whose deconstructive method undermines ideological "isms," including "centrisms," stands out as a rebel against the overarching logocentric project of European philosophy. Yet despite their critical outlooks, as philosophers Heidegger, Nietzsche, and Derrida—even Sartre—are primarily Eurocentric in practice. The scholarly sources that they use tend to be European. A break exists between this type of thinker and others of the type—Bhabha and Spivak and, before them, Fanon and Freire. The break involves, in part, the use of sources and, in part, the political stance taken by philosophers in view of their life experiences.

A SARTREAN CHALLENGE TO COLONIALISM

Sartre is an example of a philosopher whose work may be partially applicable to a postcolonial context. Although Sartre's existentialist philosophy is very Western in its basic proposals, especially that of freedom of choice for the individual, his concept of freedom is radical and critical of the status quo. As an engaged leftist intellectual, for example, he visited Cuba, along with Simone de Beauvoir, after the 1959 revolution. This visit alerted him to the realities of underdevelopment in capitalist dependent nations in the Americas. "Underdevelopment," he wrote in 1961, "must not be defined as a simple deficiency of the national economy. It is a complex relationship between a backward country and the great powers that have maintained it in this backward condition."[2] Addressing the problem of colonialism, he states, "The semicolony, delivered from its chains, again finds itself in its misery facing an irritated former mother country."[3] He adds that even if the former colonizing power were to stop overpowering its former colony, the liberated country would have to either make do on its own or subsist in a relation of dependency to the former. It seems that the first option would be difficult for a former colony. Sartre recognizes that "simply, underdevelopment is a violent tension between two nations—the amount of tension is measured in the backwardness of the one in relation to the other."[4]

While it is no longer considered acceptable to refer, as Sartre does here, to the neocolonized country as "backward," this kind of language was typical of the times in which he wrote. In this passage, Sartre was looking at Cuba through Parisian eyes. He noticed that the island's economic development is "backward," but he was clearly aware that the lag in development involved relations of dependence to powerful nations whose interests, in alliance with those of certain privileged classes in the colonized country, control the dependent nation's economy. Sartre favors the concept of the dependent country's empowerment to overcome neocolonial domination for the sake of implementing social justice. From this standpoint he accepted the justification of anti-colonial nationalist revolutions in Third World countries. He also engaged in a strong critique of racism, in both its ordinary and its violent forms, as it took place in Europe against the Jewish people. Understanding what Nietzsche called the morality of "resentment" among Aryan-identified Europeans, Sartre defined the dialectics of racial prejudice in the well-known statement, "If the Jew did not exist, the anti-Semite would invent him."[5]

In *Critique of Dialectical Reason*, Sartre theorizes about the human being as a cultural construct. He notes the effects of cultural erasure taking place in an individual, who is often unaware of the degree to which she operates within the limits of a cultural field (as he calls it) giving meaning to her life and values. If dialectical investigation is possible, he states, then,

> It is clear that *my* culture cannot be treated as a subjective accumulation of knowledge and methods "in *my* mind"; instead, this culture which I call mine must be conceived as a specific participation in interiority in the objective culture. And instead of me being a particular social atom which itself defines the cultural possibilities, this participation defines me (in a specific way). As soon as I reflexively grasp this bond of interiority which links me to the cultural totalization, I disappear as a cultivated individual and emerge as the synthetic bond between everyone and what might be called the *cultural field*.[6]

As he states, then, reflection on her cultural position allows an individual to move from a pre-critical relationship to culture to a critical one. The realization of this bond between the individual, the culture, and others situated in the cultural field leads to the awareness that the way a person situates herself in the world is inevitably linked to the culture or set of cultures that she has interacted with and that have had an impact on her life.

Sartre also claims that a person's critical understanding of her life is mediated by schemata rooted in history and culture: "I totalize myself on the basis of centuries of history and, in accordance with my culture, I totalize this experience."[7] He adds that "to the extent that critical investigation is possible, the temporal depth of the totalizing process becomes evident as soon as I reflexively interpret the operations of my individual life."[8]

From these kinds of observations about the cultural construction of subjectivity and the emergence of a critical dialectical outlook toward the cultural schemata that condition our very concept of existence, it is only a small step to the political and ethical critique of European subjectivity as the product of a colonialist culture. European culture may be considered a colonialist culture to the extent that it supported the colonizing of the American continents and other regions in Africa, Asia, and the Pacific. Lest all Europeans stand accused of being colonizers, it is worth pointing out that just as European hegemony was exercised on other peoples on Earth, as well as on minorities within Europe itself, such as the Gypsies and the Jews, there was also internal resistance among some Europeans to these hegemonic practices. Nor should we forget that other (non-European) powerful cultures have also colonized what failed to give them effective resistance. Powerful empires of one sort or another arose in ancient civilizations among peoples of different continents. Where the conditions for imperialist activity have existed, hegemonic groups and nations throughout known history have exerted such power over others. In our own times, the one superpower (the United States) exerts its force and influence throughout the world to dominate world values in terms of its own schema of understanding history and progress. The tendency of dominant cultures to impose their own values on others throughout their spheres of influence makes it all the more imperative for Continental philosophy to sharpen its critical tools with respect to the analysis of Eurocentrism and other powerful instruments of the cultural colonization of others (e.g., Anglocentrism).

What can be proposed to counter these powerful hegemonic cultural forces? The Continental tradition offers at least one possible alternative: reflecting on its own postcolonial status at the beginning of this new millennium. Before I proceed to this topic, however, I would like to make a few observations about Nietzsche.

NIETZSCHE'S APPEALS TO MONUMENTAL AND CRITICAL HISTORY

In an early essay entitled "On the Uses and Disadvantages of History for Life," Nietzsche noticed that among his contemporaries the consciousness of history did not always take the same form. He observed three different "types" of history, or of doing history, which he labeled antiquarian, monumental, and critical.[9] The antiquarian historian wants to preserve whatever he can from the past. The monumental historian looks for the high moments in history as examples of deeds worth emulating, so as to be energized for future-oriented transformative action. The critical historian annihilates a part of the past in order to undo past oppressions. Describing critical history, Nietzsche states,

> If he is to live, man must possess and from time to time employ the strength to break up and dissolve a part of the past: he does this by bringing it before the tribunal, scrupulously examining it and finally condemning it; every past, however, is worthy to be condemned—for that is the nature of human things: human violence and weakness have always played a mighty force in them. . . . Sometimes . . . life . . . wants to be clear as to how unjust the existence of anything—a privilege, a caste, a dynasty, for example—is, and how greatly this thing deserves to perish. Then its past is regarded critically, then one takes the knife to its roots, then one cruelly tramples over every kind of piety.[10]

In what follows, I will apply the term "critical" to a context underemployed by Nietzsche. Critical history, I want to claim, is not so much the destruction of the past as the reading of the past in a critical light. Nietzsche's categories do not explicitly offer this alternative reading, yet he does not rule it out. What Nietzsche calls "critical" history is a reference more to the passion to be liberated from a perceived oppression than to a balanced assessment of historical biases. His closest stand to a critical reading of history (understood as a critique of mainstream historical biases) is actually what he calls *monumental* history. For Nietzsche, this "type" allows us to reflect on the greatest moments of history—a standpoint that may then provide us with a critical distance useful for evaluating the sociocultural assumptions of the present time. Monumental (not critical) history offers Nietzsche the alternative of providing an inspiration for actions that go against the grain of the moment. "Of what use, then, is the monumentalistic conception of the past, engagement with the classic and rare of earlier times, to the man of the present? He learns from it that the greatness that once existed was in any event once *possible* and may thus be possible again."[11] Nietzsche's ideal of monumental history contains an undeniable truth—namely, that to struggle against an overarching contemporary trend one needs an even more powerful idea to serve as one's compass. If monumental history can achieve this standard for guidance, it has provided a positive meaning to a creative life. Still, what Nietzsche failed to address is that there are issues with respect to which monumental history cannot serve as our guide. Colonialism is one example. The extension of a superpower's dominion over other cultures and peoples may be a monumental enterprise, but it is not justified ethically. The building of the pyramids at the cost of the slave labor of its builders may be justifiable on monumental standards but, contra Nietzsche, others may hold that it is not ethically justified.

If colonialism were linked with monumental history, following Nietzsche's terms, only a turn to critical history would help us to justify the dissolution of colonialist oppression (whether past or present). How could the same event—say, the dissolution of a past oppression—appear justifiable under one view of history (critical history) though not necessarily justifiable under another (monumental history)? The answer lies in part in Nietzsche's inherent perspectivalism, which allows for flexibility (or at least multiplicity) in the way that events in the world are seen and interpreted. Moreover, Nietzsche's incipient perspectival epistemology[12] permits him to claim that all historically engaged action is at least partially biased. The very importance that we give to history, he claims in this early work, is a Western bias. "Our valuation of the historical may be only an occidental prejudice [okzidentalisches Vorurteil] but . . . let us at least learn better how to employ history for the purpose of *life*!"[13] Bearing this in mind, I would take Nietzsche's awareness of the West's bias toward its own history to propose that if our conversations about history become more balanced in terms of the participants' places of origin and their corresponding historical standpoints, perhaps we can reduce at least a portion of this evident "occidental prejudice." And just as we mention history, so we could also mention philosophy. Insofar as our conversations about philosophy stop requiring an exclusively Eurocentric orientation, then Nietz-schean perspectivism would grant that the force of new hybrid cultures is on the rise. It remains to those whose creativity is burdened under the weight of "occi-dental prejudice" and who perhaps have had to rise to the challenge of colonial-ism in their/our lives to apply a full-blown critique to the Eurocentrist bias as it appears in Continental thought.

So, let me move on to the work of those who, not necessarily trying to position themselves in the academy by virtue of being natives of the developing world, nevertheless have influenced our ways of reading Continental philosophy in a noncentrist direction.

POSTCOLONIAL VOICES

Actually, at the point when postcolonial subjectivity is inserted into Conti-nental philosophy, the concept of discipline and canon begins to break down. The writers I mention next are not quite considered philosophers, even though they are of interest to philosophers. Their works constitute the diaspora of philosophic ideas, as it were. This is where we see the influence of Marxism, existentialism, de-construction, and poststructuralism—all of which are philosophical theories in their own right, though, when applied, we find them intermixed with social thought or literary criticism, as the case might be. Today there is at least one field where some of this material may be housed—cultural studies. But some of it is too old to be placed in categories of recent origin.

One place to start is with Frantz Fanon. Fanon was an Afro-Latin thinker from the Caribbean—specifically, the island of Martinique. He was taught what every colonized or neocolonized subject is taught to think: that validity for all knowl-edge and social status comes from the "mother country" or the dominant "me-tropolis." In the case of Martinique, that country was France. Fanon's work *Black Skin, White Masks* documents the impact of cultural imperialism on his island ed-ucation, his attempt to prove himself in France, the pervasive racism of which he became conscious there, and his personal struggle to accept himself as a black man without succumbing to the hatred of the white race that oppressed him. Where is the Continental philosophy in this book? Fanon deals with psychoanalysis, iden-tity, and race. His work emerges out of his Caribbean/French experience as medi-ated by Freudian, Jungian, Adlerian, and other psychoanalytic concepts. He mentions Hegel's concept of the struggle for recognition and Merleau-Ponty on the phenomenology of bodily perception.[14] Clearly, as an educated Martinican, he came in contact with Continental thought if he received a good education. But why must a good education be structured by a colonialist project? One question we ask today is, To what extent were France's wealth and cultural status indebted to its colonies? Another is, Why is French philosophy oblivious to France's colo-nial role in the Caribbean? In truth, it cannot be said that there was no inter-change between France and its colonies. The colonizer is indebted to the colonized for the wealth and the labor power extracted from the colonies, at the least. Moreover, in Gayatri Spivak's words, the colonizer has performed an "epistemic violation"[15] of the colonized, insofar as all legitimizing concepts in the colony derive from the colonizer's mentality and interests.

Does Continental philosophy engage in a monologue if it does not include the voices and register the states of consciousness of those who know what it is like to have been colonized? What one finds in the texts of the postcolonial "others" is a kind of internal dialogue in which, as in the case of Fanon, conceptual threads from the Continental tradition are interwoven with ideas developed in view of experiences reaped in developing countries, to produce a different textual mosaic. I shall offer some other examples.

In Brazil, the educator Paulo Freire, another product of a Western education, became a leading figure in developing teaching methods for what he called the liberation of the oppressed. In *Pedagogy of the Oppressed*, Freire explains the methodology and philosophy of his new teaching strategy. He had read Fanon, along with the Western Continental canon of the sixties (when his book was first published)—Marx, Hegel, Heidegger, Sartre, Althusser, Buber. A Christian, Freire had also read the New Testament, along with the work of Marxists, including Third World Marxists, and developed a Christian interpretation integrating some of the keenest insights of his sources. He intended his book to serve as a handbook for revolutionary leadership. Devoted to empowering the people as they became engaged in a process of popular education, it was received throughout the developing world as a tool of liberation. In 1964, Freire was imprisoned by the Brazilian authorities on account of his freedom-oriented thinking, his solidarity with humble folk, and his subversion of authoritarian thinking.

Freire's work is a product of its time, with its strengths and limitations, but it shows a way of reading philosophy that is directly linked to the experiences of a developing people. Things that Europeans take for granted, such as reading and writing, were opportunities presented for the first time to the adult peasants with whom he worked. Freire devised a dialectical method aimed at dislodging authoritarian methods of teaching. Instead, a mutual, reciprocal method of teaching and learning was devised for the instructor and the class. In the authoritarian class, he argued, "the teacher teaches and the students are taught."[16] In the democratic class, where education reflects "the practice of freedom," everyone contributes to learning, and the teacher often learns from the students.[17] Needless to say, since the students were often illiterate peasants, this method was quite revolutionary even with respect to the elites of the developing countries, not to mention the impact it had on the centers of power in the metropolis, where much of what Freire noted about disenfranchised peasants applied to students of color, the handicapped, and economically disadvantaged students.

There is an epistemic break between postcolonial predecessors such as Fanon and Freire and some of the deconstructive criticism that takes place in the United States today. I think Fanon is closer than is Freire to our contemporary outlook because, as Homi Bhabha has noted, Fanon tried to locate the culture of a people in a performative process of continual renovation or change, a paradigm that harbors an element of unpredictability and uncertainty about the future.[18] Influenced by deconstructive strategies, contemporary postcolonial critical studies attempt to place an element of undecideability in the colonial signifier, such that the utterance is prevented from attaining a self-validating closure. In Bhabha's view (and perhaps also Spivak's), it is here, in this "interruptive" (Spivak's term) moment, in this undecideable instant, that what I earlier called the "resonance" of the postcolonial is felt in Continental thought. Somewhere in the speech of the colonizing power, a code is left imperfect, through which critical thinking can garner an Other vision, an Other language, a meaning missing in the lexicon of the dominant. Thus, reversing my earlier comment as to whether a non-Eurocentric reading of Nietzsche might be missing or lacking something, in the eyes of a Eurocentric public, the suggestion here would be: rather, it is the Eurocentric reading that misses the reality of the post-colonized world if it indeed attempts to view itself as complete in terms of its cultural roots and relevance.

Postcolonial subjectivity points to the incompleteness of Eurocentrism, not just its blindness or its arrogance. In Nietzschean terms, one could say that the Eurocentric/Anglocentric consciousness fears the loss of its individuation, along with its epistemic dominance. Faced with this threat, which becomes all the more real at the present time given the speed with which the West comes into contact with the educated elites of its former colonies and possessions, if it is not possible to silence the Other completely, the next best choice will be to appropriate the others' voices. Indeed, this is what Spivak argues that the developed world is currently doing as globalization projects envelop the lives of people in cultural and economic peripheries.

In her recent work *A Critique of Postcolonial Reason*, Spivak (who by her own admission is a literary critic, not a philosopher) takes Continental thought to a new frontier. A native of West Bengal, India, who received an elite education and has attained a position of prominence in the West, Spivak attempts neither to dialogue with Anglo-European culture nor to support the project of postmodern/postcolonial studies without qualification. In an ambitious move, she questions the entire project of capitalist globalization from a transnational and transdisciplinary perspective. Her work shatters existing conceptual frameworks, even the concept of postcolonial studies that she had previously helped to develop. As its cover notes, the book "ranges from Kant's analytic of the sublime to child labor in Bangladesh." The work is meticulously researched, as one can detect in the use of footnotes that often extend the main text's literary discussion to socioeconomic contexts. Spivak takes deconstruction beyond Derrida and Marxism well beyond Marx as she challenges the New World economic order whose object is the globalization of finance capital: "Privatization is the kingpin of economic restructuring for globalization."[19] The cost of development, she claims, is the loss of social redistribution projects that the nation-state was expected to undertake in the period prior to the collapse of the Soviet Union. "In the post-Soviet world . . . it is now more than ever impossible for the new or developing states . . . to escape the orthodox constraints of a 'neo-liberal' world economic system that, in the name of Development, and now, 'sustainable development,' removes all barriers between itself and fragile national economies, so that any possibilities of social redistribution are severely damaged."[20] Linked to this situation of economic cutbacks on the part of developing nations, the pressure to migrate to the developed world accelerates. Thus a whole sector of diasporic migrants become invested, according to Spivak, in the future of Eurocentrism. "'The new diaspora,' the new scattering of the seeds of 'developing' nations so that they can take root on developed ground, means: Eurocentric migration, labor export both male and female, border crossings, the seeking of political asylum, and the haunting-in-lace uprooting of 'comfort women' in Asia and Africa."[21] Regarding the new diaspora consisting of the intelligentsia from developing countries, Spivak is skeptical of the enthusiasm with which they have received the advent of postcolonial studies. "I will risk a generalization here. Elite 'postcolonialism' seems to be as much a strategy of differentiating oneself from the racial underclass as it is to speak in its name."[22]

I have come full circle in my excursion into the topic of Continental philosophy and postcolonial subjects. I began by decrying the absence of a consciousness of postcoloniality in much, though not all, of the discipline. I made reference to the pressure, often exerted by conservative peers and by students, to maintain an aura of Eurocentric affiliation as one engages in the teaching or scholarly production of Continental philosophy. Yet it is a fact that to do so somehow constitutes an epistemic violation, if not of our own experience as natives of the world's nondominant cultures, at least of the subaltern populations whose ways of thinking or struggles for justice may be silenced by the conceptual frameworks and methodologies on which we rely professionally. To be sure, there have been, and in all likelihood will continue to be, innumerable valuable aspects and contributions of Continental philosophy and of European culture to a life of knowledge and to the struggle for social justice. My intent is not to eradicate Continental philosophy but to expand and diversify its scope in response to the challenges posed by non-Western and Southern Hemisphere voices. The postcolonial writers I have mentioned engage with a multiplicity of aspects of Western culture, which is not only Europe's or North America's, but which is assimilated to various degrees by anyone subject to its impact around the world. In this regard, I think that assuming a hybrid perspective on postcolonial subjectivity is a healthier practice than is that of trying to establish oneself as a self-nominated official reader of European texts from the so-called periphery. Indeed, I fully sympathize with Spivak's depiction of "elite 'postcolonialism.'" It would be more appropriate to say that the postcolonial label should strictly refer to whatever invokes a critical memory of colonialism and its sequels. Such political practices have included the exploitation of the majority of the world's women with a clear conscience. However, the stipulative definition of postcolonialism that I have invoked is often overlooked in practice. Terms such as "postcolonial" and "diasporic" have become fashionable; they are appropriated for any number of uses. The "post" in "postcolonial" is used at times in order to forgo the critical sense, while "diasporic" can easily refer to those who seek to distance themselves from racialized or politically and economically discredited locations in today's global economy.

In sum, I have proposed to retake Nietzsche's perspectival project of a critical history of the world in which, for better or worse, we live. In contrast to Nietzsche, however, my kind of critical history is one whose identity need not depend on monumental history for its higher model and complement. Realizing that the concept of the monumental and of greatness itself has been colored by our historical biases (and noting the larger biases that can result when the aura of national power and wealth prevents us from attending as much as we should to such biases), I embrace a critical reading of history, and of texts in general, in order to gain freedom from multiple oppressions. This standpoint also requires an ethical project large enough to include such still-to-be-attained ideals as gender equity, economic opportunities for the disadvantaged, and the conservation of global ecosystems. To the extent that the voices of difference are heard in Continental thought, it is hoped, we will grow wiser in the theorizing and practice of philosophy.

NOTES

1. In the Eurocentric perspective, the connection between European thought and the essence of civilization may be considered either a contingent or an essential matter. My criticism is directed at the effects of either position on Continental philosophy.
2. Jean-Paul Sartre, *Sartre on Cuba* (New York: Ballantine Books, 1961), 81.
3. Ibid.
4. Ibid.
5. Jean-Paul Sartre, *Anti-Semite and Jew* (New York: Schocken Books, 1948), 13.
6. Jean-Paul Sartre, *Critique of Dialectical Reason* (London: NLB, 1976), 54.
7. Ibid.
8. Ibid.
9. Friedrich Nietzsche, "On the Uses and Disadvantages of History for Life," in F. Nietzsche, *Untimely Meditations*, trans. R. J. Hollingdale (Cambridge: Cambridge University Press, 1983), 67.
10. Ibid., 75–76.
11. Ibid., 69.
12. I call Nietzsche's perspectivalism "incipient" here insofar as he did not develop this concept until his later writings.
13. Nietzsche, "On the Uses," 66.
14. Frantz Fanon, *Black Skins, White Masks* (New York: Grove, 1967), 216–222 and 225.
15. Gayatri Spivak, *A Critique of Postcolonial Reason* (Cambridge, Mass.: Harvard University Press), 414.
16. Paulo Freire, *Pedagogy of the Oppressed* (New York: Continuum, 1993), 59.

17. Ibid., 69.
18. Homi Bhabha, *The Location of Culture* (New York: Routledge, 1994), 152.
19. Spivak, *A Critique of Postcolonial Reason*, 357.
20. Ibid.
21. Ibid.
22. Ibid., 358.

Part 4.
(Re)Discovering the Political and Ethical in History

8. On the Rights of Indigenous Peoples: The Case of Chiapas

MARÍA HERRERA LIMA

As a result of the Indian rebellion in Chiapas—or rather, one might say, as one of the achievements of the Chiapas Indians as a social movement—the debate over Indian rights has been firmly introduced into the political agenda of Mexico, in spite of political shifts and the fact that this debate has been overshadowed by more urgent concerns. Of course, it is not possible to give any final assessment of these problems, since they are changing constantly—so the possibilities of political or legal arrangements are still quite open—but it is nevertheless, in the context of the development of these problems that I want to consider some implications for political and moral theory of the idea of indigenous rights.

I will attempt to bring together two potentially controversial proposals: on the one hand is respect for cultural differences and a defense of special legal protections and guarantees for indigenous peoples in the country, justified as a remedy to past and present injustices. On the other are arguments for restrictions on the possible forms of self-government of these communities from the perspective of the principles of a constitutional democracy and a human-rights political culture.

I

The Indian rebellion in Chiapas has presented a challenge to the Mexican state at a time of transition toward democratic institutions (more credible and freer elections, political reform, and so on). This challenge is two-sided: on the one hand, the state has to justify itself to a more demanding and politically diversified domestic public opinion; on the other, because of the globalization of information and a generalized human-rights culture, the state's actions are also open to international scrutiny and criticism in ways unknown in the past.

Chiapas represents an anomalous case in the Mexican nation-state in many ways:[1] it has not had regular elections until very recently (instead, it has had a succession of substitute governors), and its political officials and local government posts exhibit a peculiar lack of independence with respect to the powerful landed oligarchy. The effects of agrarian reform in post-revolutionary Mexico were minimal in Chiapas, and the policy of linguistic assimilation of the Indians (*indigenismo*) as a tool for their gradual incorporation into the Mexican nation, through the introduction of bilingual rural teachers, was either reduced to a system for getting laborers for coffee plantations and cattle ranches, or opposed from the perspective of a conservative conception of the separation of ethnic groups. On the other hand, Chiapas also has one of the longest traditions of Indian resistance in Mexican history; in recent times, rebel groups have been present in the state since the seventies.[2] The government had known of the Zapatista rebellion since at least 1993, but it was not made public so as not to endanger the signing of the NAFTA treaty. From the beginning, the Zapatistas included in their demands not just "cultural" rights (which were already more or less contemplated in the Constitution and in local legislation in some states) but also economic rights and a concern about the anti-communal measures and privatization policies adopted by recent governments.

In spite of the fact that many proposals for legislation on these matters were discussed, only one of which—the one presented by the COCOPA (the official Commission for Peace and Reconciliation)—was consistent with the signed San Andrés agreements,[3] the one that was finally approved was an initiative of the executive branch. It amounts to a recognition of cultural rights and of the existence of indigenous groups within the nation, and it includes some welcomed provisions against discrimination (in any form), but it lacks any effective guarantee for the fulfillment of these newly recognized rights.

In the years before the presidential elections of 2000, the conflict was transformed into a situation of war, with thousands of displaced people (from eleven thousand to fourteen thousand, depending on the source), an overwhelming army presence that disrupted civilian life and interrupted agricultural work. There was a constant climate of violence caused by the growing number of armed civilian (or paramilitary) groups, which in fact, with the complicity of local and state authorities and financial support from landowners, formed a significant counter-revolutionary force that at times outnumbered the Zapatista rebels in weapons, equipment, and resources. This has changed somewhat with the new government (at the local level, a coalition of opposition parties) so some of the displaced people are beginning to return to their towns and political tensions are not as strong, but the main problems remain unsolved.

If one were to follow the logic of the past government's attempt to redefine the conflict as a simple case of insurrection that could therefore be solved by military force, why is it that this could not be done? A plausible answer is that these successive redefinitions of the Indian rebellion as, among other things, an inter-ethnic conflict, local disputes over land, or religious conflicts between Catholics and some of the Protestant groups—the evangelical church—or the characterization of the Zapatistas simply as masked guerrillas have not succeeded. This is because there is a symptomatic lack of confidence in this type of official rhetoric, and also because presenting the Zapatistas as terrorists is not supported by the facts, since their use of violence has been minimal, rather symbolic, and a way to get attention for their cause. And they continue to enjoy the support of civilian organizations and of a significant segment of public opinion, nationally and internationally.

So, in spite of the urgency of other problems, the question of Indian rights has not disappeared from public debates. If one thing is now clear, it is that peace will not be achieved unless there is recognition of the nature of the conflict—and as a consequence, an acknowledgment that the question of indigenous rights will profoundly affect power relations among the local elites, and between these groups and political parties. What makes the Zapatistas' rebellion different from previous demands by other Indian groups in Mexico is that they want to remain independent from political parties (including the left), and the form of self-administration that they are demanding is not restricted to "cultural" rights. They include what we may call, following Henry Shue, "basic rights" (subsistence and security),[4] and they are presenting these as demands to the state; they are not separatist, but they want political autonomy within the nation-state. In addition, in the San Andrés agreements the Zapatistas committed themselves to respecting human rights, especially those of women. This means that they are not as vulnerable to the usual objections that, for instance, they are not interested in respecting and upholding the gains of political liberalism.

Why is it, then, that the Zapatistas are perceived as a threat by local and central governments? After all, in the past they were largely ignored as they continued practicing their traditions and local forms of self-government, and as recently as 1998, some legislation on Indian rights—which was as radical, in some ways, as that proposed in Chiapas—was approved at the state level in Oaxaca. One might say, with Michael Walzer, that "toleration fails when the others look dangerous,"[5] and the danger here comes from the fact that these demands are presented not as grievances, resolutions for local conflicts, or calls for development aid and the like, but as demands that claim generalized validity for and implicitly reformulate the social contract with indigenous peoples in the Mexican nation-state.

This perhaps explains the reluctance on the part of the previous governments to continue the dialogue with the rebels that they had accepted and even promoted in the beginning, and the regressive character of the new law for indigenous peoples recently approved by the Senate (2001). The government could accept Indian communities and their ways as "private-collectives" (Walzer) but not as "public-collectives," so they could not be allowed "to organize autonomously and exercise jurisdiction over their fellows," as Walzer says about regimes of toleration[6]—and, I might add, they could not be expected to have privileged access to natural resources in virgin land that is potentially rich and attractive to foreign investors in the global market economy.

However, even if we can explain the reluctance to grant special rights to Indian communities, for it is indeed a thorny issue considering that there are other social groups in need of assistance in the country, what cannot be justified and is entirely at odds with the process of democratic changes in the country is the strategy of counter-revolutionary war against those communities and violations of the human rights of displaced people. After dialogue with the rebels was interrupted and the government failed to comply with the signed San Andrés agreements and with the new national legislation, it has become clear that the central government is refusing to grant legitimacy to the Indian cause, so there is no longer much room for a discussion on autonomy. Consequently, the conflict is reduced to a question of economic development to be decided by the logic of the market, without local participation in decision-making processes, and the "Indian question" becomes, once again, a matter of assimilation for the federal government. These changes in public perception have had an effect on the debates; there is a certain feeling of frustration among politicians and business people, who see the rebellion as simply an irritation, an obstacle to be overcome by military means (openly or covertly), and it has forced even the local conservative elites to accept some readjustments in power relations and the need for economic change in the region.

But all of this makes the situation of the Indians more critical, as they are increasingly divided among themselves (those who accept government aid in exchange for opposition to the rebels, and divisions among dissident religious groups), while it seems that no peace can be achieved unless some form of legislation on Indian rights is proposed and accepted by all groups—which is not the case with the new law. There is, however, continued controversy among legislators on the question of possible revisions, so the debate must go on.

II

Now, I will look at the ways in which the question of indigenous rights can be conceptualized. Indigenous rights have been characterized in several ways, including as civil and political rights of previously neglected peoples, as legal protection from external threats (landowners as abusive employers, intolerant neighbors), and as a legitimate demand to the state for survival. There may also be rights to protection *from* the state, as an instance of negative liberties, directed against forced assimilation. Both types of rights require special attention from and impose special duties on the state. In addition, in the Mexican case, these rights are now regarded as constituting a condition of democratic legitimacy for the nation-state, for the Indians were excluded from the founding political pacts of the Republic, even after their rhetorical inclusion in post-revolutionary Mexico.

Cultural rights can be understood as forms of toleration that can be accommodated within the legal framework of liberal democracies, or as legal protections for traditional ways of life that go beyond what is usually accepted in Western democracies. In the latter case, they can also be considered historical rights, or rights of restitution that apply to colonized peoples who were conquered by force.

In a more radical version, indigenous rights go beyond toleration of cultural differences and become a demand for self-government or some form of political autonomy. This is seen as an attempt to reach a form of inclusive political agreement within the nation-state by previously excluded communities. According to Will Kymlicka, we must distinguish individual rights, first, from the rights of other minorities and "stateless nations" (such as the Basques in Spain or the Québécois in Canada).[7] Even if indigenous peoples share with other national minorities a resistance to "nation-building policies" (imposition of the language and other traits of the dominant culture) and may fight for some form of self-government, they differ from other groups in that they can make an appeal based not only on their unjust incorporation into the state, but also on the fact that their cultural differences are more radical, and for that reason their marginal status and social disadvantages are greater than in the other cases. Although there is some overlapping between these two kinds of ethnic minorities, there is now a tendency in international law to consider them as distinct groups, because, as Kymlicka says, "Stateless nations would have liked to form their own states, but lost in the struggle for political power, whereas indigenous peoples existed outside the system of European states."[8]

In terms of existing international law, there are two options for indigenous minorities; however, these are either too weak or too strong to provide an adequate response to their needs. They are, respectively, Article 1 of the United Nations Charter, which states the right to self-determination, and Article 27 of the International Covenant on Civil and Political Rights, which has to do with cultural rights. Most indigenous peoples are not separatist—they do not want to form their own state—but nor are they satisfied with the reduction of their claims to a more or less arbitrarily defined gray area of "cultural" practices. For that reason, in Kymlicka's words, "Most national minorities need something in-between, and recent developments in international law regarding minority rights are precisely an attempt to codify certain standards in between articles 1 and 27."[9]

This is certainly not an easy task for many reasons. To begin with, it is not very clear what autonomy status may imply in terms of the relationship of indigenous peoples to the nation-state. On the one hand, there are demands for economic assistance and services, in the Mexican case, to aspire to be at the same general level of welfare as are all other Mexican citizens—so they require an active role from the state and not merely negative rights of non-interference—but, on the other hand, they want to be exempted from the laws of the nation in many important respects, as well as to enjoy special protections and privileges. As has been the case in other countries, this is further complicated by the problem of the criteria for inclusion in these groups, especially when there are no clear territorial limits for the traditional communities. All of this still needs to be worked out with greater precision, but assuming that some form of local self-government that is not in contradiction with constitutional principles can be found, it would have to be a new political arrangement at the national level. However, this new social contract would have to take the form of some "constitutionally mixed regime" or, in Charles Taylor's words, an "asymmetrical federalism,"[10] since these communities are not just one among many minority groups, they are not part of the Western liberal tradition; thus, their inclusion presents a different set of problems.

Defending the possibility of preserving cultural differences that include forms of local self-government and restrictions to individuals subjected to communal rule compels us to look for the kind of autonomy that could be seen as compatible with the fundamental principles of a constitutional democracy. The most serious objection to the idea of indigenous self-determination comes from its potential incompatibility with the principle of impartiality under the law, as well as from possible human-rights violations inflicted on some members of these traditional communities.

In connection with this argument, Michael Walzer discusses the problem of aboriginal peoples (in the case of Canada) as one of the complicated issues for regimes of toleration. For Walzer, "It isn't at all clear that their way of life can be sustained, even under conditions of autonomy, within liberal limits: it isn't historically a liberal way of life." The problem that he is addressing here is that of potentially intolerant practices, or of important discrepancies with civil rights and liberties. He asks regarding these non-liberal communities, Can they be tolerated as autonomous communities with coercive authority over their members?[11]

This is indeed a serious problem. In the case of indigenous groups in Mexico, there have already been instances of questionable practices, such as religious intolerance between Catholic and Protestant communities in Chiapas, and disputes over public services and facilities elsewhere. In one case, in the central area of the country (the town of Ixmiquilpan), politically dominant groups attempted to impose forced communal work for their church, denying access to municipal services, such as roads, water, and the town's cemetery, to the members of a religious minority living in the town. In this case, ethnic or cultural differences were not the issue—it was a mixture of politics and religion—but in any case municipal authorities invoked "traditional customs" (*usos y costumbres*) in their defense.

To Walzer, this would be sufficient reason to deny special protections to aboriginal peoples, since in the case he is discussing, they are Canadian citizens, so their communal authority must be limited by the higher laws of the country. He nevertheless accepts that these peoples are different from other religious or ethnic minorities: "Because of their conquest and long subordination, the Aboriginal peoples are given, and should be given, more legal and political room to organize and enact their ancient culture."[12] In spite of his recognition of old grievances that justify special treatment, this in fact amounts to a restriction of indigenous rights to cultural rights, or to those practices that can be assimilated into one of the existing liberal provisions—such as that of voluntary associations—or to other practices that may be seen as part of the exercise of private choices, or as non-harmful social (collective) activities. Most liberals would agree with this restriction, for in this way it would seem that the risk of violations to civil liberties and equal rights of citizens are avoided. This is, no doubt, something that should be part of the agenda of reasonable political pluralism, or of any multicultural regime, but it is not clear that this restriction—of indigenous rights to cultural practices—does justice either to the indigenous peoples' historical claims of restitution or to their present demands for social and political justice. This is not to say, of course, that granting special status of autonomy to some people within a nation-state may not have unintended undesirable effects. So, in case of the acceptance of such a regime, it would be reasonable to ask as well for some legal provisions to prevent abuses of minorities—indigenous peoples do not constitute a homogeneous, monolithic community—and special forms of arbitration for the resolution of conflicts among different groups.

However, we must also take into account the fact that so-called cultural rights are not so easily distinguishable from other practices that may not be regarded as acceptable—as exemplified in the above-mentioned cases in Mexico—so the restriction proposed by liberals (and assumed in the recently approved law in Mexico) is not a good solution after all. In addition, considering indigenous peoples simply to be regular citizens only masks the conditions of extreme inequality and social disadvantage in which they actually live.

This is consistent with the explicit declarations of leaders of the indigenous movement in Mexico, who have insisted that toleration is not enough. Solving security problems and eliminating extreme forms of intolerance, while necessary, is not sufficient to meet their demands for justice. We might say that these demands have to do mainly with two issues: that of public recognition, and a solution to their precarious conditions of material existence. The first has to do with the idea of a new social pact (or contract) with the nation-state; the second, with welfare demands that are not exclusive to these communities.

1. Historical Rights and the New Social Pact

The idea of a social contract has had enormous symbolic power in the political imaginary as the source of legitimate authority of the state. For liberal theory, the founding moment of the state must include an implicit agreement among the actors involved, in the form of a rational compromise, a "pact" of self-restraint and submission to a political ruler, or a voluntary "contract" in which the parties agree under conditions of equality to submit themselves to a common social order sanctioned by law. In contrast, when none of these conditions has been met historically, we have found a situation of at least potentially contested legitimacy.

Historical rights, as a sort of continuity right, are one of the oldest forms of claims over land, as well as an implicit questioning of the violence of conquest and appropriation of foreign lands by force. These rights can be stated as a morally justified demand, although they have seldom been recognized as such. We could point to cases of reparations or compensations—as in some cases of war—elsewhere, but this demand has never been accepted as valid by any Mexican postcolonial government. So, "historical" rights had to be rephrased as "traditional" rights, placing the blame for the conquest of indigenous lands in the remote past of an overthrown colonial regime. In the present context, they are seen, rather, as a de facto acceptance of cultural difference within Mexico; in turn, the existence of such radical differences is seen by some Mexicans as a failure of assimilation—this was until recently the official position—and by others, now a larger group, as justified demands that require legal codification. In part, what the Zapatistas achieved was a process of cultural "translation": to present in the language of rights their traditional beliefs about justice. In this way, their claims gained force and legitimacy as "rights," since a right, as Henry Shue remarks, is not merely a request, a plea, or a petition; it is, rather, "something that can be demanded or insisted upon without embarrassment or shame."[13] For Indian groups in Mexico, this could mean to go from asking for "gifts and favors," in Shue's words, to a position of power and recovered dignity. This is something of great value for these communities; in fact, they have not emphasized as much the idea of restitution as that of public recognition. In the San Andrés agreements the figure of *"entidades de derecho público"* (to be given a legal status as "peoples" with authority to negotiate with the state) was proposed, but in the end what was adopted was the weaker figure of *"entidades de interés público"* (public-interest groups or communities), which has no legal force. In a sense, we can say, following Shue, that these are not truly rights, for the proclamation of a right is not sufficient: it is not the fulfillment of the right, it may be at times only a promise "in the place of the fulfillment."[14]

So, even if restitution is not a possibility in the Mexican context, and the need for new legislation still has to be addressed, the idea of historical rights should be preserved as a part of a "politics of memory" that can be very important for a critical reconstruction of a national history.[15] To understand the Indian groups' contemporary demands as justified because of past injustices may contribute to creating a more favorable climate of public opinion for the solution of their problems, as well as to improving inter-ethnic relations in the country.

2. General Welfare Demands

From the perspective of those "basic rights" (subsistence and security) that Henry Shue considers the "moral minimums" that must be guaranteed by any democratic regime, and "whose possession is essential to the enjoyment of other rights"[16]—such as physical security and minimum conditions for a dignified existence—the moral deficit as things stand now with indigenous groups in Mexico falls on the side of the nation-state. The following quotation by Shue could easily be seen as a description of the situation of Indians in Chiapas: "To be more likely than other people to suffer forms of abuse—by the police or the army, or other members of privileged groups in a society."[17] Indians do not enjoy the same opportunities for free assembly or forms of self-organization as do the rest of Mexican citizens. For example, the schools and public libraries in Chiapas, small and modest community centers built with the help of civilian groups and international organizations, have been destroyed by the army; these actions can hardly be justified as acts of war. There are other cases of abuse of authority in Mexico, mostly in rural areas; although not all the groups affected are indigenous peoples, they can still be considered the most vulnerable social group. Thus, the first task in order for the Mexican state to be minimally consistent with its proclaimed liberal credo will have to be facing and correcting these abuses; for that, a change in power relations will have to take place. So, a plausible argument could be made in favor of a form of political autonomy for these communities as the only way to effectively change the balance of power and thus create the conditions for fair inter-ethnic relations.

This is also the case with "subsistence rights," or second-generation human rights. Poverty, a problem that affects groups and not only individuals, is an effect of social relations and of the unequal distribution of power and resources; it cannot be solved unless those conditions are altered, as is evidenced by the failure of governmental aid and anti-poverty programs. It is not something that can be solved by administrative means. In fact, the monumental failure of one such program (Pronasol) prepared the way for the Indian uprising in Chiapas. The problem of poverty is not exclusive to the Indians; it also affects other peasant communities and the urban proletariat—who may be part Indian—but the Indians have suffered more extensive forms of systematic abuse because these are also related to forms of cultural and racial discrimination.

In connection with this issue, I could mention the UN optional protocol on civil and political rights (1976) and the International Convention on the Elimination of All Forms of Racial Discrimination, in force since 1969. In accordance with this text, the systematic violation of the human rights of Indians in Mexico can be seen as a form of racial discrimination. This can be shown in a reconstruction of their condition from colonial times (when they were considered "minors" incapable of owning land or signing contracts) to the various redefinitions in postcolonial republican regimes, to the present day, when formal equality in the Mexican constitution is not matched by an actual recognition of their equal status as members of the polity.

It is clear that when we defend the inclusion of all the different groups in a nation-state—be that difference ethnic, religious, or other—under the protection of constitutional rule, we do so by appealing to a conception of equality that can be regarded as just by all. However, from the perspective of constitutional law, this may involve different, and even divergent, conceptions of equality. In the debate over Michael Walzer's conception of "complex equality," David Miller observes that there is no single conception of equality, not even of "simple" equality: if it is defined as the "equal possession of advantage X . . . there are as many notions of simple equality as there are possible contenders for the X in this formula: candidates include property, income, opportunity, rights, resources, capacities, and welfare."[18] Rather, the most serious problem with the idea of simple equality is the reduction of the core idea of equality to any single good, because it would not be possible to realize it empirically without the possession of some of the other goods in the above list. In other words, the interdependence or mutual imbrications of ideas of freedom with at least minimal conditions of material welfare, and of these, in turn, with opportunities and skills and the like, means that the debate cannot be decided in favor of any of these once we think of them as "goods" or, in Miller's terms, as "actual possessions" and not only as principles.[19]

Thus, the debate in political philosophy, as Miller says, is often expressed as, Equality of what? As a matter of principle? Or as a condition to achieve certain goals (freedom) or to have access to certain goods (welfare)? As we know, in most societies, and especially in multicultural or pluri-ethnic ones (following Kymlicka's distinction), we start with conditions of extreme inequality, and the challenge is that of achieving minimum conditions of distributive justice without compromising individual freedom or sacrificing cultural differences. In the case of multicultural societies, the debate has to go beyond the limits of the problem discussed by Walzer, because the problem is not only that some social goods (say, money or power) dominate over others, leading to conditions of inequality (in violation of relevant criteria for distribution), but that some social actors are not participants in the game of distribution at all. Walzer, to be sure, argues in favor of fair distribution of political power, but at the same time he understands equality as equal citizenship. For the reasons expressed above, this does not seem an adequate solution to the problems of economic and cultural segregation of indigenous peoples.

Some other solutions, such as the one proposed by Joseph Raz, seem more amenable as a conception of distributive justice for these types of societies. As reported by David Miller, Raz "argues that many so-called principles of equality are better construed as principles of entitlement [that is, as] principles asserting that everyone has a right to a certain level of X."[20] The notion of entitlement fits well with the language of traditional communities, and it is indeed used this way by members of indigenous communities in expressions such as "indigenous rights." These are understood as the conditions required for a life worth living, not just as economic conditions, but as the enjoyment of social respect for their persons and communities and for their traditional ways of life. It would not be too difficult to maintain that any social arrangement or political "pact" between culturally different social groups presupposes some form of "complex equality."

III

What, then, may be the sort of political and legal arrangement that can meet both conditions—first, respect for a human-rights culture and equality under the law (even as some version of functional or complex equality) and second, sufficient guarantees for respecting cultural differences, and an answer to the legitimate welfare demands of indigenous peoples and other vulnerable groups? These two types of demands are not easily distinguishable in practice, and they are frequently a source of conflict. Depending on the reasons given to justify demands for special rights we find different underlying conceptions of rights, in both nature and scope. One possible way of understanding special rights may be a version of what Kymlicka calls "remedial" rights—that is, legal protections aimed at correcting past abuses, or as some form of restitution that is, nevertheless, temporary, for it would cease to be required when conditions of equality (welfare) are achieved. These are sometimes called "transitional" rights; from this perspective, forms of territorial autonomy or privileged access to natural resources would not seem justified. This is in fact the position of conservative political parties in Mexico. If, on the other hand, we accept the need to grant some special legal protections to indigenous peoples as historically and morally justified, we will have to find some legal formulas that could, at the same time, meet the previously stated conditions of respect for basic freedoms.

In other words, we have to confront the problem of equality versus difference in some way other than the usual irreconcilable opposition. To do this, we have to see our constitutions as historical agreements that can be revised, and as social pacts that can be broken. The Italian jurist Luigi Ferrajoli states that a broken or a nonexistent pact amounts in fact to a return to a "state of nature,"[21] a form of political violence that may justify forms of political resistance, as was accepted, for example, in the Universal Declaration of 1789. When violence comes from those who have been excluded from protection under the laws of the country, a reworking of the national "pact" in the form of a constitutional reform may be in order. We cannot consider Ferrajoli's argument in detail here, but a few remarks on his proposal may suggest some interesting possibilities for the solution of problems of excluded minorities.

An important innovation of modern constitutional democracies that affects the very structure of the legal institution consists in the establishment of juridical limitations to legislative production—that is, "the juridical regulation of positive law itself."[22] For Ferrajoli, this affects not only the form or procedures of legislation, but also the content of what is produced. So, some substantive content is added to the procedural program in the form of binding principles and values embodied in the constitution. What is of special importance for Ferrajoli is that this requires the establishment of legal guarantees that must be satisfied. He is a critic both of legal positivism and of some versions of procedural justice in legal theory, for he wants to maintain a strong internal connection between formal and substantive aspects of rights, something that, in turn, has important consequences for the theory of democracy. To him, this means that in addition to negative limits generated by the right to freedom of individuals, democracy also gives rise to positive duties—social rights—that require guarantees for their fulfillment. These should take the form of constitutionally binding political agreements.[23] In addition, these principles establish the limits of that which is no longer the object of negotiations and is thus subtracted from the logic of the market. For Ferrajoli, these constitute the sphere of "fundamental rights" that comprises negative freedoms as well as basic social rights, in a way consistent with Henry Shue's mentioned above. As for the role of legal guarantees, Ferrajoli says that these are none other than legal provisions designed to reduce the structural distance between normativity and effectiveness, adding to the usual protections of liberal freedoms, a chapter of social rights with the rank of constitutional duties. Beyond the debate between formal versus substantive conceptions of democracy, what is interesting for us now is that

the question of the compatibility between negative liberties and positive duties of
the state (with the possibility of special rights) has to be worked out at the level
of constitutional principles and rules, and not only as political negotiations. There
are also questions of normative validity and justice.[24] For example, if subsistence
and security (Shue) were included in the chapter of fundamental rights (Ferrajoli),
to protect them would become a question of justice, a duty for the state, rather
than a question of political compromise. However, Ferrajoli accepts that this is
only a (perhaps utopian) proposal; in our times, this is indeed a political question
rather than something to be solved by the theory of rights.

Nevertheless, this is an area in need of work as well, so Ferrajoli offers a theory
of legal guarantees that introduces a distinction between "fundamental" and "patrimonial" rights, seeing the first as "the law of the weaker" and as an alternative
to the "law of the strongest" that is at work in the absence of substantive justice.
In turn, the absence of this distinction can be explained by the history of liberal
theory, according to Ferrajoli: the intermingling of heterogeneous categories, such
as freedom on the one side and property rights on the other, responds to an early
juxtaposition of natural right doctrines against the Roman civil law tradition. This
has marked, to our day, the entire liberal theory of rights, and shaped the conception of the modern constitutional state.[25] Fundamental rights (life, personal freedom, participation in public decisions) are universal in a way that patrimonial
rights cannot be; that is, the latter affect subjects in differentiated ways, and they
can be alienated, whereas the former cannot be renounced or taken away under
any circumstances. This categorical confusion has also influenced debates in political theory and philosophy; thus, we have on the liberal side a conflation of
democracy and the market, and on the side of former Marxist critics (and some
contemporary left positions) an unfortunate rejection of private property together
with civil liberties and moral universalism.

Fundamental rights set limits to the state but also to the exercise of popular sovereignty, since not even majority rule could decide over those matters. To Ferrajoli, "No political majority could dispose of fundamental freedoms and rights."[26]
So, in the case of indigenous peoples this would also be binding; we might say that
these fundamental rights are a "condition of entry" to the political pact as members of a constitutional state. They are not negotiable in the way that almost anything else can be.

This could be argued in defense of the possibility of criticizing a culture that is
not our own—avoiding the standard suspicion of cultural imperialism—for this
entrance into a new political agreement with the nation-state implies access to
rights as well as *voluntary* acceptance of duties on both sides.

In addition, those who demand the acceptance of conditions (respect for
human rights and basic freedoms) must pass an additional legitimacy "test." That
is, in order to consider the imposition of requisites that are foreign to the other
culture as legitimate, it must be demonstrated that this imposition is not to the advantage of those who dictate them (be that the state, or legislative bodies, or the
critics of non-Western cultures). There should be no hidden "agenda" of domina-

tion in their motives, and the only way to prove that would be to open these decisions to public scrutiny. There are no guarantees for this process, to be sure, but it seems that some conception of public morality as "protection" is urgent in our globalized world; in Henry Shue's words, public justice has to be, among other things, "an attempt by the powerless to restrain the powerful."[27] In addition, international (or transnational) institutions must be designed so as to secure conditions for fair arbitration—under common, binding rules—in cases of conflict, and at the nation-state level, to assure governance.

From the perspective of the public policies of Mexican government, the obvious contradiction rests in their appeal to a global market economy while at the same time they attempt to contain the flow of information and the political effects of globalization. Just as liberals ask about the limits of what can be permitted to non-Western peoples living in a constitutional democracy, we can also ask, What are the limits for the legitimate use of violence against traditional communities in a democratic regime? Is political stability sufficient justification to induce forced assimilation? Or does it condemn these peoples to extinction? All these possible outcomes are the end result of human decisions and government policies, not, as some would like it, merely "natural catastrophes" of the era.

So in the final analysis, if we see the question of indigenous rights as a problem of the legitimacy of post-colonial regimes and as an unresolved self-contradiction of the professed egalitarian ideals of liberal justice, the question becomes part of the struggle for decolonization, and as such, it does not have to be set in opposition to ideals of freedom and equality—although, admittedly, these will have to search for new formulations, or inter-cultural translations.

There would be a need as well for undertaking historical reconstructions from the perspective of all the people in our lands. They are not something external to the linear development of Western civilization, as they are presented in the narratives of official history. They have always been there, and the new simultaneity of our global situation will make it an urgent task to look for new political arrangements for the peaceful coexistence of different peoples and forms of fairer distribution of world resources.

Finally, it is interesting to point out that the Zapatista movement differs from other rebel groups in that it professes an ideology of nonviolence and has made the language of human rights its own. In the first stages of the movement, when there was more active participation by Mexican civilian groups, there was also what we may call an intensive process of mutual learning. Among the most striking results of this process was the change in attitudes toward women—mostly by the women themselves, of course, but also by the leadership of the movement, which has included women since then, and has become more open to discussion of equal rights and other issues within Indian communities. So we must not think about the question of cultural rights always as a problem of incompatible or incommensurable belief systems. Learning is possible when actual dialogue takes place and the conditions of political negotiation are perceived as fair by all social actors involved.

NOTES

1. For historical information on the region, see Antonio García de León, *Resistencia y Utopía* (México: Ediciones Era, 1997). See also Enrique Florescano, *Etnia, Estado y Nación* (Aguilar: Nuevo Siglo, 1996).

2. See Hector Díaz-Polanco, *La Rebelion Zapatista y la Autonomía* (Mexico City: Siglo XXI, 1997). See also Carlos Montemayor, *Chiapas, La Rebelion Indígena de México* (Mexico City: Joaquín Mortiz, 1997).

3. The San Andrés Larráinzar agreements were signed by the Zapatista rebels and representatives of central government in February, 1996. However, they were never implemented as laws.

4. Henry Shue, *Basic Rights: Subsistence, Affluence, and U.S. Foreign Policy* (Princeton, N.J.: Princeton University Press, 1996).

5. Michael Walzer, *On Toleration* (New Haven, Conn.: Yale University Press, 1998), 30.

6. Ibid., 26.

7. Will Kymlicka, *Politics in the Vernacular: Nationalism, Multiculturalism, and Citizenship* (New York: Oxford University Press, 2001), 120.

8. Ibid., 122.

9. Ibid., 123.

10. Quoted in Walzer, *On Toleration*, 46.

11. Ibid.

12. Ibid., 47.

13. Shue, *Basic Rights*, 14–15.

14. Ibid., 15.

15. There are many interesting recent works on this topic in the U.S. See Thomas McCarthy, *"Vergangenheitsbwätigung* in the USA: On Coming to Terms with Slavery and Its Aftermath" (unpublished manuscript).

16. Shue, *Basic Rights*, 19.

17. Ibid., 20–21.

18. David Miller, "Complex Equality," in David Miller and Michael Walzer, eds., *Pluralism, Justice, and Equality* (New York: Oxford University Press, 1995), 197.

19. Ibid., 202.

20. Ibid., 202, n.7. See Also Joseph Raz, *The Morality of Freedom* (New York: Clarendon Press, 1986).

21. For an interesting and extended discussion of these issues, see Luigi Ferrajoli, *Derechos y Garantías: La ley del más débil* (Madrid: Trotta, 1999).

22. Ibid., 19.

23. Ibid., 21–22.

24. It would be important to compare this proposal for a normative theory of law with that of Jürgen Habermas (*Between Facts and Norms: Contributions to a Discourse Theory of Law and Democracy* [Cambridge, Mass.: MIT Press, 1996]), but this is not attempted in this essay.

25. Ferrajoli, *Derechos y Garantías*, 45 (my translation from the Spanish).

26. Ibid., 51–52.

27. Shue, *Basic Rights*, 18.

9. Democratization in the Context of a Postmodern Culture

NORBERT LECHNER

I. TO CREATE A DEMOCRATIC POLITICAL CULTURE

Political struggle is always also a struggle to define the predominant conception of what is understood as politics. What does it mean to do politics? What is the field of politics? These questions refer us to political culture. This theme, in itself difficult to study, causes greater difficulties in the processes of democratization, where it is a question not merely of the analysis of existing culture(s), but of *creating* a democratic political culture. No matter how superficially we investigate the process of democratization, we can confirm that the genesis of a democratic political culture is one of its central aspects. I would like to refer to a feature not usually considered: the international context.

The importance of the international ideological-cultural environment in political struggles of individual countries is particularly notorious in the case of Latin American societies, whose organization and political development have developed, since the colonial period, under the Iberian and Anglo-Saxon traditions. There are important historical studies with respect to this issue. But the influence of Western political thought is not due solely to an intellectual tradition specific to the "cultural *mestizaje*" of our societies, which have "capitalized" so extensively and intensively that we cannot interpret the national reality without taking recourse to the explanatory categories of capitalism. Both the external setting and the internal dynamic of Latin America are conditioned by the capitalist "logic." However, whoever refers to the state or to classes knows the sui generis character of Latin American reality. Although every theory illuminates some questions and whisks others away, in the case of Latin America the difficulties are even greater. The political conceptions and practices that we elaborate in our countries cannot dispense with the political-ideological debate in the metropolitan centers, but these interpretive schema, in turn, tend to distort our formulations of the problems that we face.

Translated from Norbert Lechner, *Los patios interiores de la democracia. subjetividad y politica* (Santiago: Fondo de Cultura Económica, 1990).

I recall this well-known difficulty in order to evade extremely lineal analysis. Those who start from a "minimal definition" of democracy do not lack good reasons to investigate the factors that favor or hinder, accelerate or slow the development of a democratic regime. In fact, functionalist studies tend to be clearer and more limited. It seems more fruitful to me, however, to take a dialectical approach that broaches jointly the forms of democratization and the historical problems of a given society. I allude to the transformations that have taken place in societies under dictatorship; independently of how we evaluate such transformations, the fact is that one society has become another. The dictatorship is not a mere parenthesis and, consequently, we cannot return to prior forms. But it is neither only nor mainly a matter of considering the new social conditions. Together with ruptures, there are lines of continuity; our countries drag behind them historical problems—for instance, the "national question" or the "social question"—that were further exacerbated by military regimes. From this point of view, authoritarianism belongs to a past cycle and expresses a crisis. Its "solution" demands new forms of conceiving and making politics.

The quest for a new form of doing politics and the elaboration of new conceptions of politics fit into an international context that we could call "postmodern culture." The question is, *To what extent does "postmodern culture" contribute to the generation of a democratic political culture that would be capable of solving the historical problems of our societies?*

Without entering the debate concerning "postmodernity," I would like to point to two elements of the contemporary "cultural climate." *On the one hand, it expresses a process of disenchantment,* in particular the disenchantment of those on the left. They no longer believe in socialism as a predetermined goal or in the working class as a revolutionary subject, and they abhor an omni-comprehensive vision of reality. Intellectually, this presupposes a critique of central aspects of Marxism and, more generally, of a whole political tradition: a philosophy of history, the idea of the subject, the concept of totality. It is a critique that creates distance without aspiring to elaborate an alternative paradigm. This rather expressive character of postmodern culture manifests itself, on the other hand, in *the emergence of a new sensibility.* Noteworthy are two characteristics: first, the vanishing of affects, a chilling of emotions; second, an erosion of historical-critical distance, leveling social life into a new, featureless collage. Although these characteristics are part of a mainly aesthetic sensibility, opposed by other tendencies (an emphasis on subjectivity and, in particular, on authenticity and intimacy, or the role of political-moral fundamentalism), this (primarily youthful) "state of mind" has to be taken into account when rethinking the contemporary meaning of politics.

Put into more general and tentative terms, I believe that I see in postmodern culture the expression of a *crisis of identity.* This crisis reflects the lack or erosion of an articulation of the different aspects of social life that allow the affirmation of a vital common world. For, is disarticulation or, to use a common expression, "structural heterogeneity" not one of the great historical problems of Latin American society? Is the fragmentation of the social fabric not in fact one of the gravest effects of authoritarianism? Even when the problem of identity is a fundamental question in the constitution of the order in Latin America, and is possibly one of the causes of the convulsion in the countries of Europe and North America, the same phenomena enter the equation. This is not the place to explore and contrast the historical roots, the social framework, and the theoretical interpretations in one or another case. Nevertheless, although they involve different disarticulations, these experiences return us to a shared political problem: the elaboration of a framework for collective reference.

Although Latin American societies have to elaborate for themselves a reasonable social identity departing, above all, from their own—heterogeneous—modernity, the postmodern climate is not alien to them. The debate that is developing in Europe and the United States about postmodernity contributes, I believe, to a reflection focusing on the articulation of a new collective order through a democratic political culture. In particular, it directs our attention to two fundamental difficulties. The first is the indeterminacy of political space. Once the political space is no longer seen as a natural and/or immutable realm, there emerges the question of the borders between the political and the non-political. We must then ask ourselves what belongs to politics—and what can be expected from politics. According to how the borders are drawn, which aspects of social life can be articulated in a political identity are established. Second, it draws our attention to the precariousness of time. The politically possible depends on the available time, on our disposition toward time. If we are not able to produce temporal continuities, we are also not able to constitute "collective identities."

II. THE INDETERMINACY OF POLITICAL SPACE

After the thirties, and especially after 1945, Latin American societies went through a process of modernization with contradictory effects.[1] The dynamics of secularization and social marginalization called into question the foundations of the established order, even in countries that seemed to have solved the national and social questions. It is within this frame of reference that I see the "ideological inflation" of the sixties. Responding to a threat of social dissolution and atomization was born the quest for a totalizing vision that would be capable of unifying the social process. Although under different and antagonistic political signs, this quest for an identity followed a similar guideline. Three traits appeared to me to be characteristic.

1. The sacralization of political principles as absolute truth. This implies a double effect: inward, it encourages and consolidates strong collective identities, proper to religious communities. The price of internal cohesion is, outwardly, a rigidity in distinctions, an intransigence in negotiations. Purity fears contamination; the greater the ideological consistency of a group, the greater the tendency to demonize the adversary.

2. The sacralization of the constitutive principles of identities are closely linked with a re-signification of utopia. This is visualized as a factual goal, from which emanates a given "historical necessity." When utopia is identified with a possible future, a great social mobilization is achieved which allows the procurement of "irreversible changes" that would make reality the promised order. It is a matter of an instrumental politics, referred to a predetermined object and, therefore, blind to the production and selection of different options. The perception of the present as "transition" motivates self-denial, sacrificial behavior, and scorns for past achievements.

3. The strength of utopia rests on a notion of totality, not as articulating instance, but as fully realized identity. Divisions between classes and groups, between public and private, between theory and practice, between manual and intellectual labor, and between culture and politics thus appear to be obsolete. The result is a suggestive questioning of established spaces, but also an insecurity concerning social ordering. Instead of elaborating a new system of distinctions, the tendency is to extend a given rationality, belonging to one space, to all of social life: the quest for a totalizing vision leads to a sectarian/totalitarian position.

To complete and summarize the framework that I have outlined, all that is left is to underscore the religious baggage that is implied in this type of politics. All politics implies a theological dimension. But in these cases, in order to compensate for the experiences of radical exclusion and abandonment, the religious moment is accentuated in such a way that politics assumes, at least implicitly, the surrender of the soul. This grants revolutionary politics its mystique; on the other hand, it makes the new authoritarianism (despite the aseptic neo-liberal language) a "crusade of salvation." But this is not a phenomenon specific to Latin America. If we consider the thriving fundamentalism in the United States, we catch a glimpse of the importance of religious motivation (even as "civil religion") in countering the feeling of uncertainty. If uncertainty is a constitutive characteristic of democracy, as some maintain, then the demand for certainty ought to occupy a privileged place in the studies on democratization.

Against this background are profiled the changes that characterize the contemporary democratic climate in South America (I speak of "climate" because we know little about the precise strength of democratic convictions and behavior). From the point of view that interests us, two tendencies stand out in the construction of a democratic political system. First, there is a strong revalorization of secularization. In opposition to the messianism introduced by the revolutionary perspective of the sixties and exacerbated by authoritarianism, secularization today possesses an exclusively positive connotation, without reflection on its destabilizing potential. For democratic consolidation it appears imperative to unlink the legitimacy of truth and re-establish the sphere of the political as a space of negotiation. To establish a climate of transaction, it would be essential to relieve politics of ethical-religious compromises, which have been at the origin of prior intransigence and disproportionate expectations. It is a question, in sum, of "unburdening" an over-burdened politics. This requires not only dismantling the quest for redemption and plenitude, but also a certain withdrawal of commitment to the involved values, motivations, and emotions.

The second tendency points in the same direction: *the call to realism*. Reacting against a "principled" position, a "heroic" view of life, and a messianic approach to the future, politics is now formulated as the "art of the possible." The quest for the politically possible displaces the prior emphasis on the necessary ("historical necessity"), at the same time as it opposes the impossible: neither to repeat a past that proved nonviable nor to claim to realize an unfeasible utopia. Aside from its critical intentions, the invocation of realism is a call to a collective construction of an order. Order is not an objective reality but a social production, and it cannot be the unilateral product of one actor, but has to be undertaken collectively. Hence, the revalorization of institutions and procedures—that is, the precedence of the forms of doing politics over actual content.

Both tendencies seek to restrict the prior spaces of politics, which are considered disproportionate. What would be adequate limits to the political space? This conflict, more latent than explicit, regarding the limits of the space of politics appears to me to be one of the privileged terrains in the genesis of a new political culture. As of now, it has not crystallized more clearly. A first step has been to become aware of the prior politics of the "omnipotence complex" and, therefore, of the specificity of different social spheres. The tension between politics and morality, politics and culture, state and politics, and so on is perceived. These tensions are assumed, but not elaborated (not even caustically) due to a lack of criteria. What does postmodern culture contribute with respect to this issue?

I would like to indicate two phenomena that insinuate a certain contemporaneity between the democratic climate in Latin America and the context of international culture; both phenomena illuminate the difficulties of modern democracy.

The call for a secularization of politics can be based on postmodern culture insofar as this implies a certain dissipation of emotions, favoring "cool" and ironic behavior. In this sense, international "fashion" helps to cool the emotional load of politics, diminishing pressure and, therefore, allowing the political sphere to acquire greater autonomy. Such tendencies probably favor a democratic consolidation in our countries. But this is not why we enter "postmodernity." "Postmodern culture" does not orient a process of secularization; it is its product. More precisely, it is the expression of hyper-secularization. Perhaps we ought to understand postmodernity as a rationalization ex post of a disenchantment—but a mimetic, not reflexive, rationalization. In political terms, "postmodern culture" assumes hyper-secularization in its tendency to sunder the social aspects of value, motivational, and emotional structures. That is, it accepts a liberal vision of politics as "market": an exchange of goods. And what happens with non-exchangeable goods? I refer to human rights, to psychosocial needs with transcendental referents, but also to fears and desires for certitude. I do not see any reflection with respect to this in postmodern culture. On the contrary, its critique of the notion of a subject (without doubt, partly justified) tends to undermine the bases for the rethinking of politics. When it identifies political logic with the market and exchange, the problem of identity cannot be formulated. This problem, however, is one of the major tasks confronting a democratic political culture.

So-called realism also has, at first sight, an affinity with "postmodern culture." Both reject grand gestures and are receptive to the new, to the "street signs," to exploring the political in daily life. Above all, they dedramatize politics. Seen in this way, "postmodern culture" feeds political realism insofar as it offers a new sensibility with respect to the possible; a sensibility that could help to reduce the distance between political programs and people's daily experiences. Instead, I do not see postmodern culture reflecting on the main problem of realism: the criteria for selection. Once the possibilities have been discovered and formulated, which options do we select as the best possible? The debate concerning the possible refers us to the desirable. We need these criteria not only in order to hierarchize possibilities, but also in order to evaluate the effectiveness and success of a political gesture. What I mean is: realism not only looks to what is, but also to what can and ought to be. It demands, then, an anticipation of the future—precisely what is lacking in "postmodern culture." I will return below to the lack of future, but here I anticipate a fundamental aspect: the renunciation of an idea of emancipation. In addition to "postmodern culture's" critique of determinism and its teleological view of history, it abandons all reference to emancipation (whatever its formulation). This abandonment seems to me to be problematic. Apparently, "postmodern culture" liberates itself from Enlightenment illusions; in reality, however, it loses the notion of history and, above all, it loses all capacity to elaborate a horizon of meaning. Now, do the processes of democratization not confront precisely the task of producing a new "sense of order"? Hence the importance of political culture. If we cannot develop a new horizon of meanings, democratic institutionalization will be bereft of any roots: an empty shell.

Summarizing, I believe that the postmodern climate can help us demystify the messianism and religious character of a "culture of militancy," to relativize the centrality of the state, the political party, and politics itself; on the other hand, it introduces to political activity a less rigid *sociability* and a ludic enjoyment. In this sense, it contributes to a reformulation of the limits of politics, although it does not contribute criteria that limit the sphere. On the contrary, it increases the indeterminacy of these limits and, therefore, the conflict around them. This provides the processes of democratization with dynamism, but also with instability.

III. THE PRECARIOUSNESS OF TIME

Today it is almost a commonplace to speak of a "crisis of projects." The sixties and seventies were turned to the future, and therefore had an optimistic perspective not only with respect to the society to be made, but also, and above all, with respect to the capacity to construct a new order. After two decades of failures, that period appears to us today to have been the final, delayed, apogee of the idea of progress. In no country is the failure of the heroic, almost Promethean, vision of development as evident as it is in Chile. Neither the developmentalist politics of Frei, nor the socialist reforms of Allende, nor the neo-liberal measures of Pinochet crystallized a process of sustained and stable social transformation. It is not that there were no changes; there were, many of them radical. But they were—to use historiographical terminology—more events than processes. Even now, and each time in a more dramatic fashion, we experience time as a sequence of happenings, of crossroads, that do not accomplish the crystallization of a "duration"—a structured period of past, present, future. We live in a *continuous present*.

Although less violent, the experience of other countries in the region is not very different. Neither the purported "economic miracle" of the Brazilian military nor the populist reforms of the Peruvian military, nor even the extraordinary resources that petroleum offered to the government of Mexico and Venezuela at one time translated into a consolidated "style." I do not refer only to the already proverbial political instability of the continent. The deep problem is that no experience is able to create, beyond the rhetoric of the moment, a horizon of future. Even countries with a relatively stable social order face a lack of future. There are projections, but no projects. Inasmuch as the present is restricted to a recurring repetition, the future in turn is identified with the "beyond": messianism is the other face of self-absorption.

Perhaps the crisis of projects in Latin America is more noticeable today because this crisis is inserted into an international context that empowers the present as the only available time. This fact is bemoaned by some and celebrated by others. There are those who criticize the lack of a perspective and, thus, of criteria that would allow us to deliberately choose our future; others, instead, praise the liberation from an omnipresent foresight and an ineluctable fate that leaves no space for experimentation, adventure, and gratuitous acts. The fact is that we stand before a time without horizon, whether we speak of a radically open future where "everything is possible" or feel repeatedly trapped by the past.

"Modernity," wrote Baudelaire, "is the transitory, the fugitive, the contingent, the half of art, of which the other half is the eternal and the immutable"[2] In this almost hysterical yearning for the new, the ephemeral, the latest fashion, is expressed a rebellion against the normalizing functions of tradition, but without losing the reference to the past. Only in relation to the past is modernity conceivable; the discovery of what is modern is fed by memory. This tension is broken in "postmodernity." The past is erased, along with the historical distance that put current events in relief. With the condensation of time into a sole present, social life becomes a flat surface, a collage. With both the perspective and the in-depth look thus eliminated, all is equal: *anything goes*. And precisely because everything is possible, every possibility is ephemeral, consumed in an instant.

In this acceleration of time nothing is affirmed; even *identity succumbs to vertigo*. In this sense, I referred to "postmodern culture" as an expression of a crisis of identity. In reality, how can an identity be affirmed in a recurring present? It is not accidental that schizophrenia is evoked as the emblematic figure. The loss of identity that characterizes schizophrenia can be understood as the result of a disarticulated experience in which the different isolated elements, disconnected, discontinuous, are not structured into a coherent sequence. The schizophrenic does not know an "I" because "the schizophrenic . . . does not have our experience of temporal continuity . . . but is condemned to live a perpetual present with which the various moments of his or her past have little connection and for which there is no conceivable future on the horizon."[3] Due to the lack of a sense of identity that endures through time, the schizophrenic not only is no one, but also does nothing. In order to have a sense of identity, the schizophrenic would have to have a project, and this implies a commitment to a certain continuity. When the temporal continuities through which we select and order the different aspects of life are ruptured, our view of the world becomes undifferentiated: an unlimited summation of juxtaposed elements. The schizophrenic does not "filter" the present, and for this reason he has a much more intense experience, but in the end it is overwhelming. He lives intensely in the instant, but at the cost of his petrification. Without putting limits on the present, giving dimensions to it, the schizophrenic drowns himself in an immediacy without depth.

IV. THE CREATIVITY OF POLITICAL CULTURE

Can we derive from the above an elaboration of a democratic political culture in Latin America? We have seen, on the one hand, the difficulties in determining what encompasses a democratic politics, which is space. The identification of politics with the state or the party, or of the political space with the public sphere, is no longer accepted. The cloistering of politics is rejected, but the notion that everything is politics is also not accepted. Social life has been rendered de-centered; however, it requires structuring. It not only demands norms that distinguish the good from the bad, the legal from the prohibited; equally important are criteria that define the possible and the desirable, the legitimate and the rational, the normal and the efficient. On the elaboration of such criteria depends—in form and content—what politics we make. I believe that these criteria are not determined, even in countries where there is agreement on the constitutional "rules of game." These are necessary but not sufficient to limit the sphere of the politically decidable and discernable.

On the other hand, we have seen the precariousness of time. We do not have at our disposal a strong concept of time, capable of structuring the past, present, and future as historical "development," nor do we share commensurate horizons of temporality. Our consciousness of time proves to be extremely volatile, thus making it difficult to determine periods and synchronize expectations. In summary, our capacities to calculate and control time are extremely weak.

The uncertainty with respect to space and time allows for the revelation of the *growing doubts concerning how much power and effect we can have*. What degree of real incidence, of rational and effective control over social processes, do men and women have today? Long gone are the days in which humanity felt called upon to "transform the world." The feeling of omnipotence that reigned in the sixties has given way to a feeling of powerlessness. We do not have to go to the extreme of neo-liberalism, but its current offensive not only against state intervention, but also against the very idea of popular sovereignty, is a sign of this epoch. When questioning the deliberate construction of society, not only is democracy itself questioned but all of modern politics is also questioned. The faith that we once placed in the strength of political will has dissolved. But not only does voluntarism disappear; there is a tendency to lessen the importance of political action itself. Latin American society is already too complex, too entwined in an excessively rigid international context for the possibility to introduce radical changes to be allowed. Even a reform government would finally have to be satisfied with some "symbolic changes." That this image of lack of productivity emerges from "postmodern culture" remains a paradox. Precisely the culture that topples/dismantles determinism and opens itself radically to an exploration of the horizon of the possible leads to a vision of what exists as what is necessary.

Probably the phenomena outlined above are not constitutive elements of a "long wave," but the gyrations of the needle of a compass of hope. But meanwhile, the processes of democratization also find themselves in a "compass of hope."

TRANSLATED BY EDUARDO MENDIETA

NOTES

1. See Gino Germani, "Democracia y autoritarismo en la sociedad moderna," in G. Germani et al., eds., *Los límites de la democracia*, vol. 1 (Buenos Aires: CLASCO, 1985).

2. "La modernité, c'est le transitoire, le fugitif, le contingent, la moitié, de l'art, dont l'autre moitié est l'éternel et l'immuable." Quoted by David Frisby, *Fragments of Modernity: Theories of Modernity in the Work of Simmel, Kracauer and Benjamin* (Cambridge, Mass.: MIT Press, 1986), 14. See also Lois Boe Hyslop and Francis E. Hyslop, Jr., trans. and ed., *Baudelaire as Literary Critic: Selected Essays* (University Park: Pennsylvania State University Press, 1964), 296.

3. Fredric Jameson, "Postmodernism and Consumer Society," in Hal Foster, ed., *The Anti-Aesthetic: Essays on Postmodern Culture* (Port Townsend, Wash.: Bay Press, 1983), 119.

10. On Citizenship: The Grammatology of the Body-Politic

BEATRIZ GONZÁLEZ STEPHAN

Perhaps the borderline situation caused by the postmodern and postcolonial debates allows us to visualize—and to question—the true foundational and expansive moments of knowledge and legality. These undoubtedly were entwined with the culture of the book, which validated a certain type of logocentric power as well as vertical functioning patterns. From another perspective, provided by new experiences that imply the disintegration of many "strong" paradigms, it means standing outside the panoptic city model,[1] a project that is very dear to modern liberal utopias, and disassembling the formidable state machinery into its most insignificant pieces, its apparently innocuous and innocent details, the imperceptible gears of everyday life, which are nevertheless essential not only for its functioning, but also for consolidation and reproduction of the power that supports it.

The intense study of national issues, citizenship, the relationship between public and private issues, the creation of an individual and a social body, and the validity of the democratic legal order takes into account only the cultural and historical character (in a provisional sense) of these categories, which have created the identities that are still recognized as national states. Knowing that we are living within the limits of the law or, better yet, in a limited situation, feeling the expressive possibilities of body and language, imagining similar others and different others, feeling that we belong to a land whose existence seems to be verified in cartographic representations, trusting that we ascribe to an order whose legitimacy lies in words: these are some of the many challenges that the post-independent state—just to mention the Latin American case—has had to face and design.

The political space that opened with the new republics forced a careful reappraisal of the distribution and implementation of power mechanisms which, in view of the recent citizen's legal status, and due to the ideas brought about by the Enlightenment, had to be less punitive and overt than during colonialism. The violence inflicted upon Indians, blacks, mulattos, slaves, Masons, native dissidents and emancipators, aboriginals and fugitives, by governors and commissioners, members of the Holy Office, foremen and landowners, is well known; they made a public spectacle of tortures and broken limbs in the name of the King and of

God. We must not forget the unlimited rights of teachers, parents, and husbands to inflict physical punishment upon their disciples, children, and wives; authority and the law were violently enforced through a systematic policy of physical punishment—public and domestic—in which sores, scars, and even death were part of an interplay of mixed signals: guilt and power.

However, in other areas of social life, at least well until into the nineteenth century, the intensity of passions prevailed, as did violence in games, family relationships, parties, carnivals, the theater, the treatment of servants, uninhibited sexuality, in bodily gestures, sensuality, wantonness, clamor, and laughter. In sum, there was a sensibility that was not prone to restraint, was qualified by modern culture as "barbarian," and was identified with an archaic and shameful past as well as with incivility, unlawfulness, and guilt. The new learned individuals of the republic regarded violence in prisons and in punishment as an excess of "instincts," a "savagery" that needed to be tamed or, preferably, prevented by activating control and subjection mechanisms that would oversee every detail of daily life—deploying a written system of "micropenalties" that would watch each movement, gesture, and word, thus saving strength by making "barbarians" docile and useful.

In this sense, we can illustrate this new sensibility with the polemics that unraveled in Caracas in 1790, due to the creation of a "House of Mercy" to provide shelter to the growing number of foundlings. Project supporters argued that since this was a women's problem, it was more urgent to "correct their habits"—that is, the function of the new institution would be to reeducate them: "To guide those women who vilified an occupation which should honor them, putting them to spin, weave, work with cotton and in other activities that could help support the household."[2] Violent punishment and unrestrained passions had to be redirected to build the *homo economicus* and the domestic(ated) woman, subjects of the new bourgeois society, the required prototypes for the utopia of progress and modernization. The new direction of a free and explosive vitality within the republican legal order assumed a new relationship between power and a body founded on discipline, productivity, and hygiene.[3] Not in vain did national constitutions, catechisms, and behavioral guides insist that idleness is the source of all vices and that public vagrancy should be persecuted.

The founding project of the nation was to civilize. It did this, first, by endowing the *written word* with the power to legalize and standardize practices and individuals whose identity was limited to the written space. Second, it organized a multiplicitous, automatic, and anonymous *power* that controlled individuals constantly and discreetly, making them citizens of the *polis* and restraining them within an invisible web of laws, rules, and policing texts—the watching and the watched in a mutual complicity that harbored possible transgressions. The written word was to be the decisive civilizing tool upon which the power to tame savagery and the softening of customs would rest. Words (laws, norms, books, manuals, catechisms) were to constrain passions and contain violence. A dichotomy between reality and words led José Martí to point out, in a critical view of Latin American modernity at the end of the century, that "a collision with a horse cannot be avoided with a decree by Hamilton," and that "the clotted Indian blood cannot be unclotted with a phrase by Sieyés." But this is a topic for another time.

Evidently, the nation was to emerge from a purely written reality—the *ciudad escrituraria* (written city), a phrase coined by Angel Rama[4]—reserved for a strict minority of learned men. Only in this way could the effect of that "imaginary community" be achieved,[5] as it was thought to be similar to the circuit established by the print culture which pretended, for reasons that are far from being simple, to ignore the contradictions and the multicultural character of potential readers and of a world society. However, this did not mean that communities with a strong oral tradition did not have other rules for creating cohesion in an imaginary group.

The liberal model of the nation basically followed the Western formula: a strong, centralized power in a state that "uses violence without war; instead of warriors, it uses policemen and wardens; it has no arms and has no need for them, it seizes immediately and magically, 'capturing' and 'combining,' thus avoiding combat." It established and secured the work force because it created corporations, workshops, and factories, and because it recruited a labor force among the indigent. It regulated all movements. It limited, distributed, classified, and arranged hierarchically territories and individuals. It created a unified and meaningful interior that faced a savage and irrational exterior. It put an end to *wandering bands* and to *nomadic behavior*. It identified history and books with its victory.[6]

The creation of the national state was a slow process that started before the nineteenth century, when some social practices anticipated modalities of the future disciplinary and liberal society. In eighteenth-century Venezuela, the uprisings of slaves and mulattos and the increasingly unbearable situation of deviants, vagrants, and beggars led the economic elites to finance a variety of establishments—a Correction House for mulattos, blacks, and particularly unruly slaves, a jail-hospice for white and mulatto women "with a dissolute life," and jails for Indians—to lock up and, in some cases, isolate a population whose "idleness" led to "crime" and "terrible vices."[7] Another example was the founding by the Colonel of Engineers, Don Nicolás de Castro, of an Academy of Geometry and Fortification in Caracas around the same time. This spurred a growing interest in institutionalizing mathematics, topography, and algebra in the country's universities, an interest that was closely linked to the scientific development of cartography and to an aggressive border policy.[8] It is obvious that the Creole elites also saw themselves as the subjects of a new project, in which the strategies of scientific knowledge—calculations and measurements—and the policy of reeducating labor would serve, on the one hand, to channel their hidden fears of a population filled with "evil otherness" and, on the other, to formalize their historic right as members of civilized society and beneficiaries of modern wealth and to redirect violence toward the increased value of capital.

Modern societies—or those trying to be modern—wielded power through a series of institutions (workshops, schools, prisons, hospices, sanitariums, jails) and discursive practices (constitutions, registries, censuses, maps, grammars, dictionaries, behavior manuals, and hygiene guides). These formed a set of "specialized technologies" and institutions of public order that coerced, controlled, subjected, and softly regulated the movement of bodies to make them tamed subjectivities— subjects of the state—and neutralize the dangers of decentralized agents. It was known as "discipline," and its power lay precisely in a written surveillance.[9]

Specifically, *constitutions, grammars,* and *manuals* (to mention only the paradigmatic forms) comprised a system of surveillance and orthopedia which seized and immobilized the citizen through laws and norms. Here, the "power of words" not only shaped but also created and held the object that it prescribed. In these cases, the identification between words/discipline/power and surveillance ran parallel to the creation of citizenship. Conversely, the prerequisite for an individual to be recognized as a citizen was that he could exist only within the framework of the disciplinary writings of the constitution.

The proliferation of these disciplinary writings in their many formats—from a newspaper article, a leaflet, or a brochure, to a book—spanned the nineteenth century and became stronger toward its end, when modernization was tangible in the already large Latin American cities, and the population density demanded a greater propagation of these texts and a more thorough surveillance. This does not mean that the violence of passions—the brazenness of body and language—was ruled immediately by the constitutions, grammars, and manuals created during earlier decades. Rather, there were tensions and a struggle, not always comfortably resolved, between the universes postulated by the ruling words and the dynamics of reality. Nevertheless, it is a fact that the concepts of "nation" and "citizenship" were the idea of a minority, a project postulated to be expansive, which could include and domesticate different communities that offered resistance to difficult negotiations. The dual task (centripetal and centrifugal) of written disciplines— including constitutions—was to incorporate and shape social groups and to expel those who could not adapt to the norms. Several times, the scholastic programs of the "learned" governments of the last third of the century ran parallel to the policies of exterminating Indians (Argentina and Mexico) or peasant nomads (the Canudos in Brazil). In addition, the concern to rid the city of dogs, hogs, and stray animals gave rise to a more generalized plan: hospices and sanitariums were used to lock up vagrants and delinquents, who lacked a stable job (and thus property and a permanent address), with the excuse of caring for the "mentally ill" and fostering the medical sciences. And in a very particular sense, literature often served as a disciplinary practice. On the one hand, peasant "delinquents" were legally recruited as labor for landowners and as soldiers for the army; landowners and the military were clear disciplinary institutions that considered being different to be illegal and sought to contain the "barbaric" masses within the law. On the other hand, the gaucho genre—as suggested by Josefina Ludmer—included the voice of the illegal peasant in the written culture, turning it "civilized" and hoping to integrate it into the disciplined body of the fatherland. Books and reading were the disciplinary exercises of the new legal order.[10]

Of all these heterogeneous sets of normative texts, the specific group of *constitutions, grammars,* and *behavior manuals* represent a particular modality of discipline and written surveillance. During the nineteenth century, there were hundreds of them in every Latin American country, and their reproduction was usually part of their function and nature. To read one constitution or manual is to read them all. Therefore, to speed up the purpose of this work, I am going to refer to the Venezuelan constitutions[11] of the last century, the *Gramática de la Lengua Castellana Destinada al Uso de los Americanos* (Castillian Grammar for Americans) by Andrés Bello (1847), and the *Manual de Urbanidad y Buenas Maneras* (Manual of urbanity and good manners), also by a Venezuelan, Manuel Antonio Carreño (1853). The *Constitución Federal para los Estados de Venezuela* (Federal Constitution for Venezuelan States), of 1811, is the first in the Hispanic world; Bello's grammar book and Carreño's manual became the main guides to proper language and good manners. It isn't necessary to mention the reasons for choosing them as examples of normative and disciplinary genres.[12]

1. THE SUBJECTIVE POLICE CORPS

Constitutions, grammars, and manuals are all forms of discourse that, as laws, rules, and regulations, not only prevent infractions and mistakes, punishment and guilt, but also form a subjective police corps that is systematically assumed by each individual through constant use, a repression that is internalized. These forms of discourse pursue prevention rather than punishment. They move into the area of prohibition and systematic threat to instill in every individual an adequate dose of fear of possible exclusion from or discrimination by the areas deemed legal by state authorities.

It can also be said that they are basically antonomastic writings because they constitute the core that gives rise to state laws (constitutions), national language (grammars), and citizenship (manuals). From their own perspective, each determines the subject's profile and requirements according to the needs of the new legal environment. They build the legal framework within which the individual is acknowledged and accepted as a subject of the *ciudad escrituraria*, and as an agent of the reproductive and moral forces of the national project. At this level, the modern era made a strong commitment with a *written legal order*, whose policies for binding body and language were at the service of a new economy that was more socially profitable. The police writings—writings that guided the social movement of the polis—included ethically different areas: on the one hand, city, state, industry, progress; on the other, rural areas, caudillos, and estates. But the new order, the "police" order, not only put these areas in opposition, it also discredited the latter: "After creating a society men relinquished the *unlimited and licentious freedom* which guided their passions and belonged to *the barbaric state*. The establishment of society assumes giving up these ill-fated rights, the acquisition of others, sweeter and more peaceful, and the subjection to certain mutual duties." Later in the Constitution of 1811, quoted above, it says, "Property is the right that everyone has to enjoy and use the goods acquired through work and industry."[13]

Labeling rural society "barbaric" automatically conferred on the written law and, in turn, on society/citizen/property the quality of natural values. Evidently, controlling idleness and lack of restraint also implied a new ethic in which virtue lay in saving passions as well as wealth. The desire to accumulate goods was considered in police writings, which modeled the passions of body and of language.

2. THE CREATION OF CITIZENSHIP

Among other things, the legal-political function of constitutions—and, to a certain extent, grammars and manuals—is the creation of citizenship, in the sense of creating an identity that had to be built as a homogeneous space so that governing it will be more viable. As Julio Ramos states, "An identity . . . had to be built upon the transformation of the population's 'barbaric' and undisciplined materials, mostly peasants and subordinates, who resisted the political and cultural centralization required by the nation."[14]

The constitution of a symbolic space that identifies *similar subjects*, whether because they use a *common language* or because their *symmetrical bodies* adjust to the same pattern, is among the conditions that will allow the establishment of a commercial order among the nation's regions and link the nation to international trade. In the nineteenth century, as railroads, telegraphy, and steamships drew lands and cities closer to each other, the new forms of communication demanded standardization of bodies and languages.

One of the attractions of the modernizing project was the efficiency of rationality, which implied a standardizing or "uniformizing" strategy at all levels for the benefit of the national state. Although there were many complex factors exhibited in the creation of citizenship, one of the most critical was grammar, because, as Andrés Bello said, it is one of the ethical, legal, and political authorities with the greatest power of intervention to create citizenship and the founding discourse of the modern state. Standardizing language through compulsory education would not only eradicate "nasty habits," "defects," and "rude barbarisms" from "people with little education," but also prevent the proliferation of a "host of irregular, licentious and barbaric dialects" in the Hispanic American continent "which block the diffusion of enlightenment, execution of the law, administration of the state, and national unity."[15]

Evidently, Bello thought that grammar had a civilizing mission, because when linguistic norms were distributed regularly, links between the several national regions were created not only for commercial purposes, but also for the written law (the constitution) to be divulged and fulfilled unequivocally. Establishing language rules would allow, through a transparent code, for the language of trade to be conditioned by legal language.[16] Written law therefore required linguistic stability for proper enforcement of law.

The legal-political function of grammar created the conditions for proclaiming the new legal subject, as it provided the structural framework for the ethics of proper language. The relationship between language and citizenship assumed the disciplinary intervention of authority—teachers and heads of family—on the "vicious practices of popular language" in order to correct the "defective" language of the "populace" and form citizens who "can read and write."[17] On the contrary, the constitution demanded that citizens be competent in written language, and those citizens who were closest to the law of language (to grammar) had the authority to write the laws. Thus, the power of grammar permeated constitutions and manuals as a determining authority because it determined the language of the law and the norm for bodies.

3. PUBLIC AND PRIVATE SPACE

Constitutions, grammars, and manuals shared, although not exclusively, the field of regulating the civilian individual. Constitutions, as the term suggests, are in and of themselves the constitution of the Great Law. Intrinsically, they are a self-reflexive discourse on the law, the impersonal authority of the state—the written word that is its own boundary, the voice that designs national spaces, territories, and subjects. In this sense, the constitution is the discourse that should intervene to delimit the *public space* of the new legal order. Its restrictions affect the *social body* of the fatherland, whose vast territory is apprehended as a geographic body which must be delimited, studied, and divided so that it is controlled by the war machine. Constitutions model the great physical body of nationality, the macro-subject. We are Venezuelan or Paraguayan because that identity is linked to the land whose imaginary borders are always designed in writing.

By expressing great disciplinary power, constitutions had the substance of patriarchal tradition. They served the possibilities of the masculine subject—or better yet, of a particular masculine subject—as the single privileged agent of public life (of the state's administration, elections, education, morality, jobs, goods, and freedom of expression).[18] From this perspective, according to the constitutions, the founding of nations was basically a phallic project, because, for example, citizenship was built upon *male* citizens, senators, teachers, scholars, and parents. Constitutions opened a space—a public space—as a zone of emergence for a particular masculine subject, who ended up legalizing rules and norms that would govern invisible areas. *In general*, the law did not rule the feminine subject but excluded her from public life—that is, she was a *non*-citizen.

Although constitutions ruled the public aspects and official dimension of civilian life, manuals acted upon the *physical body* of the individual, and particularly upon the *private and familiar spaces*, with their countless behavioral and hygienic rules. The civilizing project of the modern state could organize only the public sphere, where it implemented many small courts in all the nooks and crannies of daily life. The great legal machine—which remained outside—was divided into a varied anthropology of discipline. Norms—which controlled the slightest insinuation of body, sight, desires, any inopportune emotion or word—penetrated homes

through the school and the press, and were installed with subtlety and persever-
ance not only in the core of the family or the workplace, but also in the intimacy
of the individual.[19]

The creation of citizenship, necessary for the new commercial situation, was
heavily based upon disciplining the body and its passions, and upon distributing
sexual roles from within the family. It is not by chance that in disciplinary texts
the greater punitive stigmas fell upon the woman: the severe taming of her body
and will was closely related to the property of her womb—the imbrication between
family, property, and state—not only to safeguard an education that reproduced
containment and docility in her children, but also to monitor the private estate.
A "good housewife," besides being discreet—which is equivalent to going unnoticed—had to be thrifty in two senses: with material goods and with the desires of
her body.[20] The cost of making women into objects was inversely related to the increase in private wealth—the axis of the new liberal society—and of male descendants, which would enlarge the demos of the republican state as a literate body.

And grammars, as mentioned above, leveled out in one code the language of
the streets and the language of the home. They were the hinge that articulated
public and private issues into one project, as the two essential scenarios for the citizen's good performance. On the other hand, manuals reinforced the need to know
rules of grammar and to have good pronunciation, a pleasant tone of voice, calm
gestures, and studied movements to guarantee social success.

Therefore, these texts distributed, organized, and complemented each other in
the areas of national identity, public territories, private zones, and communication
channels. They directly affected the *body* (physical and psychic, individual and
collective) and *language*, with preventive, penalizing, and corrective measures.
They shaped the operative and enunciative conditions of the legal subject of culture. They decided the language and the body of the civilizing agent. The home
prepared the citizen for the great theater of the world.

4. STATE, SCHOOL, AND FAMILY:
SUBJECTS OF AUTHORITY

The institutions that articulated and supported a large portion of disciplinary
devices were the state—with all its legal and judicial machinery—the school, and
the family. Therefore, the model individuals called upon to implement and fulfill
the constitutional, linguistic, and behavioral order were the *judge*, the *teacher*, and
the *father*—agents authorized to oversee the fulfillment of written forms. Therefore, *obedience* became a key exercise for body and mind, for hegemony to be exerted over the individual. The modern era brought readjustments between sexes
and power. The man still had the knowledge of language, the language of the law,
and thus the authority. From another perspective, the figures of the physician and
the psychiatrist replaced those of the midwife and the priest as the two authorities
that were to rule the cleanliness of the body and the coaction of Eros.

The acquisition of citizenship was a sieve through which only those men who were competent in language, over twenty-one, married, "owners of real estate whose annual rent is two hundred pesos, or who have a profession, job or useful industry that produces three hundred pesos a year, or who have a yearly salary of four hundred pesos," could pass. Therefore, the written laws and norms outlined a field that gave authority to the masculine subject who was white, Catholic, married, literate, a proprietor and/or businessman, and who recorded in the grooves of his mind the silence of subordinate subjects, those who were at the backside of citizenship. For example, women were referred to only as the "woman *institutor*," the governess in charge of girls, "but under the rule of her husband," who was elected by the Chamber "among the most virtuous and wise of men."[21] The governess (in the constitution), or the housewife (in the manuals), was subordinated, with no right to speak or to be a citizen, and, together with a host of equals—children, servants, the deranged, the infirm, the poor, Indians, blacks, slaves, laborers, illiterate people, homosexuals, Jews—was regarded as a minor.

The violence of these individuals' authority banished abuse and physical punishment for the sake of a greater, though apparent, softening of customs.[22] Now violence passed through the filters of several disciplines or bodies of knowledge that modified—repressed—bodies, languages, and emotions, as well as the appearance of the land. Pedagogy was the great preventer: the knowledge it imparted—grammar, geography, history, arithmetic, calculus, Latin—distributed elsewhere the "pulsations of savagery." Education was the spur of progress, and the figure of the teacher held the keys to the participation of a literate citizenship.

5. GEOMETRIZATION OF AREAS: BOUNDARIES AND FRONTIERS

The foundation of an order ruled by writing brings about a double movement: the construction of a space closed within itself—the polis with all its educational and correctional buildings—which can be controlled and whose members can be counted; and the establishment of boundaries that outline rigid borders which create "transparent" identity zones and "dark" and incomprehensible zones, the open space of chaos and chance. Even though the written word outlines one field over the others—for example, over cultural systems that are not centered around a graphic legality, such as oral communities—its limits shape a boundary that not only separates the *inside* from the *outside*, but also provides the space that rules the area of a careful territorial geometry. In the words of Deleuze and Guattari, it is like a chess game: the power of the state encodes and decodes the space, charting it and layering it from its center of gravity.[23]

One of the tactics for taming nature was rationalization, which in this case meant fractionalization, division, detachment, classification, not only of the land (agronomy, geography) but also of the individual body (medicine, biology), the social body (census, statistics, sociology) and language (grammars, dictionaries).

Geometrization transformed matter into a gridded surface than could be measured in order to optimize its use, whether for natural wealth or for a human labor force. Exercise—consubstantial to discipline—worked land, body, and language by sections. Arithmetic, mathematics, geometry, and algebra were now essential to the controlling power of the state and the liberal bourgeoisie.

Contrary to a great variety of genres, from novels, photographs, and travel chronicles to painting, which delivered the printed illusion of a geography of "natural," "untamed," and "savage" territories, constitutions divided territories, multiplying borders within its even continuum. As "police" writings, they had to be able to filter the free movement of masses and individuals and to rule their contact. They "mapped" a territory that had to be subdivided into multiple legal authorities (states, governments, municipalities, mayor's offices) where customs houses oversaw, inspected, and taxed goods and stopped the constant flow of humans and animals. Charting the territory—and not in vain did mapping and traveler's relations have a great effect on it—prepared the field for the immediate establishment of a communications network: which river was the best for the draft of large steamers; which land was the most level and the farthest from savages so that railroads could be built. The space-nation was counted numerically, by regions, inhabitants, sex, occupation, abilities. To quantify was to know the potential for future wealth.

Constitutions, grammars, and manuals were, each in their own right, founding discourses for borders. Their language was forged from prohibition, a chain of gates that allowed and forbade citizens the right to have and to hide a body, to have a language that could be modified or silenced. The continuity of human space was separated into public and private, the individual body parts separated to control or inhibit their function, language dissected into prolific morphological classifications. As genres of the normalizing power, these were exercises in imposing boundaries.

Disciplines delimited spaces; they enclosed. Laws bound and centered. On the other hand, manuals, in their eagerness to discipline the human body, tamed it part by part; parts that should not touch each other—fingers and hands to the mouth, ears, nose, eyes, head, legs, feet—areas, flows, gestures, and expressions that had to be covered ("we should never leave our rooms if we are not fully dressed" [Carreño, *Manual*, 53]), eliminated ("the habit of getting up at night to relieve our physical needs is highly censurable" [48]), or modified ("we should not touch our head, or put our hands under our clothes for no reason whatsoever, not even to scratch. All these acts are always filthy and highly uncivilized when performed in front of other people" [23]) in order to achieve an aseptic, hieratic, serious, distant, and contained body. Written rules suppressed passions ("we must dominate our emotions and our countenance, and must always show an affable and jovial mood" [198]; "we must sacrifice our taste, our dislikes and even our comfort" [217]) until they were circumscribed to areas considered abject and guilt-ridden.

When constitutions allocate territories, they create reservoirs for nomadic populations—such as the North American Indians, or our Goajiros and Yanomamis—

to confine them and thus be able to locate them. On the other hand, manuals stash Eros and emotions in the bottom of the dark box of the unconscious or in mental institutions, where psychiatry is challenged to channel these repressed impulses in a civilized manner.

Civilization is an internal act with contained spaces that are carefully delineated by the written word. The monumental dimensions of public works and buildings, theaters and racetracks, squares and beach resorts, schools and academies, mansions and slaughterhouses, aqueducts and cemeteries, parcel out life in all its dimensions. Life outside the polis is "barbaric," the even surface that has not yet been stigmatized by the signs of disciplinary writings.

6. THE MACHINERY OF OTHERNESS (DIFFERENCES)

On the flip side of writing—that is, what the written word did not name— emerges a threatening dimension which strains the logic that acknowledges only an imitation of the prewritten order (on this side), and negotiated "otherness" in legal, ethical, and cultural terms (on the other side), built upon a series of operations in which "the other" assumes legal *penalty*, inquiry, judgment, and exclusion, ethical and cultural *degradation* ("filthy," "repugnant," "uncivil," "unpleasant," "vicious"), and social and economic *failure*.

Norms and laws seemed to have a specular nature. Those who did not obey them ("Every individual must live under the law"; "It is an important rule of urbanity to strictly follow the uses of etiquette") were regarded as uncivilized individuals, languages, or territories. They represented the anti-law, the guilty body of a non-state, prosecuted by the written word, which expelled and later punished them. The power of the state forged *otherness* because otherwise, disciplinary and taming practices would not make any sense. It was the test by fire of the efficiency of the new power technologies: discipline removed inadequate excrescences (leftovers) from individuals (because they were unmanageable), languages, and differences in the body itself.

An indeterminate otherness accumulated on the edges of legal writing, a strange sort of "deformity" which constitutions barely named as vagrancy, insanity, banditry, or criminality, and it referred only to subjects whose way of life was basically nomadic or not exactly sedentary, because they practiced itinerant trade or cattle trade (in the case of *llaneros*, gauchos, and *canganceiros*). In other words, if being a citizen (always masculine) implied having an annual income of between one hundred and six hundred pesos, owning real estate, and practicing a profession or a useful industry, then almost 90 percent of the population was part of that "otherness," because of insolvency (the poor, craftsmen, small urban and rural businessmen, debtors), inadequate professional skills (servants, slaves, peasants, illiterates), ethnic inadequacies (Indians, blacks, mulattos, sexual differences (women, homosexuals—because formal marriage was required), or physical or mental deficiencies (the sick, the inebriated, and the insane).

Discipline is limiting because it is limited. It is ruled by a logocentric dynamic that does not accept another logic. The edges become a wall of contention against the threats from the "outside." This must be previously invalidated through a disqualifying language. The "other" becomes vulgar, rude, sick, savage, dirty: in the words of Dominique Laporte, "It is a place of shit."[24] It was a privileged place occupied by the Indians because, since the state could not exterminate them, it had to "provide them with schools, academies, and colleges where they can learn the principles of religion, morals, politics, sciences, and useful arts . . . and try by all means to lure those natural citizens to these houses of enlightenment . . . to eliminate their dejection and rusticity."[25] Otherwise, they would continue to be the social excrement of citizenship—together with the domestic servants—riddled with "defects" and "natural deformities."[26]

Perhaps one of the most worrisome aspects of the founding of nations was the handling of *difference*. To legalize its project, the monolithic rationality imposed within the homogenizing and expansive categories could only procure several devices that quickly canceled the articulation of heterogeneity, expelling them to the area of (im)possible "savagery." I mean that the term "other" is an unfortunate construct, which from the core of its enunciative locus rarifies *difference* as such. Power must also manufacture "otherness," because when it crushes and obliterates it, it becomes stronger and legitimized.

If we compare some semantic areas of constitutions and manuals and establish some basic similarities, we see that one of the main tasks of reeducating an individual to be fit for society was the taming of his emotions, which in terms of good manners (sanity) was equal not only to the avoidance of shouting, clapping, laughing, spitting, blowing the nose, and sucking the fingers, but also getting used to "being somewhat discreet"; in the face of offenses "we must be serenely intransigent, and must restrain ourselves to the point where our anger is not even noticed on our faces" (Carreño, *Manual*, 260). That is, and getting closer to *constitutions*, any citizen who disputed, thought out loud, argued, opposed, or unleashed his rage and hate was considered insane or inebriated. Citizens who had "neutralized as much as possible the exaltations of their spirit" (256) and conquered an "elegant exterior" (254) would have political rights. Everything else—sweat, smells, approaches, hybridizations—was to be called the "other."

7. HYGIENIZATION POLICIES: CLEANLINESS AND CONTROLLED CONTACT

The modern era was intimately linked to hygienization policies for individuals, languages, and territories, which complemented the anatomy of surveillance and coercion, imposing pure and non-polluted categories.[27] It is in this sense that constitutions, grammars, and manuals (including those on sexual hygiene) created pure fields of work, because they established boundaries. It is easier to rule what has been homologated, or to control units that have been previously expunged of ethnic, linguistic, sexual, or social contamination. Dominique Laporte states, "The writer and the grammarian, no less than the prince, clean language just as they clean a city 'filled with mud, garbage, rubble and other filth:' they go down to the latrine to clean it. . . . A treasure emerges from shit: the treasure of language, of the king, and of the state."[28]

Filth—understood as humors and bodily contact, open sexuality, masturbation, carnivals, physical punishment, cockfights, bullfights, popular jargon, and the dramatization of funerals—represented one of the metaphors that complemented the great axiom of "barbarism." The *asepsis* and *cleanliness* of streets, language, body, and habits appeared as the panaceas of progress and materialization in a modern nation—to cleanse the public *res* of transient "unproductive" groups, of insane and sick people (that is, Indians, mulattos, free blacks, and "rebels"), the language of "vicious" expressions ("bad words" soil the language), and the body of odors and spontaneous impulses. In this sense, the "other" appeared as an illness, and it was feared because it could be contagious.

Hygiene was taught in concert with coercion policies, isolation, and disinfection of any contaminating element or individual. As part of a new sensibility, there was a phobia regarding the cultural complex of "barbarism," and a compulsion for correctness and cleanliness. Carreño reminds his readers that they should "never offer food or drink that we have touched with our lips" or "drink from a glass that was used by someone else, or eat what he left in his plate," or "wear soiled clothes," to avoid not only contact with fluids, but also a familiarity that was inappropriate for the order that was to be imposed. The body itself was to be subject to a series of sterilizations—and fashion was to have an important role in this area—because all matter, particularly the female body, was associated with dirt, vulgarity, ugliness, and corruption. These modern times did not free the body, they made it the center of abjection: "It is not permitted to mention in society the different limbs or areas of the body, except for those that are never covered" (Carreño, *Manual*, 124). Bodies were not the only things that should be disinfected. The modern city plan redesigned Latin American cities by redistributing buildings into discreet units, removing waste and the "vulgar" bustle of social life from the urban centers. For example, among the many redesigns made by Antonio Guzmán Blanco during his long presidential term (1870–88), he sanitized Caracas by building the slaughterhouse and the main cemetery outside the city, as well as a sewer system, aqueducts, and the municipal dump; by instituting the extermination of stray dogs; by opening a leprosarium sixty kilometers away from the city; and, in another sense, by founding the Academies of Language, History, and Medicine—because the purity of the language and of patriotic heroes had to be preserved as bequeathed from the times of the colony and independence. In fact, the creation of schools throughout the national territory acquired an obsessive nature in his political agenda.[29] Not in vain did Guzman's government seriously commit to the demands of civilization: *cleanliness, order,* and *beauty.* We can assume that Freud would have been pleased.

As part of this general cleansing program, a series of strategies were implemented which introduced controlled contact in all areas of public and private life. This implied a discreet distance between bodies ("We should never get so close to the person we are talking with that they can feel our breath"; or "The woman who touches a man not only commits an uncivil act, but will also appear immodest and easy; yet this fault is even worse and more vulgar if it is the man who touches a woman" [Carreño, *Manual*, 32, 120]). It also confined certain undesirable ethnic groups to specific territories (such as the Amazon and the Goajira), and confined individuals with behaviors considered abnormal by the disciplines in prisons, hospices, jails, and workshops.

Regardless of the levels of hygiene reached to improve social life, hygienization policies were often handled with irrational zeal, closer to the police methods of order and confinement than to the cleanliness itself. From another perspective, this zeal for cleanliness was manifested in dogmatic and conservative—and perhaps pre-fascist—solutions in which the obtaining of purity (of body, language, and blood) gave rise to the European immigration policies to "improve the race" as well as the development of Hispanicity toward the end of the century, as if the whitening of the population and the canonization of Castilian Spanish would guarantee the utopia of progress.[30]

8. AN ECONOMICS OF IMITATION

To quote Carreño (rather than Foucault), "Domestic habits, due to their daily and constant repetition, acquire an irresistible power in men, dominating him forever, rising above the speculative knowledge of his chores, and finally creating a second will that subjects him to purely mechanical acts" (Carreño, *Manual*, 227–228). In order to implement the normative aspect of disciplines it is necessary to repeat movements, gestures, and attitudes mechanically, to correct the operations of body and language, thus containing force and enabling it to be docile and useful.

Laws (constitutions) and norms (grammars and manuals) claimed to achieve a maximum collective efficiency, because they operated from the singularization of individuals. They worked thoroughly on parts of the individual and social body. They separated, distanced, classified, and regrouped analogous units. They created *groups in series* which, in their homogeneity, were ordered progressively according to age, sex, class, knowledge, behavior, and abilities: children were placed in different classrooms and buildings according to their age, sex, and wealth, and the "insane" and the "incompetent" were placed in prisons and mental institutions. They classified *homogeneous units into hierarchically organized series*. They watched for differences in order to relocate them in the corresponding social scale. Within the human race (the taxonomy brush was to sweep all the crevices of knowledge and life), they neutralized disparity so that the individual would become similar to the group. They regulated body movements and language use through endless repetition of exercises. Orthography and grammar were learned only through the daily assignments that the teacher gave at school: it was the best place to level out irregularities of expression and restlessness in the body. Therefore, keeping quiet, remaining seated, and standing in line became the mold for the school orthopedia which is still in use.

Discipline normalized the arrhythmia of social life, establishing an economics of imitation that distributed *asymmetrical relationships* into a hierarchic scale. The hierarchy was maintained and every step of the hierarchy was serialized through imitation. This attempt at leveling out society in post-colonial times was just a reinstatement of monarchic power. Violence and punishment were replaced by the standardization of mechanisms that controlled analogies and watched over hierarchies. The "arboreal" system that ruled the logos of the new states distributed its loads—previously washed—into differentiated compartments that were reciprocally subordinated.

It created overlapping singularities within the new order, isolated individualities—discreet and similar units—easily located and interchanged within a unit—barracks, school, workshop, factory—to increase productivity or punitive efficiency. A single dimension has the advantage of creating a horizon where anomalies stand out.

9. VIGILANT EYE/PUNITIVE EYE

The Venezuelan constitution written by Simón Bolívar in 1819 proposed a "fourth power," "moral power," formed by the forty most virtuous citizens of the city. This "Areopagus," regarded as a court of honor, was to be in charge of watching over public morality and "proclaiming the names of virtuous citizens and moral educated acts, and denouncing with shame and disgrace the names of the depraved and those acts of corruption and indecency."[31] Even though this element was not included in later constitutions, the spirit of censorship and surveillance was adopted by other social practices, among them manuals, which invisibly disseminated within the community an anonymous body of micropenalties that acted as a sort of infra-law. The teacher observed, the physician examined, the father watched, each looking upon the other earnestly. Constitutions permanently invited socialized spying and denunciation ("every citizen is capable of accusing"). On the other hand, manuals suggested discreet observation and elegant surveillance ("We should never stare at the people we meet, nor those who are at their windows, nor turn our heads to see those who have gone by" [Carreño, *Manual*, 82). Public and domestic life were destined to be a great theater in which the actors and the audience are constantly under observation.

The gradual disappearance of physical punishment—or at least its diminution—and open and embarrassing public derision were gradually replaced by a new punitive sensibility, more subtle and imperceptible: the development of the vigilant eye.[32] Perhaps it was a sort of police voyeurism that repressed desire, disorganized behavior, unusual uses of body and voice. Perhaps it was the flagellated eye of Thanatos. Police mechanisms, now subjectively individualized, turned each individual into a small court of inquisition. There was the fear of being seen, the shame of being observed. In any event, norms and laws also wove an imaginary control in which every eye became a judge: written norms forged watchful and watched individuals. The eyes of the judge, the teacher, the father, and the physician were disseminated among many other eyes that constantly control the slightest transgression of public, private, and intimate boundaries. Thus, individuals must watch forms, appearances, emotions, physical contact, and good rhetoric, because the eye of another person always remembers boundaries that are only imaginary.[33]

Although watching and being watched turned urban life into a great masquerade, it is also true that the turn-of-the-century city became a huge observatory, not only criminal, clinical, and pedagogical, but also linguistic and literary. Modern knowledge opened its doors under an omnipresent eye that examined and classified everything, placing individuals in a written net that seized, explained, cured, corrected, and adapted them. The purpose of science was just as disciplinary.

The new legal regime of nationalities also assumed a new relationship between power and modern categories of productivity. This implied a redefinition of the implementation of power between individuals, in terms of a better use of effort, the "useful" channeling of energy, and the inspection of free movements, in order to fulfill the desired and utopian agenda of progress.

Regardless of how the writings of the fatherland interacted with the dynamics of each respective Latin American situation, these disciplinary texts were proposed as bastions of civilization and as such, those who wrote them believed in the taming ability of words and placed their faith in the power of the patriarchal literate individual and in the diffusion of pedagogy as a machine to seize/capture/castrate "inorganic" autonomies and the "confused force of barbarism." All the controlling and supervising tactics—establishing boundaries, geometrization, divisions, exclusions, serializations, and symmetrization—were never enough to build the dreamed-of nations and the bleached, aseptic citizens prescribed by overseas models.

NOTES

General note: All quotations in this chapter were translated by Eduardo Mendieta.

1. A concept taken by Michel Foucault from the *Panopticon* by Jeremiah Bentham (1748–1832), and developed in his books *Vigilar y castigar, Nacimiento de la prisión* (Mexico City: Siglo XXI, 1976, 1988), and *La verdad y las formas jurídicas* (Barcelona: Gedisa, 1980, 1991), as a metaphor of disciplinary power that is best represented in the circular architectural figure of the "Panoptic," with concentric rings filled with cells and windows

204 Beatriz González Stephan

which face the inside as well as the outside of the building. From the central tower, the prisoner is constantly watched, not knowing who is watching him. The advantage of this construction is that power becomes both visible and unverifiable. The individual knows he is being observed, but not by whom or when.

2. Frédérique Langue, "Desterrar el Vicio y Serenar las Conciencias: Mendicidad y Pobreza en la Caracas del siglo XVIII," *Revista de Indias,* no. 201 (1994): 367.

3. See José Pedro Barrán, *Historia de la Sensibilidad Uruguaya,* vol. 1, *La Cultura "Bárbara"* (1800–1860), vol. 2, *El Disciplinamiento* (1860–1920) (Montevideo: Edics. de la Banda Oriental, 1990, 1992). This work is very instructive regarding documented research that explains the change in sensibilities, from bold and spontaneous forms to more contained and constrained attitudes.

4. See Angel Rama, *La Ciudad Letrada* (Montevideo: F. I. A. R., 1984), which gave rise to other important research; in my case, the research performed by Julio Ramos in *Desencuentros de la Modernidad en América Latina. Literatura y Política en el Siglo XIX* (Mexico City: Fondo de Cultura Económica, 1989).

5. Benedict Anderson, *Imagined Communities: Reflections on the Origin and Spread of Nationalism* (New York: Verso, 1983).

6. See Gilles Deleuze and Félix Guattari, *Mil Mesetas. Capitalismo y Esquizofrenia* (Valencia: Pre-Textos, 1988), specifically chapters 1, "Introducción: Rizoma," and 12, "Tratado de Nomadología: La Máquina de Guerra."

7. Langue, "Desterrar el vicio."

8. See Hernán González and Manuel Alberto Donis Ríos, "Cartografía y cartógrafos en la Venezuela Colonial. Siglo XVIII," in *Memoria del Quinto Congreso Venezolano de Historia* (Caracas: Academia Nacional de la Historia, 1992), vol. 2, 61–85.

9. See, in particular, Foucault, *Vigilar y Castigar,* 139–230 (the chapter entitled "Disciplina").

10. See Josefina Ludmer, *El Género Gauchesco. Un tratado sobre la patria* (Buenos Aires: Editorial Sudamericana, 1988).

11. The facsimile version of the compiled and edited Venezuelan constitutions was published in Luis Marinas Otero, *Las Constituciones de Venezuela* (Madrid: Ediciones Cultura Hispánica, 1965), volume 17 in a collection entitled *Las Constituciones Hispanoamericanas,* edited by Manuel Fraga Iribarne (published by the Centro de Estudios Jurídicos Hispanoamericanos de Instituto de Cultura Hispánica). In this chapter, I have used the constitutions of 1811 and 1819 (by Simón Bolívar), 1830 (by José Antonio Páez), 1857 (by Jose Tadeo Monagas), and 1874 (by Guzmán Blanco). In the nineteenth century, Venezuela had about twelve constitutions. All references to and quotations from constitutions are from the above work.

12. The first edition of Andrés Bello's *Gramática de la Lengua Castellana Destinada al Uso de los Americanos* was published in Chile in 1847. I use the version in Ramón Trujillo, ed., *Antología de Andrés Bello* (Tenerife: Instituto Universitario de Lingüística Andrés Bello, 1981). Manuel Antonio Carreño's *Manual* was first published as a brochure in 1853, and was published in book form in 1854; on March 14, 1855, the National Congress recommended its use. I will quote from the 1927 edition: *Manual de Urbanidad y Beunas Maneras* (Paris: Éditions Garnier Brothers, Corrected and Enlarged Edition, 1927). Throughout the present chapter, I will use the generic terms *constitutions, grammars,* and *manuals* to create specific written typologies. However, concrete examples will be taken from the above-mentioned Venezuelan models.

13. *Constitución de 1811,* 149–151.

14. Julio Ramos, "El Don de la Lengua," *Casa de Las Américas*, no. 193 (1993): 21. This work by Julio Ramos clearly establishes the relationship between language and the policies of purity within the new legal regime of the republic.

15. See A. Bello, "Advertencias Sobre el Uso de la Lengua Castellana," in Raúl Silva Castro, ed., *Antología de Andrés Bello* (Santiago: Edit. Zig-Zag, 1965), 184, 199, 187, 200 (this was originally a series of articles published between 1833 and 1834), and A. Bello, "Prólogo," in Castro, *Antología de Andrés Bello*, 207–216.

16. Ramos, "El Don de la Lengua."

17. A. Bello, "Prólogo." Being competent in reading and writing was consubstantial with citizenship. Also, constitutions regarded as "legal subjects" those who were proficient in good language: "It is the exclusive domain of the Chamber to establish, organize, and direct primary schools for boys and girls, seeing that they are taught to pronounce, read, and write correctly, together with the most common rules of arithmetic and the principles of grammar" (*Constitución de 1819*, Art. 7, section 3, 193). In this sense, a learned individual was the citizen par excellence: a "representative" of citizenship.

18. "Active" citizens—those who could vote—were those "who are more than 25 years old and know how to read and write"; "those who own real estate whose annual rent is two hundred pesos, or those who have a profession, job, or useful industry that produces three hundred pesos a year, or those who have a yearly salary of four hundred pesos" (*Constitución de 1830*, Art. 27, title VII, 227). These requirements remained unchanged until the constitutions of 1870.

19. The scope of this taming/repression reached the most unsuspected areas. Carreño's *Manual* states that "a man is not allowed to be home without his tie on, wearing a shirt, with no socks, or with bad shoes" (55) and "he may not touch his head or put his hand under his clothes, for any reason whatsoever, not even to scratch. All these acts are filthy and highly uncivilized" (23).

20. Carreño states, "The method is perhaps more important for women than for men, because . . . her destiny is to perform some special functions . . . lest she bring about great harm of high transcendence. We are talking about governing a home, about directing domestic matters, the daily investment of money, and the serious and delicate assignment of the early education of children, on which their future and that of society greatly depends."

21. *Constitución de 1819*, p. 194.

22. Even in the *Constitución de 1819*, physical violence is restricted in punishment: "The use of torture is permanently abolished" (Art. 173, p. 153). Later, "Torment and any treatment that worsens the punishment established by the law will never be used" (*Constitución de 1830*, Art. 207, 252). Manuals also contain a section on the "treatment of servants," suggesting that homeowners abstain from abuse, blows, and humiliation. Apparently, it was very frequent for servants to suffer thrashings by their masters.

23. In *Mil Mesetas*. Deleuze and Guattari continue, "One of the main tasks of the state is to striate the space it rules, or to use the even spaces as a means of communication for a chartered space. For any state it is essential to overcome nomadism as well as to control migrations and, more generally, to recover its rights, mostly 'exterior,' over what flows through the inhabited and cultivated areas. Indeed, the state cannot be separated, even where possible, from the seizure of all types of flows, populations, goods or trade, money or capital, etc." (389). For this reason, constitutional law "promotes and decrees the creation of roads, channels, and inns; the construction of bridges, highways, and hospitals. . . . To enable easy and speedy navigation and the promotion of agriculture and trade" (*Constitución de 1830*, 248).

24. Dominique Laporte, *Historia de la Mierda* (Valencia: Pre-Textos, 1980).

25. *Constitución de 1811*, 157. According to this quote, the Indian population is degraded, morally deviated, promiscuous, idle, useless, depressed, and savage.

26. Cf. Carreño, *Manual*, the section titled "Modo de conducirnos con nuestros domésticos" (68–70).

27. Cf. Ramos, "El Don de la Lengua" and Julio Ramos, "Cuerpo, Lengua, Subjetividad," *Revista de Crítica Literaria Latinoamericana*, no. 38 (1993): 225–237, to which I owe many of the ideas that I posit in this chapter.

28. Laporte, *Historia de la Mierda*, 15 and 25.

29. In the constitution, the ideas of school and hygiene and of teacher and physician go hand in hand: "The Chamber will give special care to the shape, proportion, and location of our schools . . . taking into consideration not only their stability and scope, but also the elegance, cleanliness, comfort and recreation of the youth" (*Constitución de 1819*, 193). Later, in the same section: "Every year, the Chamber will publish accurate charts or balance sheets of children born and died, their physical condition, health and diseases, their improvement, inclinations, qualities, and particular talents. To do all these observations, it will use *institutors*, priests, physicians, department agents, and learned citizens" (194).

30. In "Prólogo," Bello states that the language models to follow are "the works of the Spanish Academy and the Grammar by D. Vicente Salvá," and he mentions his debts to Juan Antonio Puignlanch and Garcés. Although his grammar is for Hispanic Americans, "I think that preserving the language of our fathers as purely as possible is very important," to avoid, according to Bello, hybrids such as "irregular, licentious and barbaric dialects" of the Latin American languages, which would muddle communication channels, just like rubbish on the streets (128, 129, 130).

31. See *Constitución de 1819*, 189.

32. Foucault says about this, "Traditionally, power is what you see, what is open, what is evident. . . . Disciplinary power is invisible. . . . In discipline, those who need to be seen are subjected. Their illumination guarantees the power that is exerted over them. Being constantly watched, or the possibility of being constantly watched, keeps the disciplined individual subjected" (*Vigilar y castigar*, 192).

33. This punitive eye was interjected to the point where the most intimate privacy was controlled. This was now an internal police: "It is also a bad habit to move violently while we sleep, because it sometimes makes the bed covers fall down, and makes us assume offensive positions that go against honesty and propriety." (Carreño, 48).

Contributors

Santiago Castro-Gómez is a professor in the faculty of social science at the Javeriana University in Bogotá, Colombia, and a member of the Institute for Social and Cultural Studies, PENSAR, at the same university. He is the author of *Crítica de la razón latinoamericana* (1992); and he has edited with Eduardo Mendieta, *Teorías sin disciplinas* (1998), and with Oscar Guardiola and Carmen Millan, *Pensar (en) los intersticios* (1999), and *La reestructuración de las ciencias sociales en América Latina* (2000). He is the director of the postgraduate program in cultural studies at Javeriana University.

Enrique Dussel is a professor of philosophy at the Universidad Autonoma Metropolitana-Iztapalapa, and the Universidad Nacional Autónoma de México. He has written more than twenty books on religion, sociology, history, theology, and philosophy, some of which have been translated into English, including *The Invention of the Americas* (1995), *The Underside of Modernity* (1996), *Ethics and Community* (1988), *Philosophy of Liberation* (1985), and *Ethics and the Theology of Liberation* (1978). His most recent works are *Ética de la Liberación: en la edad de la globalización y de la exclusión* (1998) and *Hacia una Filosofía Política Crítica* (2001). His work was the subject of a collection edited by Linda Martín Alcoff and Eduardo Mendieta, *Thinking from the Underside of History: Enrique Dussel's Philosophy of Liberation* (2000).

Beatriz González Stephan is a professor at the Universidad Simón Bolivar and, since 2001, the Lee Hage Jamail Chair Professor in the Department of Hispanic and Classical Studies at Rice University. She has served as the director of the journal *Estudios: Revista de Investigaciones Literarias y Culturales* since 1993. In 1987, her book *La historiografía literaria del liberalismo hispanoamericano del siglo XIX* was awarded the Casa de la Américas Prize. Her books include *La duda del Escorpión: la tradición heterodoxa en la narrativa latinoamericana* (1992), *Crítica y descolonización: el sujecto colonial en la cultura latinoamericana* (1992, in collaboration with Lúcia Helena Costigan), *Esplendores y miserias del siglo XIX: Cultura y sociedad en América Latina* (in collaboration with Javier Lasarte and Graciela Montaldo, 1995), and *Cultura y Tercer Mundo* (1996). Two books are forthcoming: *Fundaciones: Canon, Historia y Cultura Nacional* and *Escribir la historia literaria: capital simbólico y monumento cultural*.

Jorge J. E. Gracia is the Samuel P. Capen Chair and SUNY Distinguished Professor of Philosophy at the State University of New York at Buffalo. He is a graduate of Wheaton College, the University of Chicago, the Pontifical Institute of Medieval Studies, and the University of Toronto. He has written thirteen books, including *Old Wine in New Skins: The Role of Tradition in Communication, Knowledge,* and *Group Identity* (forthcoming 2003), *How Can We Know What God Means? The Interpretation of Revelation* (2001), *Hispanic/Latino Identity: A Philosophical Perspective* (2000), *Metaphysics and Its Task: The Search for the Categorial Foundations of Knowledge* (1999), *Texts: Ontological Status, Identity, Author, Audience* (1996), and *A Theory of Textuality: The Logic and Epistemology* (1995),as well as nearly 200 articles. He is the editor or co-editor of more than a dozen books, including the *Blackwell Companion to Philosophy in the Middle Ages* (2002, with T. Noone) and *The Classics of Western Philosophy* (2002, with G. Reichberg and B. Schumaker). His book *Individuality* received the John Findlay Prize in Metaphysics in 1992, and he received the Aquinas Medal from the University of Dallas in 2002. He is currently working on a book entitled *Surviving Race, Ethnicity, and Nationality: A Foundational Analysis for the Twenty-First Century*, and is preparing the Marquette Aquinas Lecture for 2003.

María Herrera Lima is a professor at the Universidad Nacional Autónoma de México, and a researcher at the Instituto de Investigaciones Filosóficas in the same university. She has written on political philosophy, aesthetics, and moral philosophy. She is the editor of *Jürgen Habermas, Moralidad, Ética y Política: Propuestas y críticas* (1993) and *Teorías de la Interpretación: Ensayos sobre Filosofía, Arte y Literatura* (1998).

Norbert Lechner was director of FLACSO (Latin American Faculty of Social Sciences in Santiago de Chile). He is the editor of *Estado y política en América Latina* (1981) and *Cultura política y democratización* (1988). He is the author of *La conflictiva y nunca acabada construcción del order deseado* (1984) and *Pastios interiories de la democracia* (1988)

Eduardo Mendieta is an associate professor of philosophy at the State University of New York at Stony Brook. He is the author of *The Adventures of Transcendental Philosophy* (2002); he co-edited, with Linda Martín Alcoff, *Thinking from the Underside of History: Enrique Dussel's Philosophy of Liberation* (2000) and *Identities: Race, Class, Gender, Nationality* (2002); with David Batstone, *The Good Citizen* (1999); and with Pedro Lange-Churión, *Latin America and Postmodernity: A Contemporary Reader* (2001).

Walter D. Mignolo is William H. Wannamaker Professor of Romance Studies and a professor of literature and cultural anthropology at Duke University. His recent publications include *The Darker Side of the Renaissance: Literacy, Territoriality, and Colonization* (1995) and *Local Histories/Global Designs: Coloniality, Subaltern Knowledge, and Border Thinking* (2000). With Elizabeth Boone, he co-edited *Writing without Words: Alternative Literacies in Mesoamerica and the Andes* (1994). He is the founder and co-editor of *Dispositio/n: American Journal of Comparative and Cultural Studies* and cofounder and coeditor of *Nepantla: Views from South*.

Amós Nascimento has studied music, sociology of religion, and philosophy in Buenos Aires, São Paulo, and Frankfurt. He has published a series of articles on these subjects and edited *Grenzen der Moderne* (1997, with Kirsten Witte), *A Matter of Discourse* (1998), and *Brasil: perspectivas internacionais* (2002). Presently he heads the Office for International Affairs at the Universidade Metodista de Piracicaba (UNIMEP), Brazil.

Ofelia Schutte is a professor of women's studies and philosophy at the University of South Florida. Her areas of teaching and research are feminist theory, Latin American philosophy and social thought, philosophy of culture, and Continental philosophy. She is the author of *Beyond Nihilism: Nietzsche without Masks, Cultural Identity and Social Liberation in Latin American Thought*, and numerous articles on feminist, Latin American, and Continental philosophy. Her current interests include all the above with a focus on theorizing Latin American, postcolonial, and transnational feminisms. Her work was the subject of a special "Scholar's session" at the 2001 meeting of the Society for Phenomenological and Existential Philosophy. The papers presented there will appear in the feminist journal *Hypatia*.

Alfonso de Toro is professor of romance philology in the fields of semiotics, literary theory, and theater at the University of Leipzig, where he is also the director of the Center for Iberoamerican Research at the Center for Romance Studies. He has taught at the universities of Kiel and Hamburg. He is the author of *Zeitstruktur im Gegenwartsroman* (1985), *Von den Ähnlichkeiten und Differenzen: Das Drama der Ehre des 16. und 17. Jahrhunderts in Italien und Spanien* (1993), and *Los laberintos del tiempo* (1992). He also has edited the following works: *Gustav Flaubert* (1987), *Texte-Kontexte-Strukturen* (1987), *Texto-Mensaje-Recipiente* (1988), *Jorge Luis Borges* (1992, with K. A. Blüher), and *Jorge Luis Borges: Pensamiento y saber en el siglo XX* (1999, with Fernando de Toro).

Index